THE BROKEN WELCOME MAT

THE BROKEN WELCOME MAT
2nd Edition
Copyright © Helen Raleigh, 2023
All rights reserved

Book cover design by ebooklaunch.com

ALSO BY HELEN RALEIGH

Confucius Never Said

Backlash: How China's Aggression Has Backfired

Invest Like a Zen Master and Live Happily Ever After

THE
BROKEN
WELCOME MAT

Second Edition

HELEN RALEIGH

For my husband Mike
and our beloved children,
Lucas and Allie

CONTENTS

THE BROKEN WELCOME MAT

FOREWORD TO THE
SECOND EDITION

It has been six years since the first edition of *The Broken Welcome Mat* went into print. During this period, I went through an emotional rollercoaster with America's immigration system. Initially, I became despondent when Donald Trump was elected President of the United States, and his harsh rhetoric on immigrants bothered me.

In May 2019, President Trump announced a proposal to change our nation's immigration system from emphasizing family reunion to emphasizing skill-based immigration. I was simultaneously surprised and delighted because a skill-based immigration system was the centerpiece of my recommendations in the book. I sincerely believe a skill-based immigration system will better serve America's national interests and immigrants' needs.

A few months later, a White House official called me to discuss skill-based immigration reform because he had read my book. I thought it was a prank call and demanded that he prove his identity. He was legit, and his attitude was sincere. I'm a person who will work with anyone as long as it is for the right idea. Thus, I flew to Washington, D.C., and had a long and productive discussion with him and his staff. I became hopeful that long-awaited sensible immigration reform might have arrived at last.

Unfortunately, the Democrats who controlled the U.S. Congress were under the spell of Trump derangement syndrome (irrational and adverse reactions to all things related to Trump). They rejected all Trump policies and proposals, regardless of merit. Trump's skill-based immigration proposal went nowhere. Then, the COVID-19 pandemic consumed all of our attention and resources. Immigration reform was the last thing on everybody's mind.

When Joe Biden became President of the United States, he reversed most of Trump's policies, signaling that he would embrace an open border policy and be lenient with illegal border crossings. Americans watched in horror as the worst border crisis occurred under the Biden presidency. About 5.5 million illegal immigrants were encountered at the U.S.-Mexico border between 2021 and 2020, including 98 on the FBI's terrorist watch list. In 2022 alone, border agents confiscated enough fentanyl to kill all Americans.

Human and drug trafficking across the southern border have enriched the cartels and stretched border cities and states' economic and security resources. Yet, the Democrats only began acknowledging our nation's border crisis after a few Republican governors sent some migrants to Democrat-led cities such as Martha's Vineyard and New York City. There is finally a bi-partisan consensus that America can't afford to ignore our broken immigration system any longer.

Winston Churchill once said: "Never let a good crisis go to waste." Maybe the current border crisis will, at last, motivate Americans to have an honest national debate on how to make our immigration system better. I still believe that the reform ideas I presented in the first edition of this book will improve our nation's immigration system. I have incorporated more recent studies and data in this second edition to strengthen my arguments. What I wrote six years ago is worth repeating: The time for sagacious immigration reform is now, and doing nothing is not an option. I'm willing to work with anyone serious about common-sense immigration reform.

Helen Raleigh

January 2023

INTRODUCTION FROM THE
FIRST EDITION

The year 2016 marks my 20th anniversary in the United States. I was born and raised in Communist China and came to the U.S. on a student visa. I knew no one and had nothing except $100 in my pocket. Like millions of immigrants before me, my pocket was light but my dream was rich.

Even in my wildest imagination, I never expected that the legal path to U.S. citizenship would take 17 long years—years full of encounters with some of the worst bureaucracy and most insanely complex laws in America. I didn't imagine that the process would be so expensive or that it would take such a high emotional toll on my family.

Or that my long, expensive, and unpleasant experience was normal.

Most native-born Americans know very little about what a legal immigrant has to go through to become an American. This means that the immigration reform debate largely ignores legal immigration, preferring to focus solely on illegal immigration.

Of course, there's no denying that we, as a nation, have a serious illegal immigration problem. Over the last 30 years, many politicians have tried to fix the situation but only succeeded in making matters worse. The illegal immigrant population was about 3 million when President Reagan signed his Immigration and Control Act of 1986 to grant illegal immigrants amnesty. Today, it is 11-12 million.

How did our immigration system become such a mess? We used to be proud of being a nation of immigrants. We used to gladly roll out a welcome mat to all newcomers ... but now that welcome mat is broken. People who want to come to the U.S. legally can expect long delays, huge backlogs, strict quotas, absurdly complex rules, and high costs. We don't do enough to keep those who intend to harm America out, and we make it difficult for hardworking, America-loving, law-abiding people to come and stay.

My immigration experience turned me into an activist, but that doesn't mean I want to spend my days complaining about how bad our immigration policy is. Instead, I want to identify solutions. That's the American way: if you don't like something, roll up your sleeves and do something about it.

I have spent the last few years researching legal and illegal immigration issues and formulating solutions, and this book is the result. It will answer these questions:

- How did we get into today's immigration mess?

- Why is our immigration system broken?

- Is immigration good for America?

- Why do we have an illegal immigration problem?

- What can we do to fix our immigration policy?

By answering these questions, I aim to achieve two objectives. My first is to inform. Throughout my research, it has become clear that most Americans don't know much of our nation's immigration history. I firmly believe that if we want to define our future, we have to learn from the past. History tends to repeat itself, and by examining what worked and didn't work in our nation's past, we can make informed decisions about its future.

My second objective is to advocate for meaningful immigration reform. First, I present data provided by organizations throughout the political spectrum in order to give as objective a picture as possible of why immigration is and has been good for America and why our legal immigration system is broken. Second, I propose solutions rooted in free markets and America's founding principles. My solutions are win-win: they are good for America, good for immigrants, and they maintain law and order.

The 2016 presidential race has turned immigration into *the* hotly debated issue. The debate has a lot of emotion but little factual support. As William Butler Yeats said, we truly live at a time, when: "The best lack all conviction, while the worst are full of passionate intensity." However, with the history, information, and reform ideas I present in this book, we can turn the immigration debate into informed, spirited, and fact-based discussions to repair our broken welcome mat.

The time for action is now. Doing nothing is not an option.

Helen Raleigh

May 2016

CHAPTER 1

The Foundation of Our National Identity

1.1 A Nation of Migrants

Jamestown was founded by immigrants in 1607 and is generally considered the first successful English colony in the U.S. In November 2013, archeologists exhumed four human remains in the oldest church in Jamestown, where Captain John Rolfe married Pocahontas in 1614. After two years of extensive forensic analysis, scientists identified that the remains belonged to four of Jamestown's early leaders.[1] Among them were Reverend Robert Hunt, the first Anglican minister in Jamestown, and Sir Ferdinando Wainman, the first English knight to die in the New World (whose cousin Sir Thomas West later became the governor of Virginia).

This archeological discovery reaffirms an undisputable fact: our nation is a nation of immigrants, and it has been since its earliest days.

Immigrants from England were not the first Europeans to set foot in North America. Between A.D. 997 and 1002, five centuries before Christopher Columbus was born, a group of Viking sailors led by Leif Eriksson, sailed from Iceland to North America. According to Viking legend, they built a settlement called Leifsbudir. In the 1960s, in

1

Newfoundland, Canada, archeologist Dr. Anne Stine Ingstad and her husband, Helge Ingstad, excavated artifacts of Viking origin dating from around A.D. 1000. Later, other archeologists discovered Viking artifacts in Maine, Minnesota, and Oklahoma. In 1964, President Lyndon Johnson declared October 9 Leif Eriksson Day.

After the Vikings came the Spanish and the French. In the 1500s, the Spanish and French began to establish settlements in North America thanks to Christopher Columbus's historic voyage in 1492. Early expeditions from the U.K. were out of military necessity. On November 6, 1577, Sir Humphrey Gilbert submitted to Queen Elizabeth I *A Discourse How Her Majesty May Meet with and Annoy the King of Spain.* Persuaded by Sir Gilbert's argument, Queen Elizabeth I granted him a six-year charter to plant a colony and be its governor. Sir Gilbert made several unsuccessful attempts and was eventually reported dead during his last endeavor in 1583. Sir Gilbert's half-brother, Sir Walter Raleigh, inherited Gilbert's coveted charter in March 1584, and sent his first expedition to North America in April. In 1585, based on the information he'd learned, Sir Walter sent a second expedition to North America. One of the captains of the voyage, Ralph Lane, established a military base on Roanoke Island (today's Dare County, North Carolina).

Figure 1.1. Sir Walter Raleigh (1552-1618)

In 1587, Sir Raleigh dispatched a third voyage with 115 colonists to establish a new English colony on the Chesapeake Bay in North America. This last voyage was different in two significant ways:

First, participation was voluntary. Would-be colonists chose to join in the voyage willingly.

Second, named as the City of Raleigh, the new colony was structured as a "joint-stock corporation, and the individual colonists were expected to invest their own money. In return, each was to receive a grant of at least five hundred acres to a man."[2] The commercial nature of the expedition shows that these settlers were not indentured laborers; they had to have had some financial means in order to become colony shareholders and journey to the New World. They took a great risk by leaving England, hoping their investments would pay off.

Under the leadership of Governor John White, 115 colonists settled on Roanoke Island. Shortly after their arrival, the colonists joyfully welcomed a new life to the New World. Virginia Dare, John White's granddaughter, was the first English child born in North America. Later that year, White returned to England to obtain supplies, but because of England's continuing war with Spain, three years passed before he managed to return to the New World in 1590. He was shocked to discover that all of the colonists, including his grand-daughter, had vanished without a trace. Since then, Roanoke Island has been known as the Lost Colony, and the fate of those colonists remains one of the oldest unsolved mysteries in America. For centuries, investigations of what might have happened haven't yielded any satisfactory answers.

In 1606, King James granted a charter to a new joint venture called the Virginia Company. On May 14, 1607, about a hundred colonists from the Virginia Company founded the first permanent English settlement in North America: Jamestown. Unfortunately, "famine, disease and conflict with local Native American tribes in the first two years brought Jamestown to the brink of failure before the arrival of a new group of settlers and supplies in 1610."[3]

1.2 Why Did Early Settlers Come to America?

The early settlers' life in North America was strenuous. Why did they choose to leave England in the first place? Generally speaking, they left England for one of two reasons. The first reason was economic. From 1520 to 1630, the population of England more than doubled, from 2.3 million to 4.8 million.[4] This meant that many people could not find opportunities in England. Like today's immigrants, these English settlers hoped to make a better life for themselves and their families on a new continent. Those with means became shareholders of the colonies; others were skilled immigrants who came to America as contract laborers or indentured servants.

The second reason colonists chose to leave England was religion.

1.3 Religion and Reform in Europe

The popular belief today is that early settlers came to America to escape religious persecution, which is an overly simplistic assumption as history is much more complicated. To understand early settlers' motivation from the religious aspect, we must take a step back to 14th century Europe. A new movement known as the Renaissance was born in Florence, Italy. The Renaissance's intellectual basis was humanism, which was derived from the redis-covery of the classical Greek philosophy that "man is the measure of all things" (Protago-ras).* This new thinking emphasized personal independence and individual expression and was widely represented in art, architecture, politics, science, and literature.

Figure 1.2. Statue of David by Michelangelo

In the meantime, the Catholic Church had "entrenched and linked *membership* in the Church with salvation."[5] It used proceeds from indulgence sales to finance Church activities, such as wars or building new cathedrals, and told people that purchasing indulgences would give them absolution from sin.† The Bible was not widely available, so few questioned the Catholic Church's interpretation of the Holy Scrip-tures. But in 1516, Desiderius Erasmus, a famous humanist, published his Greek translation of the New Testament, dismantling the Catholic Church's monopoly on interpreting the Bible. Following Erasmus's example, other enlightened Europeans began translating the Bible from Latin into their native languages. In 1453, Johannes Gutenberg

---

* Protagoras (c. 490–c. 420 BC) was an ancient Greek philosopher, pre-Socrates and Plato.

† Indulgences are part of Catholic teaching, but the *abuses* of indulgences that took place in the 1500s are not. The Catechism of the Catholic Church states, "An indulgence is obtained through the Church who, by virtue of the power of binding and loosing granted her by Christ Jesus, intervenes in favor of individual Christians and opens for them the treasury of the merits of Christ and the saints to obtain from the Father of mercies the remission of the temporal punishment due for their sins."
Retrieved from http://www.catholic.com/tracts/primer-on-indulgences.

invented a printing process using moveable type to print Bibles. The new printing process gave birth to a grassroots book publishing industry, which allowed the holy text to reach a much wider audience, including commoners. When more people gained direct access to the Bible and other scientific and philosophical texts, their dissatisfaction with traditional Catholic Church authority grew.

Martin Luther, a German monk, led the charge against the Catholic Church's authority. As a theologian, Luther saw the church's corruption as a symptom of something more serious. Based on his own readings of Scripture, he believed salvation is not something that can be bought and sold—or granted by the Catholic Church. On the contrary, salvation is a free gift from God.[6]* Luther's message went viral, thanks largely to a new book-publishing industry in Wittenberg.

The Reformation movement swept through Europe. John Calvin (1509–1564), a generation younger than Luther, led the Reformation movement in France. Calvin believed "the gospel is not a doctrine of the tongue, but of life. It cannot be grasped by reason and memory only, but it is fully understood when it possesses the whole soul and penetrates to the inner recesses of the heart."[7]

In England, after the Pope refused to annul King Henry VIII's marriage to Catherine of Aragon, Henry broke away from the Catholic Church in 1525. Nine years later, the British parliament passed the Act of Supremacy, declaring Henry Head of the Church of England.

For some British Protestants, the Church of England was just as corrupt as the Roman Catholic Church. These Protestants were called Puritans, because they advocated purifying English Christianity and reforming the Church of England. Their beliefs were rooted in Calvinistic theology, which emphasizes "God's sovereignty over the universe, predestination (election), and salvation by God's grace

---

* The Catholic Church says that when you have faith and perform good works, you will be saved. Luther said faith would save you and motivate you to perform good works.

    Luther expressed this concept as *Sola fide* (faith alone) and *Sola gratia* (grace alone): people are declared righteous before God by their faith alone, not by their works; and they are saved by God's grace alone, not by anything they did to earn salvation.

alone."[8] They also believed that "hard work was a Christian duty as well as a form of worship to God."[9]

After Henry VIII passed away, his son, Edward VI, became King of England. When Edward died at age 15, Henry's daughter, Mary Tudor, assumed the throne. Mary was a devout Catholic. She mended England's relationship with the Pope and reinstated Catholicism in England. She also brutally persecuted Protestants and burned hundreds of them to death, earning herself the nickname "Bloody Mary."

The persecution of Protestants lightened after Queen Elizabeth I came into power. She was raised Protestant, and knew only Protestants recognized the marriage of her mother, Lady Ann Boleyn, to King Henry VIII. In addition, her tutors, including Roger Ascham, were famous Cambridge humanists who supported the Protestant cause.

Although sympathetic to Protestants, Elizabeth never openly endorsed them because she was concerned that such an endorsement would further divide England.[10] Her priority was the peace and stability of the realm, so she advocated religious tolerance. She only resorted to the persecution of English Catholics when they threatened her rule. When the Protestant King James came to power after Elizabeth, religious persecution still existed, and Englishmen were still forbidden from worshiping outside of the Church of England.[11]

The Puritans believed they could establish God's Kingdom on Earth, but they disagreed on how. Some wanted to reform at home and called themselves "non-separating Puritans", and others who wanted to leave to found a new church called themselves "separating Puritans."

Non-separating Puritans. This group of Puritans tried to reform the Church of England and British politics from within. Several members became leading forces in the British Parliament in 1630 under the leadership of Oliver Cromwell. Cromwell believed in religious tolerance, except for Catholics.* King Charles I, the ruling monarch,

---

* It was a widespread view among Protestants that Catholics swore loyalty to a foreign prince—the Pope. Thus, Catholics can't be trusted. Cromwell didn't believe religious tolerance applied to Catholics. His army slaughtered many

preferred to rule without Parliament. He "alienated many people by his policies of raising extra-parliamentary taxes and imposing his Catholicized vision of Protestantism on the Church of England."[12] When Charles I was forced to reopen Parliament in 1640 because he wanted to raise taxes to finance a war, Cromwell led other Puritan members of Parliament to reject the king's request and bring up the issue of taxation vs. representation.* King Charles responded by dissolving Parliament. The dispute between the king and Parliament eventually led to a civil war between Royalists and Parliamentarians.[13]

Cromwell and the Parliamentarians wanted to reach a compromise with King Charles, but the king rejected any solution other than recognition of his divine power. After being tried for treason in 1649, King Charles was executed. Cromwell agonized over the king's execution, but firmly believed that when a king broke faith or his covenant with the people, "the king may be deposed."

After the king's execution, England became a republic, known as the Commonwealth of England from 1649 to 1653. Several English colonies later adopted the name "Commonwealth." Cromwell was credited with "laying the foundation for Parliamentary democracy."[14] The English Civil War and the idea of no taxation without representation would have a profound impact on the American Revolutionary War.

Unfortunately, power corrupted Cromwell. In 1653, he dissolved Parliament and became a Julius Caesar-style military dictator. After his death in 1658, Parliament restored Charles II as King of England. By then, England was largely a Protestant nation, but both Charles II and his brother James II took initiatives to promote religious tolerance toward Catholics. After James II's wife gave birth to their son, a group of James's Protestant opponents feared a Catholic succession to the

---

Irish Catholic soldiers and civilians at Drogheda and Wexford during the English Civil War (1642–1651). This atrocity left many Irish people with bitter memories that continue today.
Retrieved from
http://www.newworldencyclopedia.org/entry/Oliver_Cromwell

*History tends to repeat itself. Similar issues regarding taxation vs. representation led to America's war for independence against King George III in the 1700s.

crown. They therefore secretly invited William of Orange, husband of James II's Protestant daughter Mary, to invade England and oust his father-in-law. William landed in Devon in November 1688, and James fled to France. In 1689, the British Parliament formally offered William and Mary the throne as joint monarchs. This event was later known as the Glorious Revolution. It not only marked England's transition to the parliamentary rule we know today, but it also ensured the dominance of Protestantism in England.[15]

Separating Puritans. Not all Puritans wanted to reform from within the system. Many were eager to break away from the Church of England and physically settle—and establish God's Kingdom on Earth—somewhere else. John Winthrop, a Puritan minister and the future governor of Massachusetts, famously declared that the goal of migration to the New World was that: "We shall be as a city upon a hill, the eyes of all people are upon us."*

One subset of the separating Puritans, led by Reverend John Robinson, formed an independent congregation known as the Separatist church. In 1609, the Separatists migrated from England to the Netherlands, the new center of Europe after the discovery of a sea trade route to India. After 12 years, however, they were concerned that their children might become too Dutch, so they decided to migrate to the New World—a place with vast land, where they could have a fresh start and establish a new place, adhering to God's teachings.

The Separatists sent two representatives, Robert Cushman and John Carver, to London to secure a land patent in the existing Virginia colony. A London merchant, Thomas Weston, probably one of the earliest venture capitalists, led a group of investors and offered the Separatists a deal they couldn't refuse. The deal stipulated that everything the colonists produced would belong to a "commonwealth." At the end of seven years, everything would be equally divided between investors and colonists. Since the investors wanted to get their money back first, this deal forbade colonists from having any personal time to

---

* John Winthrop came to North America in 1630, later than the Separatists who boarded the *Mayflower*.

US History website. Retrieved from http://www.ushistory.org/us/3c.asp.

work on their private business during the seven-year contract term. The terms of this deal seem harsh today but are understandable if we put ourselves in these investors' shoes. It was a highly risky business. Lending money to a group of people traveling to a faraway land was a precarious proposition. There was no guarantee the travelers would make it, and even if they did, the investors would have no control over what happened next.

The representatives of the Separatist church accepted the deal without telling their congregation all the details.[16] In July, William Brewster, a church elder, led a group of pilgrims aboard the *Speedwell* and traveled from the Netherlands to England. When the pilgrims said goodbye to their families and loved ones, "Tears did gush from every eye, and pithy speeches pierced each other's heart, that sundry of the Dutch strangers that stood on the Key as spectators could not refrain from tears."[17]

In England, the *Speedwell* met a ship called the *Mayflower*, which carried another group of colonists hired by investors. The ships set out for the New World together on August 15, 1620. Unfortunately, the *Speedwell* started leaking shortly after the voyage began. After several failed repairs, they had to consolidate crews and passengers onto the *Mayflower*.[18] On September 6, the Mayflower departed from England with 102 passengers onboard, including 18 women.[19] Among them, only 44 were members of the Separatist church. These passengers called themselves the "Saints." They named the other passengers (a group that included tradesmen, servants, and adventurers)[20] the "Strangers."

The 66-day journey must have been excruciating for both groups. Not surprisingly, squabbles broke out. Fortunately, the Saints and Strangers didn't resort to violence (as far as we know). Maybe their survival instincts got the better of them. Probably, they realized that no matter how much they disliked one another, they had to depend on each other to survive in the New World, a "desolate wilderness, full of wild beasts and wild men," and that a mighty ocean "was now as a main bar or gulph to separate them from all the civil parts of the world."[21]

1.4 The Mayflower Compact

While the *Mayflower* was anchoring at Cape Cod for repairs, the two groups drew up an agreement establishing rules of conduct. On November 11, 1620, when they arrived at Provincetown Harbor, Plymouth Colony (what is now Massachusetts), 41 men out of the 102 passengers signed the agreement before leaving the ship.[22]

This agreement was later called the Mayflower Compact. The original document was lost; below is the modern version of the text based on a transcript by William Bradford.

In the name of God, Amen. We, whose names are underwritten, the Loyal Subjects of our dread Sovereign Lord King James, by the Grace of God, of Great Britain, France, and Ireland, King, defender of the Faith, etc.:

Having undertaken, for the Glory of God, and advancements of the Christian faith, and the honor of our King and Country, a voyage to plant the first colony in the Northern parts of Virginia; do by these presents, solemnly and mutually, in the presence of God, and one another; covenant and combine ourselves together into a civil body politic; **for our better ordering, and preservation and furtherance of the ends aforesaid; and by virtue hereof to enact, constitute, and frame, such just and equal laws, ordinances, acts, constitutions, and offices, from time to time, as shall be thought most meet and convenient for the general good of the colony; unto which we promise all due submission and obedience** [bold by author].

In witness whereof we have hereunto subscribed our names at Cape Cod the 11th of November, in the year of the reign of our Sovereign Lord King James, of England, France, and Ireland, the eighteenth, and of Scotland the fifty-fourth, 1620.

This compact has fewer words than Lincoln's Gettysburg address, but it sets the tone and foundation of what America was to become. The colonists agreed that in order to achieve the general good of the colony, they must create laws that offer equal protection to all, elect political officers to enforce the law, and promise their submission. Using this agreement, the settlers formed a governing body by consensus and elected their first governor.

The Mayflower Compact is an early embodiment of ideas that were later enshrined in the Declaration of Independence and U.S. Constitution: political order rests on consent; liberty can coexist with political order only as long as the political order is just and offers equal protection to all.

William Bradford (1590-1657), one of the signers of the Mayflower Compact, was an exemplary figure. He was born in Yorkshire, England, and demonstrated nonconformist religious susceptibility at a young age. At 17, he joined the Separatist church. In 1609, he emigrated to the Netherlands with the church congregation. In 1620, he and some fellow church members boarded the *Mayflower* bound for North America. He was a leading architect behind the Mayflower Compact. Later, he was unanimously voted governor of the Plymouth settlement.

The early settlers' lives were arduous. During the winter of 1620, only 44 out of the original 102 passengers survived. The survivors probably wondered whether it had been wise to come to the New World — and how long the rest of them would stay alive. Fortunately, an Indian named Squanto came to their rescue.

Squanto was no ordinary Indian. He had been captured by early settlers in 1610 and sold into slavery. A group of Catholic friars freed him and brought him to England, where he learned to speak English. In 1618, serving as an interpreter on an English ship, he was brought back to the New World. Since he couldn't find his own tribe, he chose to live in the woods alone around the Plymouth area until the *Mayflower* pilgrims arrived. Squanto taught the pilgrims how to plant and fish. He even brokered a peace treaty between the pilgrims and other Indian tribes. Without him, the pilgrims would never have survived and thrived. Many pilgrims thought Squanto was sent by God to help them. The fall of 1621 saw a great harvest. Indian tribes and pilgrims joined together for a harvest festival. The tradition later evolved into the Thanksgiving holiday.[23]

Even with the help of the Indians, the colonists had a hard time surviving. The communal social and economic structure that the investors demanded proved disastrous. Not all colonists were willing to work hard or work at all for the "common wealth." Bradford had to admit that "some do it not willingly, & others not honestly."[24] Many resented that whatever they produced went into a common pot and was divided among them equally. Knowing that at the end of the seven-year term, they were required to surrender half the wealth they'd accumulated to investors in England offered no incentive. Since not everyone was pulling the same weight, the colony was constantly running out of food. Jean Bodin pointed out: "For nothing could properly be regarded as public if there were nothing at all to distinguish it from what was private. Nothing can be thought of as shared in common, except by contrast with what is privately owned."[25]

Conceding the problem, Bradford wisely recognized that a change must take place. He gathered the settlers to a brainstorming session:

> So they began to think how they might raise as much corn as they could, and obtain a better crop than they had done, that they might not still thus languish in misery. At length, after much debate of things, the Governor (with the advice of the chiefest amongst them) gave way that they should set corn every man for his own particular, and in that regard trust to themselves; in all other things to go on in the general way as before. And so assigned to every family a parcel of land, according to the proportion of their number, for that end, only for present use (but made no division for inheritance) and ranged all boys and youth under some family.[26]

By turning the communal property into private property, the colony was transformed, in Bradford's words, into a

> Great success, for it made all hands very industrious, so as much more corn was planted than otherwise would have been by any means the Governor or any other could use, and saved him a great deal of trouble, and gave far better content. The women now went willingly into the field, and took their little ones with them to set corn; which before would allege

weakness and inability; whom to have compelled would have been thought great tyranny and oppression.[27]

William Bradford was re-elected governor of the Plymouth settlement 30 times, and served for all but five years until 1656. In addition to a long and successful political career, he wrote the book *Of Plymouth Plantation*, one of the most important early chronicles of the settlement of New England. His descendants include such well-known names as Noah Webster, Julia Child, and Supreme Court Chief Justice William Rehnquist.[28]

Between 1620 and 1640, America saw more English migrants arrive on the northeast coast and establish colonies in Massachusetts, Connecticut, Rhode Island, and New Hampshire—what we today refer to as the New England region. Not all the settlers were Puritan, but Puritans were the majority and the leading force of the new colonies. By the 1630s, almost 14,000 Puritans had emigrated to North America. Around the same time and thereafter, the Dutch set up settlements along the Hudson River and founded the city of New Amsterdam (now New York City);* the French established a stronghold along the Mississippi River and the Gulf Coast; Scottish, Irish, and German immigrants settled in Pennsylvania, Delaware, and Maryland. The only group of arrivals who were brought the New World completely against their will were enslaved people from Africa.† By 1770, there were 13 colonies, English language was the official language, and English law was the law of the land.

Although there was a clear separation between church and state and Christianity was never designated as an official religion, Christianity and Puritan ethics were central to America's identity. A final interesting story for all the history buffs: Following William Bradford's death on May 9, 1657, his manuscript *Of Plymouth Plantation* was

---

* The British captured New York from the Dutch in 1664.

† Since my objective is to write about history and issues of voluntary immigration, I won't explore the subject of slavery in this book. Nevertheless, slavery is an important part of our nation's history. There are many literary works and resources devoted to slavery. I highly encourage readers to explore this subject further on their own.

passed to his second son. After changing hands several generations later, the manuscript was nowhere to be found. Then in 1855, the manuscript reappeared in the library of Fulham Palace in London, the Bishop of London's residence. After a tremendous effort between the American Antiquarian Society, the Pilgrim Society, and the New England Society of New York, Ambassador Bayard brought the manuscript to a joint convention of both houses of the Commonwealth of Massachusetts on May 26, 1897.

U.S. Senator George Frisbie Hoar proclaimed that there's been nothing like Bradford's manuscript "in the annals since the Story of Bethlehem." He went on to promise that "Massachusetts will preserve it until the time shall come that her children are unworthy of it; and that time shall come—never."[29] This was more than a promise for the manuscript. It's a pledge on behalf of our nation—that we shall never forget where we came from and the great values passed down to us. We ought to do everything we can to ensure that we continue to be worthy of this great nation.

CHAPTER 2

Did Our Founders Support or Oppose Open-Border Immigration?

The early migration from England and other parts of Europe reached a peak at the beginning of the American Revolutionary War (1775-1783). The war naturally slowed down the influx of immigrants. At the birth of our new nation, under the fourth Article of Confederation, each state had its own jurisdiction on the naturalization of aliens.* The Articles of Confederation declared

> That the *free inhabitants* of each of these States, Paupers, vagabonds, and fugitives from justice excepted, shall be entitled to *all privileges and immunities* of *free citizens* in the several States; and the people of each State shall, in every other, enjoy *all the privileges of trade and commerce.*[30]

---

* The word "alien" comes from the Old French *alien*: "alien, strange, foreign; an alien, stranger, foreigner"; and from Latin *alienus* "of or belonging to another, foreign, alien, strange" — a word that also, as a noun, means a person owing allegiance to a country other than that in which he lives; foreigner.

This language was confusing, and, as James Madison remarked, it was "a fault in our system, and as laying a foundation for intricate and delicate questions."[31] Alexander Hamilton also expressed his concern that if "each state had power to prescribe a distinct rule, there could not be a uniform rule"[32] for our new nation. An alien in one state could be entitled to different rights and privileges in another state.

Furthermore, the founders expressed concern over the ease of foreign sailors' ability to vote in the U.S. Keep in mind that the 18th century was an age of exploration. Ships from Europe regularly carried thousands of sailors to U.S. harbors. Sailors often chose their own allegiances. Since most of them didn't bring papers to identify their citizenship, sea captains had no way to verify sailors' claims other than educated guesses based on their ship's design and the language and clothes of her crew. Consequently, there were documented instances of foreign sailors voting in local elections.

Our founders determined to correct this situation at the Constitutional Convention in 1787 by moving the nationalization power from individual states to the federal government, so Congress would "have power to establish a Uniform Rule of naturalization throughout the United States."[33] Our founders had very spirited debates on immigration principles and policies. Whether you are for or against immigration, you can probably easily find a quote or two from our founding fathers to bolster your position.

2.1 Where Exactly Did Our Founding Fathers Stand on Immigration?

Plenty of historical documents show that our founders generally supported immigration for ideological and practical reasons.

The ideological reason, stemming from the earlier English Puritan settlers' dream to establish a "city on the hill" as a beacon of hope for all, continued to be echoed by luminaries such as Thomas Jefferson and Thomas Paine, albeit in less religious tones. The founders wanted to establish a nation as the "admiration of the world" (Jefferson). Jefferson reminded King George III that,

Our ancestors, before their emigration to America, were the free inhabitants of the British dominions in Europe, and possessed a right, which nature has given to all men, of departing from the country in which chance, not choice has placed them, of going in quest of new habitations, and of there establishing new societies, under such laws and regulations as to them shall seem most likely to promote public happiness.[34]

Thomas Paine, an immigrant from England,* declared in his famous work *Common Sense* that America's destiny was to be "the asylum for the persecuted lovers of civil and religious liberty."

The practical reason for supporting immigration was that America was a vast land with plenty of resources that needed inhabitants and labor. Before the Revolutionary War, England's imperial economic system imposed restrictions on manufacturing in the U.S. and forced Americans to send raw materials back to England. In addition, English laws forbade the export of tools and technological know-how to America. In his *Report on the Subject of Manufactures*, Alexander Hamilton argued that the United States needed to develop domestic manufacturing to protect its freedom and break away from economic dependence on England. Hamilton was keenly aware that

Figure 2.1. Alexander Hamilton (1789-1795)

developing manufacturing requires skilled laborers. He looked to immigration to fill the labor void because "immigrants exhibit a large proportion of ingenious and valuable workmen, who by expatriating from Europe improved their own condition, and added to the industry and wealth of the United States."[35] James Madison also recognized the practical need for immigration. He pointed out that "America was indebted to immigration for her settlement and prosperity."

---

* Paine first immigrated to America in 1774. He went back to Europe (first to England and then to France) in 1787 and returned to America in 1802 at the invitation of Thomas Jefferson. He died in 1809 in New York City.

But the founders' support of immigration didn't mean they intended an open door for anyone. James Madison made that clear: "When we are considering the advantages that may result from an easy mode of naturalization, we ought also to consider the cautions necessary to guard against abuses."[36] From the very beginning, even in the absence of immigration law, the founders knew that America had to set boundaries. Their top three concerns were the qualifications, assimilation, and allegiance of newcomers.

2.2 The Qualifications of New Immigrants

There is little evidence that the founders advocated a free-for-all, open-door immigration policy. Instead, they emphasized the moral character and contribution that newcomers would bring. They said that moral character is important, because the "nation cannot long remain strong when each man in it is individually weak, and that neither social forms nor political schemes have yet been found that can make a people energetic by composing it of pusillanimous and soft citizens" (Tocqueville). Not only should the new migrants have good moral character; they should also place "high importance to the respectability and character of the American name" and do their best to "preserve its good fame from injury."[37] The founders didn't want convicts and criminals as new immigrants.*

George Washington preferred skilled new immigrants, such as "useful mechanics and some particular descriptions of men or professions."[38] James Madison wanted the "worthy part of mankind to come and settle amongst us," so they can "increase the wealth and strength of the community; and those who acquire the rights of citizenship, without adding to the strength or wealth of the community are not the people we are in want of."[39]

---

* Based on quotes by Mr. Burke at the rule of naturalization debate: "There is another class also that I would interdict, that is, the convicts and criminals which they pour out of British jails. I wish sincerely some mode could be adopted to prevent the importation of such; but that, perhaps, is not in our power; the introduction of them ought to be considered as a high misdemeanor."

Retrieved from http://press-pubs.uchicago.edu/founders/print_documents/a1_8_4_citizenships8.html.

How can a new immigrant increase wealth and strength of the community? Mr. Lawrence, one of Madison's compatriots, clarified that:

> Every person who comes among us must do one or the other; if he brings money, or other property with him, he evidently increases the general mass of wealth, and if he brings an able body, his labor will be productive of national wealth, and an addition to our domestic strength. Consequently, every person, rich or poor, must add to our wealth and strength, in a greater or less degree.[40]

2.3 Assimilation is Both Necessary and Important

The United States was founded upon specific ideas and moral principles, as expressed by the eloquent words of the Declaration of Independence. Thomas Jefferson believed that "it is for the happiness of those united in society to harmonize as much as possible in matters which they must of necessity transact together."[41] He feared that if new immigrants affixed to different ideas, "with their language, they will transmit to their children. In proportion to their numbers, they will share with us the legislation. They will infuse into it their spirit, warp and bias its direction, and tender it a heterogeneous, incoherent, distracted mass."[42]

Benjamin Franklin shared Jefferson's concerns. Some people today accuse Benjamin Franklin of being anti-immigration because of the disparaging words he said about German immigrants. In fact, Franklin was anything but—he was the one who published the first German newspaper in America, the *Philadelphische Zeitung,* in 1732.[43] Franklin wasn't against immigration; he was concerned that a lack of assimilation would be harmful to immigrants' happiness and damning to the unity and longevity of the republic.

George Washington expressed a similar concern—that it is not beneficial for America if immigrants congregate and "retain their language, habits and principles (good or bad) which they bring with them."[44] Instead, he firmly believed that new immigrants, "by an intermixture with our people, they, or their descendants, get assimilated to our customs, measures and laws: in a word, soon become one people."[45]

2.4 Allegiance to America is Both Essential and Imperative

No matter what drives them to America, some immigrants may retain residual loyalty to their countries of birth and cultures. To become Americans, the founders believed that immigrants needed to give up prior allegiances and pledge an oath of fidelity to the U.S. because, in Alexander Hamilton's words,

> The safety of a republic depends essentially on the energy of a common national sentiment; on a uniformity of principles and habits; on the exemption of citizens from foreign bias and prejudice; and on the love of country which will almost invariably be found to be closely connected with birth, education, and family.[46]

John Quincy Adams, in an 1819 letter to Moritz von Furstenwarther, a German citizen who was considering moving to the U.S. and had asked Adams for a job, stated that the U.S. is a land "not of privileges, but of equal rights." Thus, Adams warned Furstenwarther that new immigrants like him

> Must cast off the European skin, never to resume it. They must look forward to their posterity, rather than backward to their ancestors; they must be sure that whatever their own feelings may be, those of their children will cling to the prejudices of this country, and will partake of that proud spirit.[47]

2.5 Citizenship Needs to Be Earned, Not Granted Cheaply

While some founders believed an oath of allegiance and a declaration to stay in America were sufficient, others didn't want to give out citizenship too cheaply. They pointed out that some foreign sailors had voted for assembly elections in Philadelphia after taking oaths of allegiance—and had then left America, having never had any intention of remaining. This kind of practice not only results in election fraud but also threatens the "safety of a republic" (Hamilton) because a foreigner who rejects American principles and ideas would vote accordingly. Therefore, some founders deemed "some security for their [immigrants'] fidelity and allegiance were requisite besides the bare oath."[48] The additional security the founders sought was property ownership or residency. Property ownership has been used to distinguish citizens from aliens since the Roman Empire.* Some founders wanted to "see the title of a citizen of America as highly venerated and respected as was that of a citizen of old Rome."[49]

During the Philadelphia Constitutional Convention, the majority of the founders regarded it as essential that an individual have a period of residency in the U.S. prior to gaining citizenship. Residency achieved two purposes:

> First, that he should have an opportunity of knowing the circumstances of our Government, and in consequence thereof, shall have admitted the truth of the principles we hold. Second, that he shall have acquired a taste for this kind of Government. And in order that both these things may take place, in such a full manner as to make him worthy of admission into our society.[50]

How long the residency should be was debated extensively. Some suggested two years, while others suggested five years or even longer. But all agreed the residency requirement should be long enough to "give a man an opportunity of esteeming the Government from knowing its intrinsic value, was essentially necessary to assure us of a man's becoming a good citizen."[51]

Hamilton, the most famous immigrant to America, opposed limiting any congressional office to either native-born Americans or immigrants who met the residency requirement. People suspected later that he was trying to make himself eligible for the U.S. presidency. Hamilton's actual argument at the Constitutional Convention

---

* In the early days of the Roman Empire, the Roman army consisted of only citizens who owned land. The Romans believed that an army made up of property owners would fight harder because they were protecting their property.

showed he was more concerned about ordinary immigrants. He pointed out, "Persons in Europe of moderate fortunes will be fond of
coming here, where they will be on a level with the first citizens. I
move that the section be so altered as to require merely citizenship and
inhabitancy."[52] The majority overruled Hamilton's proposal by requiring future U.S. House Representatives to meet a seven-year residency
requirement, U.S. Senators a nine-year residency, and presidents a
fourteen-year residency.

2.6 The Uniform Rule of Naturalization of 1790

These discussions among the founders finally led to the first naturalization law in our nation's history — the Uniform Rule of Naturalization
of 1790. The law contained fewer than 260 words and set simple but
effective criteria for U.S. citizenship. It stated that "any Alien being a
free white person" can become a U.S. citizen if the person had resided
"within the limits and under the jurisdiction of the United States for
the term of two years," could prove that he or she was "a person of
good character," and took a court-administered oath. This law also
spelled out the citizenship status of children of naturalized citizens. It
stated that the children of a naturalized citizen who resided in the U.S.
and were younger than 21 years of age should be considered U.S. citizens when their parent was. The children of U.S. citizens who were
born outside the U.S. were to be considered as natural born citizens,
except "that the right of citizenship shall not descend to persons whose
fathers have never been residents in the United States."[53]

1794 was the year the new nation faced the challenges of dealing
with immigrants on two fronts. On one side, was the influx of refugees
from France. After the French Revolution turned into a wholesale killing of aristocrats, many French refugees escaped to the U.S. One in
every ten residents of Philadelphia was French, and most of them had
lost their wealth and prestige. There were no government refugee
resettlement programs back then, but many Americans, including
Hamilton and his wife, Eliza, stepped up and organized relief efforts.

The other challenge came from Western Pennsylvania's Scottish
and Irish immigrants, who rose in armed rebellion against the new
federal government's whiskey tax, an excise tax on domestic distilled

spirits. The whiskey tax was highly unpopular, and the rebels used violence to intimidate tax collectors. President Washington and Treasury Secretary Hamilton had to raise a federal militia to suppress the Whiskey Rebellion. Fortunately, both men exercised great restraint and quashed the rebellion without causing much bloodshed. Nevertheless, according to Hamilton's biographer, Ron Chernow, this event became a turning point in Hamilton's attitude towards immigrants. Hamilton had advocated unrestricted immigration before, but he began to think some restrictions were necessary after the Whiskey Rebellion.

Our nation's first immigration law, the Uniform Rule of Naturalization of 1790, was repealed five years later, in 1795, when George Washington was in his second term as President of the United States. The Naturalization Act of 1795 increased the residency requirement from two to five years. In addition, a person who wished to become a U.S. citizen was required to renounce any foreign "title or order of nobility" and "renounce forever all allegiance and fidelity to any foreign prince, potentate, state, or sovereignty whatever, and particularly, by name, the prince, potentate, state or sovereignty and whereof such alien may, at that time, be a citizen or subject."[54] Since Washington was keen on ensuring every migrant who came to the U.S. became part of one people—Americans, he regarded demanding immigrants give up former loyalties as a must.

The naturalization law of 1795 kept the phrase "free white person," which many people today would find offensive or at least troubling. However, it is essential to keep it in its historical perspective. Yes, our founders had their historical limitations and biases. But that shouldn't diminish the nobility of their efforts to live up to a lofty ideal: that the U.S. is a sanctuary for all who embrace liberty and self-government. The laws of 1790 and 1795 were probably the most progressive at the time they were passed because they didn't deny anyone's application for U.S. citizenship based on gender, religion, social class, or birth. All they looked for in immigrants were people with good character and ability—attributes that would preserve the unified national character and enhance national well-being in addition to immigrants' well-being. The racial bias in the law was a blemish that only four scores and seven years later, we as a nation fought a bloody civil war and passed several constitutional amendments to remedy.

For some African Americans, relief came as early as 1796. When Britain and France went to war in 1793, Britain's Royal Navy turned to impressments to fill the shortage of sailors. Even George Washington's kinsman, Charles Lewis, an American citizen and a sailor, was impressed. The impressments of American citizens prompted the creation of custom house protection certificates in 1796. These certificates "marked something new in the Atlantic world: the wide dissemination of national identity documentation to ordinary people."[55] These certificates were issued to all American sailors, including thousands of black sailors, because "the value of sailors to the nation made it crucial to look past race and birthplace—even to look past enslavement—in order to enfold these men within the state's protection."[56]

Like a baby who tries to learn how to walk, setbacks followed every time our new nation made some progress. Partisan spats between the Federalist Party and Jeffersonian Republicans reached a high point during John Adams's presidency (1797-1801). During the 1790s, the number of newspapers in America more than doubled. Both the Federalist Party (led by Alexander Hamilton and John Adams) and the Republican Party (led by Thomas Jefferson and James Madison) employed the press to promote vicious attacks against political opponents. Some of the language they used to attack each other would never make it to publication in modern times. Abigail Adams, the wife of President John Adams and one of the most enlightened women in that era, considered the people in the press who were against her husband "traitors" to America.

Since new immigrants, especially non-English ethnic groups, had been among the core supporters of the Democratic-Republicans in 1796, Abigail demanded "a more careful and attentive watch out to be kept over foreigners."[57] Even Hamilton wanted to slow down the flow of new immigrants. It was true, then as now, that even enlightened people could have a hard time dealing with dissenting voices despite revering freedom of speech as an "inalienable" right.

America's undeclared naval war with France in 1798 gave the Federalists a convenient excuse. The U.S. Congress, dominated by the Federalists, passed the Alien and Sedition Acts, which consisted of a series of bills that were signed into law by President John Adams. The most notable bills included the following:

- **The Naturalization Act of 1798**, which increased the residency requirement for U.S. citizenship from five years to fourteen years.

- **The Alien Friends Act**, which authorized the president to deport, without hearing, any resident immigrant considered "dangerous to the peace and safety of the United States."[58]

- **The Alien Enemy Act**, which authorized the president to apprehend and deport resident aliens if their home countries were at war with the United States of America.

- An additional act that made it a crime to "write, print, utter, or publish . . . any false, scandalous and malicious writing" against the government and government officials.[59]

Even though the Alien and Sedition Acts were passed in the name of national security (an argument often cited today), many believed the real intent of the Acts was to strengthen the Federalist Party and weaken the Democratic-Republican Party by curbing an influx of Irish immigrants who tended to vote for the Democratic-Republican Party. Congressman Harrison Gray Otis of Boston, a Federalist, famously declared that America should no longer "wish to invite hordes of wild Irishmen, nor the turbulent and disorderly parts of the world, to come here with a view to disturb our tranquility after having succeeded in the overthrow of their own governments."[60]

These Acts marked the first time, but certainly not the last time, that immigration laws and laws regarding foreigners were enacted for political purposes. Rather than advancing liberty for all and strengthening the American ideals the founders held so dearly at the birth of our nation, the immigration law was used to promote a political party's interests.

The worst feature of the Alien and Sedition Acts was that they allowed the government to punish anyone who did "write, print, utter, or publish . . . any false, scandalous and malicious writing" against the government. This language was clearly unconstitutional because it violated the First Amendment. Even the leader of the Federalist Party, Alexander Hamilton, protested to Treasury Secretary Wolcott, saying, "I hope sincerely the thing may not be hurried through. Let us not establish a tyranny."[61] James Madison, one of the leaders of the Democratic-Republican Party and the Father of our Constitution, called the Alien and Sedition Acts "a monster that must forever disgrace its parents."[62] The first victim of this Act was none other than Benjamin Franklin Bache, the grandson of Benjamin Franklin and publisher of the *Aurora*. He was arrested for "libeling the president and executive government in a manner tending to excite sedition and opposition to the law."[63] The Alien and Sedition Acts were so un-American that most of the country was uneasy about them

Some states, such as Virginia and Kentucky, declared the Alien and Sedition Acts invalid in their states.* John Adams lost his second presidential run to Thomas Jefferson in 1801. The Naturalization Act of 1798 was repealed in 1802. Jefferson and Madison's victory on this front shows that although our nation drifts away from its founding principles from time to time, we have the ability to self-correct and get back on the right path.

---

* Jefferson drafted the resolution for the Kentucky legislature, and Madison did the same for Virginia.

CHAPTER 3

The 19th Century:

"Give me your tired, your poor,

Your huddled masses yearning to breathe free"

After Thomas Jefferson became President of the United States in 1801, he advocated for a revision of the naturalization policy. Jefferson agreed that "a residence shall be required sufficient to develop character and design [of the immigrant]," but he deemed the 14-year residency requirement, enacted by the naturalization law of 1795, too harsh. In his annual message to Congress in December 1801, Jefferson stated:

> Considering the ordinary chances of human life, a denial of citizenship under a residence of fourteen years is a denial to a great proportion of those who ask it, and controls a policy pursued from their first settlement by many of these States, and still believed of consequence to their prosperity.

Jefferson reminded Congress of the unique role America plays by asking, "Shall we refuse the unhappy fugitives from distress that hospitality which the savages of the wilderness extended to our fathers arriving in this land? Shall oppressed humanity find no asylum on this globe?" While he advocated for America's role as a sanctuary for humanity, Jefferson didn't support open borders. Instead, he wisely affirmed that restrictions should be put in place "to guard against the fraudulent usurpation of our flag; an abuse which brings so much embarrassment and loss on the genuine citizen, and so much danger to the nation of being involved in war, that no endeavor should be spared to detect and suppress it."[64]

With Jefferson's support, Congress passed the Naturalization Act of 1802, which reduced the residency requirement for naturalization from fourteen years to five. This new law required immigrants who wished to become naturalized citizens to give a three-year period of notice of intent to renounce their allegiances to foreign sovereigns, foreign princes, and any hereditary titles or nobility.[65] Like all past immigration laws, the new immigration act also asked prospective citizens to demonstrate their "good moral character." Unfortunately, the new law kept the language that restricted any prospective citizen to "a free white person."

There was no explicit education requirement under the 1802 Act except that it required applicants to show "attachment to the principles of the Constitution." Since local courts administered naturalization, local judges had plenty of leeway to determine how they wanted to quiz an aspiring applicant for citizenship Since local courts administered naturalization, local judges had plenty of leeway to determine how they wanted to quiz an aspiring applicant for citizenship. Some judges would probe an applicant's knowledge of the U.S. Constitution, history, and civics in an open court, and the applicant had to give oral answers.[66] This later evolved into the civics test, which is an integral part of the naturalization process today.

The Naturalization Act of 1802 governed the United States for several decades. No other major immigration act was enacted until 1882. During this period, especially in the second half of the 19th century, America's policy towards immigration and the American people's attitude toward immigrants were contradictory, shaped by powerful forces such as the Civil War, the westward expansion, post-war urbanization and industrial revolution, and a more centralized and powerful federal government.[67]

For example, during the Civil War, the U.S. government encouraged immigration as a means to replace men enlisted in the army. After the conclusion of the Civil War, many in the federal government felt they had not only won the war, but had also gained indisputable moral authority to apply sweeping policy changes. Congress passed the 13th Amendment in January 1865 to abolish slavery and involuntary servitude in the U.S., except as a punishment for crime.* The 13th Amendment was ratified by the required number of states in December 1865.

Congress then passed the Civil Rights Act of 1866, with nearly unanimous Republican support, to protect the essential rights of former slaves. The 1866 Act contains a vital citizenship clause, which states "that all persons born in the United States and not subject to any foreign power, excluding Indians not taxed, are hereby declared to be citizens of the United States."[68] President Andrew Johnson vetoed the Act with the assertion that giving black citizenship was no different than "favor of the colored and against the white race."[69] Nevertheless, the Republican-led Congress had enough votes to override him.

Concerned that the Civil Rights Act of 1866 might be struck down as unconstitutional, the same Republican-led Congress passed the 14th Amendment to the Constitution, which declares that "all persons born or naturalized in the United States, and subject to the jurisdiction thereof, are citizens of the United States and of the State wherein they reside." The politicians who created this Amendment probably didn't foresee many heated debates about this sentence's meaning later. But no doubt, many future immigrants from other races and regions benefited from this birthright citizenship clause and became U.S. citizens.

---

* The original text of the 13th Amendment: "Neither slavery nor involuntary servitude, except as a punishment for crime whereof the party shall have been duly convicted, shall exist within the United States, or any place subject to their jurisdiction."

Retrieved from the website of the Library of Congress:
www.loc.gov/rr/program/bib/ourdocs/13thamendment.html.

From 1790 to 1870, the U.S. saw an immigrant surge, with an estimated nine million immigrants arriving. "The census of 1860 revealed that there were slightly more foreign-born residents — 4,138,697 — than there were slaves, a rise of nearly 2,000,000 since 1850."[70] By the end of 1870, the immigration population was about 14.4% of the U.S. population. In 1870 alone, the U.S. received 387,000 immigrants, which was equal to over 1% of the U.S. population. The majority of the immigrants came from Ireland, Germany, and China. Let's explore these three groups' immigration histories in more detail.

3.1 A Brief History of German Immigrants

The Germans were among the earliest European settlers in America. Historical evidence confirms that several German immigrants were among the English colonists in Jamestown in 1602.[71] Written records show that "on October 6, 1683, thirteen Quaker families from Krefeld arrived in Philadelphia. From the outset, their settlement on the northern outskirts of Philadelphia was called Germantown."[72] From then on, small groups of German immigrants, most belonging to the Lutheran and Reformed churches, continued settling in America, mainly congregating in the Philadelphia area. Today, many German Americans commemorate October 6 as German-American Day. Almost every major U.S. city celebrates the traditional German fall festival Oktoberfest, serving plenty of beer and German food like bratwurst and knockwurst.

But back in the 17th century, the concentration of German immigrants in Pennsylvania caused alarm for the English-speaking colonists, including Benjamin Franklin. Franklin was brutally honest about his frustration with some German immigrants' resistance to assimilation. He wrote, "I am not against the admission of Germans in general, for they have their Virtues, their industry and frugality is exemplary; They are excellent husbandmen and contribute greatly to the improvement of a Country."[73] One of the Germans' noticeable contributions was the Conestoga wagon, which was designed and built by German immigrants and helped in the opening of the American frontier. By 1790, German immigrants made up 8.8% of the U.S. population; in Philadelphia, they made up 33% of the population.

One prominent German immigrant was John Jacob Astor (1763-1848). Astor left his village of Waldorf in Germany and arrived in the United States in 1784 with $25 and seven flutes. In a typical rags-to-riches American story, he became wealthy through trading fur; by the time he passed away, he had left a fortune worth $25 million. Another prominent German businessman was Henry J. Heinz, born in Pittsburgh in 1844, the son of a German immigrant from Kallstadt. He went on to found the food giant Heinz, which is known today for its ketchup and spaghetti sauce. He credited his business success to lessons he'd learned from his parents, such as being thrifty and avoiding waste. He famously said, "To do a common thing uncommonly well brings success."

By the 1860s, there were over two million German immigrants in the U.S. After many working-age American men enlisted in the Union Army to fight the Civil War, there was a worker shortage. Thus, the federal government encouraged immigrants under labor contracts to work in the U.S. agriculture industry. German immigrants were desirable due to their knowledge and experience in farming. U.S. railroad companies often had large land grants available, so they advertised in German cities to attract farmers to the U.S., promising them cheap transportation and farmland sales on easy terms. The Santa Fe railroad hired its own commissioner for immigration and sold over 300,000 acres to German-speaking farmers.[74] While most German immigrants congregated in the Midwest, in cities like Cincinnati and St. Louis, some migrated to the West and settled in Nebraska and Colorado, incentivized by the Homestead Act of 1862, which allowed "any U.S. citizen, or intended citizen, who had never borne arms against the U.S. Government could file an application and lay claim to 160 acres of surveyed Government land."[75]

German immigrants were active in civic life too. Politicians had long recognized the importance of capturing German immigrants' votes.

In the 1840s, it was the general practice to advertise in the German papers of New York just before the Election Day that all Germans wishing to be naturalized should apply to the German committee of Tammany Hall, where they would receive their citizenship papers gratis.[76]

One of the prominent German immigrants during this time was Hermann Raster. He published anti-slavery pamphlets and was the editor of the *New York Abendzeitung*, the most influential German-language newspaper in America at the time. An active member of the Republican Party, he helped convince German Americans across the United States to vote for Abraham Lincoln.

Most German immigrants were anti-slavery. German immigrants were the largest immigrant group to volunteer to fight for the Union Army in the American Civil War. At the beginning of the Civil War, Brigadier General Samuel R. Curtis, commander of the newly formed military of the District of Southwest Missouri, appointed Franz Sigel as his second-in-command, in charge of the 1st and 2nd Divisions, which were made up overwhelmingly of German immigrants.

Sigel was the highest-ranking German officer in the Union Army, and his appointment was no coincidence. He graduated from the Karlsruhe Military Academy and participated in the failed revolutionary movements in Germany in 1849. Though the Battle of Pea Ridge (1862) showed that Sigel wasn't a military genius, he kept being shuttled around to divisions with large numbers of German immigrants due to his popularity with German-speaking soldiers and the immense political influence associated with such popularity. The federal government and Union Army leaders recognized "Sigel's symbolic importance to the large German population in the North."[77]

Political maneuvers or not, Sigel and German-speaking soldiers demonstrated their patriotism to this new nation. When a German farmer's son in the 94th Ohio regiment heard that his sister was dating someone who supported slavery, he wrote to their mother, who blessed the relationship:

Shame on you all abuse your dear son for fighting for your liberty, why did you leave germina and come to this country . . . you would do better to go back to germina and liver there . . . it appears you are dissatisfied with a free government . . . I shall never want to see any of my relations that worked against me while I was in the surves.[78]

After the Civil War, some German immigrants moved to the South. There, they made up the "largest bloc of immigrant Southern Republicans."[79] They elected a German refugee and critic of the Confederacy and slavery, Edward Degener, as a Republican U.S. House Representative from Texas in 1866.

In the late 19th century, it was common for wealthy American students to go to Germany to experience German universities' cutting-edge learning and research models. In 1876, Johns Hopkins University was founded and modeled after Germany's Heidelberg University. Johns Hopkins was the first university to integrate research and teaching. Other prestigious American universities quickly followed suit and jointly brought the modern German education model to America.

Probably no one summarized the appreciation of German immigrants better than Fredrick Douglass. In one of his famous speeches in 1869, he said:

> To no class of our population are we more indebted to valuable qualities of head, heart and hand than the German. Say what we will of their lager, their smoke and their metaphysics they have brought to us a fresh, vigorous and child-like nature; a boundless facility in the acquisition of knowledge; a subtle and far reaching intellect, and a fearless love of truth. Though remarkable for patient and laborious thought the true German is a joyous child of freedom, fond of manly sports, a lover of music, and a happy man generally. Though he never forgets that he is a German, he never fails to remember that he is an American.[80]

German immigration to the U.S. continued steadily until the early 20th century. The two world wars and the Immigration Act of 1924 limited the influx of immigrants in general. Between 1950 and 1960, however, more than a quarter million new German immigrants came to America. Today, about 49 million Americans claim some German ancestry,[81] including the 2016 presidential candidate Donald Trump, whose paternal grandfather, Friedrich Trump, immigrated from Kallstadt, Germany, in 1885 at age 16. Friedrich arrived in the U.S. without passport. He probably would never have become a naturalized U.S. citizen had his grandson been in the White House in 1885.

3.2 A Brief History of Irish Immigrants

Just like the Germans, Irish immigrants started settling in America in colonial times. Charles Carroll of Carrollton, grandson of a wealthy early Irish settler, was one of the signers of the Declaration of Independence. Between 1820 and 1860, the Irish constituted over one-third of all immigrants to the United States.[82] The city of Boston was called the "Dublin of America" because one in every three people living there was Irish. During the Irish Potato Famine (1845-1852), over one million Irish migrants came to the U.S., three-quarters settling in New York City. Immigrants tended to congregate in big cities because the Industrial Revolution helped turn these cities into booming economic centers, where employment opportunities were abundant. Unfortunately, not everyone in the big cities thrived. Many Irish immigrants were poor and uneducated, so they lived in slums. Their presence exacerbated the poverty problem in U.S. cities.

In the 19th century, government welfare support for the poor was nonexistent. Private charities' relief operations were limited in terms of both scale and duration, because the popular belief was that too much assistance would undermine independence, as a governmental injunction issued in 1865 declared: "A man who can work has no right to support by the government. No really respectable person wishes to be supported by others."[83] Americans in the 19th century viewed the cause and thus the cure of poverty very differently than Americans today — "They tended to see moral failings as the root cause of squalor and to insist that religion, temperance, and thrift were the cures" (Ronald G. Walters).[84] Thus, some native-born Americans looked down on poor Irish immigrants or were even outright hostile.

James McPherson wrote about immigrants in the 1850s in his book *Battle Cry of Freedom*:

> Immigration during the first five years of the 1850s reached a level five times greater than a decade earlier. Most of the new arrivals were poor Catholic peasants or laborers from Ireland and Germany who crowded into the tenements of large cities. Crime and welfare costs soared. Cincinnati's crime rate, for example, tripled between 1846 and 1853 and its murder rate increased sevenfold. Boston's expenditures for poor relief rose threefold during the same period.[85]

Native-born Americans often regarded these immigrants as unwanted competition for jobs, especially low-paying jobs. In addition, many Americans viewed Irish Catholic immigrants as threats to the republic's values because they feared Catholics would be more loyal to the Pope than to the president.

The rising population of Irish immigrants prompted a nativist movement. A group of anti-immigrants, native-born Americans formed the Native American Party, commonly known as the Know Nothing Party, because their party members' standard reply to questions about their activities was, "I know nothing about it." The Know Nothing Party advocated severe restrictions on immigration, the exclusion of the foreign-born from voting or holding public office in the U.S., and a 21-year residency requirement for citizenship. In addition, they argued that the nation's business owners should employ true Americans by denying employment to immigrants. Riding popular anti-immigrant sentiment, the Know Nothing Party won several local and congressional elections. It nominated Millard Fillmore as its presidential candidate for the 1856 election. Fillmore lost the election, carrying only one state: Maryland. The party hastily declined after that.

Yet, the anti-Irish sentiment didn't swiftly disappear. "Throughout America, anti-Irish sentiment was becoming fashionable. Newspaper advertisements for jobs and housing in Boston, New York, and other places routinely ended with 'Positively No Irish Need Apply'."[86] Sometimes, discrimination against the Irish turned into violence. For example, during a riot in 1831, St. Mary's Catholic Church in New York City was burned down. In 1844, riots in Philadelphia left 13 Irish immigrants dead.

At other times, discrimination against Irish Catholics was more disguised. A good example pertains to public education reform. Prior to 1860, wealthy kids either went to private schools or were taught by private tutors, while kids from families of lesser economic means went to public schools by either paying fees or being accepted on a charitable basis. By 1860, free public-school education had become widely supported by Americans, who saw the increasing presence of immigrants as threatening the republic with declining virtue. Naturally, some viewed education as the answer to indoctrinating immigrants with Protestant moral values. In 19th-century America, public schools were religious and dominated by Protestant teachings. Reading the Bible, reciting Protestant prayers, and singing Protestant hymns were mandatory activities for all students. Not surprisingly, new Catholic Irish immigrants opposed compulsory Protestant teachings in public schools. They regarded the public schools "as bastions of middle-class Protestantism," because "the Bible used [in public schools], and the theology, were Protestant — a fact that angered Catholics."[87]

Catholics resisted, and their efforts to preserve their faith elicited harsh responses from native-born American Protestants. There are many accounts of Catholic children being harassed, beaten, or even expelled for refusing to read Protestant Bibles or say Protestant prayers. To preserve their faith and educate their youth the way they wanted, Catholic immigrants started their own schools and pleaded for a portion of public funds, just as Protestant schools received. This prompted the Protestant majority to seek legislative measures to preserve the Protestant nature of the public schools.

In 1875, Congressman James Blaine proposed a constitutional amendment to exclude government funding from schools that taught "sectarian" faiths. Anthony R. Picarello, Jr., Vice President and General Counsel of the Becket Fund for Religious Liberty, explained that "the term *sectarian* both expressed and implemented hostility to the faiths of those immigrants (especially, but not only, Catholics) who resisted assimilation to the *nonsectarian* Protestantism then taught as the *common faith* in the *common schools*."[88] Even the U.S. Supreme Court recognized that "it was an open secret that 'sectarian' was code for 'Catholic'."[89] Although this amendment failed to pass the U.S. Congress, 38 states adopted it in their constitutions. Many people today are probably unaware of the discriminatory nature of the Blaine Amendments. As a matter of fact, groups who are against school choice regularly rely on the Blaine Amendments as their legal basis.

For example, in 2015, the Colorado Supreme Court ruled against a scholarship program in Douglas County Public Schools that would allow students to use scholarships to attend schools (religious or non-religious) of their parents' choosing. The court reasoned that the possibility of public funds being used for religious-affiliated schools violated Colorado's Blaine Amendment. Considering the historical context and the discriminating nature of the Blaine Amendment, this ruling is truly regrettable!*

Despite these discriminations, more than 150,000 Irish immigrants, many of whom were not yet U.S. citizens, demonstrated their unequivocal love for their adopted home by enlisting in the Union Army during the Civil War. They formed the famous "Irish Brigade," made up of only-Irish infantries: the 63rd, 69th, and 88th New York Infantry regiments. In 1862, the 28th Massachusetts Infantry Regiment and 116th Pennsylvania Infantry Regiment were added. The Irish Brigade was known for its valor in many Civil War battles and suffered heavy casualties. When Robert E. Lee observed the 69th Irish

Figure 3.1. Irish Brigade Memorial, Antietam

---

* The U.S. Supreme Court vacated the Colorado Supreme Court's ruling against vouchers in June 2017. But, Douglas County's newly-elected anti-voucher school board canceled the voucher program and dismissed the case entirely on January 25, 2018.

Infantry, led by Irish hero Thomas Francis Meagher,* launching charge after charge during the battle at Fredericksburg, Lee called them "The Fighting 69th." The Fighting 69th marched under an emerald banner with these words: "They shall not retreat from the clash of spears."

Many Irish soldiers fought fearlessly because they saw a parallel between defending the union and their historic fight against the British in Ireland. A young Irish soldier of the 28th Massachusetts Infantry regiment wrote to his wife in 1863:

> This is my country as much as the man who was born on the soil ... I have as much interest in the maintenance of ... the integrity of the nation as any other man ... Irishmen and their descendents [sic] have ... a stake in (this) nation ... America is Irelands refuge Irelands last hope destroy this republic and her hopes are blasted.[90]

He gave his young life to this new nation in 1864. If you visit Antietam Battlefield today, you will find a monument dedicated to the Irish Brigade. The front of the monument shows the charge of the regiment, and the reverse side shows a bas-relief of General Thomas Francis Meagher.

After the Civil War, Irish immigrants gradually improved their economic situation as well as their political influence. Political patronage was prevalent in 19th-century America. Tammany Hall, a Democratic political organization in New York, played a key role in not only helping Irish immigrants rise in American politics but also helping eager politicians secure immigrants' votes, sometimes by means of political corruption. Generations of "bosses" of Tammany Hall became the king-makers in New York City and New York State. Politicians made sure to capture Irish votes by making the naturalization of Irish

---

* Thomas Francis Meagher was one of the leaders who led the fight against the British. He immigrated to the U.S. in 1852. He joined another Irish American, Michael Corcoran, to lead the Irish regiment during the Civil War. He became Corcoran's successor after Corcoran was captured, and commanded the Irish regiment until 1863. After the war, Meagher died mysteriously while serving as Secretary of Montana Territory. If you want to know more about him, I recommend the book *The Immortal Irishman* by Timothy Egan.

immigrants so easy that sometimes "Irish immigrants landing in the morning might be voters by nightfall."[91] The most notorious case occurred right before New York City's 1868 election. William M. Tweed, boss of Tammany Hall, ensured "between 20,000 and 30,000 [Irish immigrants] were naturalized in New York City courts in the six weeks before the election. Both Democrats and Republicans paid the necessary fees. One judge naturalized over 10,000 in two weeks."[92]

Tweed eventually went to jail in 1873 after he was exposed for defrauding New York City of at least $365 million in today's dollars.[93] His political demise didn't bring down Tammany Hall entirely. Tammany Hall played a strong political hand until the 1930s and ceased to exist in the 1950s.

The post-Civil War economic boom in America attracted more immigrants. In 1886, the French people gave the American people a wonderful gift—the Statue of Liberty. It was dedicated on October 28, 1886, at Liberty Island. From then on, the Statue was a symbol of freedom and the United States, and a welcoming sign to many immigrants. In 1890, President Benjamin Harrison designated Ellis Island, near York Harbor, a federal immigration station. On January 1, 1892, Annie Moore, an Irish teenager, became the first immigrant processed at Ellis Island. After a grueling two-week sea journey, the sight of the Statue of Liberty near Ellis Island must have been a comforting sign to her and her two young brothers.[94]

From 1892 to 1954, more than 12 million immigrants were processed through Ellis Island, among them a young man named Gibbon Raleigh.

Gibbon was born in the village of Castle-

Figure 3.2. Mary and Gibbon Raleigh's wedding photo (they're in the center).

mahon in Limerick County. At the age of 20, in 1903, he set out for the port of Queenstown and made his way to New York. Family lore holds that he came as part of an arranged marriage to Mary Ellen Clark of Chicago. Mary Ellen was the daughter of an alderman, and a marriage to an Irishman would serve her family well in winning the increasingly important Irish vote. The arranged marriage worked out for Gibbon Raleigh, too. Mary was a beautiful and talented young lady, and she played piano for silent movies. Thus, Gibbon Raleigh started the tradition of Raleigh men marrying beautiful women.

Unfortunately, Gibbon's stay in America would not be a long one. In 1913, nine months after the birth of his first son, Gibbon passed away. The connection to Ireland would remain in the family, however. Gibbon's son John would go on to marry an Irish beauty, Veronica O'Donnell, and finally settle in Omaha, Nebraska. Veronica owned a book of Irish surnames. When a member of the family brought someone home, Veronica would check the guest's surname in the book to validate the extent of his or her Irish blood. She felt a special kinship to anyone who bore an Irish name. John and Veronica had six children: four sons and two daughters. Their second son, James Raleigh, is the father of my husband, Mike Raleigh. Veronica and I never met because she passed away before Mike and I started dating. I can't help but wonder what might have happened if I had met her, because I came from China, and certainly her book would not have contained my maiden name— "Zhou." However, Mike assures me that Veronica and I would have gotten along fine because we are both petite but strong-willed and unapologetically straight shooters.

3.3 A Brief History of Chinese Immigrants

The mid-19th century was a very difficult period in China's history. For a long time, the Middle Kingdom enjoyed wealth, a strong military, and a sophisticated culture. By the mid-19th century, however, China had been on a steady decline due to corruption, internal conflicts, and self-imposed isolation from the rest of the world. The only silver lining for China was trade. The West developed an unconstrained appetite for China's tea and silk. But China wanted almost nothing from the West.

The trade imbalance devastated the coffers of China's trading partners, so the British began smuggling opium into China. By 1850, the opium trade from the British-controlled East Indian Company accounted for 15-20% of the British Empire's revenue, even though the drug was outlawed in both Britain and China.[95] Soon, American merchants joined in the opium trade, and they had a monopoly on the Turkey-to-China opium trade. Some of the famous American traders included Samuel Russell and Warren Delano.* The profits from the opium trade helped fund railroads, mines, hospitals, and several prominent institutions in the U.S., including Yale University, which sits on the land provided by Samuel Russell's family.

The opium trade benefited western powers but drained China's treasury and caused severe social and economic destruction. The trade dispute eventually led to war. Between 1839 and 1860, China and western powers — including England, France, and the United States — engaged in two wars, historically called the "Opium Wars."† China lost both wars and was forced to sign humiliating treaties, which included granting all western powers the most-favored-nation clause and China having to pay an indemnity of millions.‡ Years of war and the financial burden resulting from those wars forced many Chinese people to find other ways to survive — somewhere else.

On January 24, 1848, James Wilson Marshall was building a mill for John Sutter, a German immigrant and founder of the colony of Nueva Helvetia (today's city of Sacramento). Suddenly, James noticed

---

* Warren Delano's daughter Sara Delano Roosevelt was the mother of Franklin D. Roosevelt, the 32nd President of the United States.

† The Opium War broke out in 1839 after the Chinese government tried to suppress the opium trade, and the British Navy attacked Canton in return. The first opium war ended in 1842 when the British and the Chinese signed the Treaty of Nanjing.

‡ According to the Treaty of Nanjing (signed after the first opium war from 1839 to 1842), China had to pay the British government 21 million silver dollars over three years. See text from the Treaty of Nanjing.
Retrieved from http://afe.easia.columbia.edu/ps/china/nanjing.pdf.

something shining in the American River. As he later recalled of his historic discovery, "It made my heart thump, for I was certain it was gold."[96] Just days after Marshall's historic discovery, Mexico signed the Treaty of Guadalupe Hidalgo, which ended the Mexican-American War and left California to the United States. As the news of gold discovery spread, many Americans traveled to California, hoping to strike a fortune, and eventually, gold fever spread across the ocean. When word of gold being discovered on the west coast of America reached China, many young Chinese men jumped at the opportunity. San Francisco in Chinese means "the gold mountain."

A majority of Chinese immigrants during the Gold Rush era were poor and unskilled laborers. Like some of the 17th-century English immigrants, their passage to the U.S. was paid for by rich Chinese merchants, and these Chinese laborers had to earn money in whatever ways they could to pay back the debt. Chinese immigrants were often called "coolies," a derogatory term that generally refers to indentured unskilled laborers. It's not an accurate description, because most Chinese laborers came to the U.S. voluntarily. They wanted a better life for themselves and their families. Their wages were low by American standards but quite high by Chinese standards. They shared a hard-working attitude and were willing to take low-wage jobs that the locals considered "dirty." Frederick Douglass, the famed abolitionist, praised the Chinese as being "industrious, docile, cleanly, frugal; they are dexterous of hand, patient of toil, marvelously gifted in the power of imitation, and have but few wants."[97] When there was

Figure 3.3. Chinese immigrants working on the transcontinental railroad

plenty of gold to be mined, these Chinese workers' strong work ethic was welcomed by Californians. John McDougal, governor of California during most of the Gold Rush, even praised Chinese laborers as being "one of the most worthy of our [California's] newly adopted citizens."[98]

However, when the gold mines began to be exhausted and people from other parts of the U.S. as well as overseas kept coming, the welcome turned into hatred. The Chinese laborers were specifically targeted because of their unique culture, language, living habits, dress codes, and especially their willingness to take on "dirty" jobs for less. Chinese laborers were accused of stealing American jobs and driving down wages. They soon became "the constant victims of cruel harshness and brutal violence" (Frederick Douglass, 1869). For instance, 200 Chinese miners were robbed and four were murdered at Rich Gulch, California, in 1852.[99]

Even the government of California used its legislative power against Chinese immigrants. In 1852, California demanded a special foreign miner tax from non-U.S. citizen miners. Since Chinese immigrants were the largest non-citizen miner group, they bore most of the tax burden. This tax required a payment of three dollars each month at a time when Chinese miners were making approximately six dollars a month. Tax collectors could legally take and sell the property of those miners who refused to or could not pay the tax.[100] Consequently, many Chinese immigrants were forced out of the mining industry and took on work in other fields.

In 1861, California passed the Swamp and Overflow Act to encourage levee building. Building levees was strenuous work. It required workers to stand in waist-deep water for long hours in an area where malaria was endemic. Only Chinese workers were willing to take up this kind of labor. Consequently, American developers hired several thousand Chinese workers to build hundreds of miles of levees in the Sacramento-San Joaquin Delta region. These Chinese workers were referred to as the "wheelbarrow brigade" because they used mostly primitive hand tools, earning less than one dollar per person per day. Thanks to their hard work, a total of 88,000 acres of fertile farmland were reclaimed from the swamps between 1860 and 1880.[101] Besides building levees, Chinese workers also helped American landowners cultivate various fruits and vegetables, such as asparagus and Bing cherries, on that reclaimed farmland. It is fair to say that without these Chinese immigrants, California would not have become the agricultural powerhouse it is today.

Although the majority of early Chinese immigrants settled on the West Coast and slogged through various types of manual labor, some of them made it to the East Coast around the time of the Civil War. Historian Ruthanne Lum McCunn estimates that about 50 Chinese immigrants participated in the Civil War, mainly for the Union Army. One of them was John Tomney. He joined the New York Infantry in 1861, and gave his life at the Battle of Gettysburg in 1863. Also, in 1863, William Ah Hang became the first Asian American to enlist in the U.S. Navy. The highest ranked Chinese-American in the Union Army was Joseph Pierce, a corporal in the Army of the Potomac.[102]

Unfortunately, no matter how hard Chinese immigrants worked, and sacrificed for this nation, some Americans still viewed and treated them with utter hostility. Naturally, politicians often touted their anti-Chinese immigrant rhetoric to appeal to their electorates. In 1867, Democrats won a congressional election on the west coast by proclaiming the Republican Party's ideal of racial equality would "lead to an 'Asiatic' influx and control of the state by an alliance of 'the Mongolian, Indian, and African.'"[103]

Yet when the Central Pacific Railroad couldn't find many willing Americans to take on the back-breaking and often dangerous work of building the transcontinental railroad, it turned to the group it knew it could depend on—Chinese immigrants.

To secure Chinese laborers, the United States and the Chinese government-run by the Manchu emperor*, signed a new treaty that "promised the Chinese the right to free immigration and travel within the United States, and allowed for the protection of Chinese citizens in the United States in accordance with the most-favored-nation principle."[104] The treaty was often referred to as the Burlingame-Seward Treaty, which was named after two chief negotiators: U.S. Secretary of State William Seward and Anson Burlingame, an American diplomat who gave up his post to negotiate on behalf of the Chinese govern-

---

* Manchu were a minority group in China that defeated the last Han ruler of the Ming dynasty and ruled China from 1638 to 1911.

ment.* The Burlingame Treaty was the first international agreement signed since the Opium War (1839-42) that dealt with Chinese on equal terms.

Chinese workers soon became the majority of the labor force of the Central Pacific Railroad Company (CPRC). For working six days a week and 10-12 hours a day, each Chinese worker earned a wage of only $26 per month, less than half of what a white worker made:

> By the summer of 1868, 4,000 workers, two thirds of which were Chinese, had built the transcontinental railroad over the Sierras and into the interior plains ... Without the efforts of the Chinese workers in the building of America's railroads, our development and progress as a nation would have been delayed by years. Their toil in severe weather, cruel working conditions and for meager wages cannot be under appreciated.[105]

We don't know how many Chinese workers died during the construction of the railroad. We do know that they encountered some of the worst winter weather while building tunnels deep in the Sierra Nevada, and many of them lost their lives in avalanches.[106] When the railroad was completed on May 10, 1869, a Chinese crew was selected and joined an Irish crew to place the last 10 miles of rail, as a symbol to honor their hard work. But images of Chinese railroad workers are nowhere to be found in Andrew Russell's famous photo that commemorates this historic achievement, *East and West Shaking Hands at Laying Last Rail*. The Chinese workers' sacrifice and contribution had

---

* Anson Burlingame was a member of the U.S. House of Representatives (1855-61). He served as the U.S. Minister to China under President Abraham Lincoln and advocated for a policy of cooperation between the Western powers and China. Upon his resignation from his U.S. post, the Chinese government named him an imperial envoy, responsible for managing China's relations with the West. Retrieved from:
https://www.britannica.com/biography/Anson-Burlingame

been all but forgotten until recently, when scholars and documentary film makers sought to recover and retell this neglected history.*

Not all Chinese immigrants were poor and uneducated laborers. Yung Wing (1828-1912) was the first-known Chinese student to graduate from Yale College in 1854. According to Yale's website:

> A native of Guangdong Province, Yung excelled in his studies and impressed Samuel Robbins Brown, a Yale-educated missionary, who brought him to the United States for preparatory school at Monson Academy and then sent him to Yale in 1850. At Yale, Yung Wing was a member of the choir, played football, was a member of the Boat Club, and won academic prizes for English competition.[107]

He persuaded the Chinese government to send a Chinese Education Mission (1872-1881) to the U.S., which allowed about 120 young Chinese students to study science and engineering in the United States. Later, many of these students returned to China, and became leaders in education, engineering, and science, and helped modernize China by building factories and railroads. Yung was awarded an

honorary Doctor of Law degree by Yale University in 1876. He married Mary Kellogg, an American, in the same year. Two years later, Yung, in appreciation of his Yale education, donated many of the 1,237 volumes of his Chinese book collection to his alma mater. This gift formed the basis of Yale University's East Asia Library.

Figure 3.4 An 1892 poster

Goodwill toward Chinese immigrants quickly faded after the completion of the transcontinental railroad. Chinese immigrants were viewed not only as an inferior and undesirable population but also as an actual threat to American culture, the American government, and even the Caucasian race. They were referred to as the "Yellow Perils" and were often

---

* To know more about Chinese railroad workers' stories, please check out independent filmmaker Min Zhou's short film trilogy, "Iron Road Builder." Retrieved from https://nvmuseums.org/railroad-museum-features-film-trilogy-on-chinese-railroad-workers/

targets of violence. Some brave Americans, like the famed abolitionist Frederick Douglass, stood up to the bigotry against Chinese immigrants. In one of his speeches in 1869, he eloquently explained why Americans shouldn't worry that Chinese immigration could "swamp" American culture:

> Though they come as the waves come, we shall be stronger if we receive them as friends and give them a reason for loving our country and our institutions ... They will come in their weakness, we shall meet them in our strength. They will come as individuals, we will meet them in multitudes, and with all the advantages of organization. Chinese children are in American schools in San Francisco, none of our children are in Chinese schools, and probably never will be, though in some things they might well teach us valuable lessons ... The fact that the Chinese and other nations desire to come and do come, is a proof of their capacity for improvement and of their fitness to come...Let the Chinaman come; he will help to augment the national wealth. He will help to develop our boundless resources; he will help to pay off our national debt. He will help to lighten the burden of national taxation. He will give us the benefit of his skill as a manufacturer and tiller of the soil, in which he is unsurpassed.[108]

Douglass was a visionary beyond his time.

The U.S. experienced an economic boom after the Civil War, but post-war economic expansion was interrupted by a financial panic in 1873. The main culprit was Jay Cooke & Co., a well-known bank that overextended itself to fund the completion of the Northern Pacific Railroad. The bank declared bankruptcy on September 18th. Within days, several other financial intuitions failed, the stock market crashed and was temporarily suspended, and unemployment spread like wildfire. About a quarter of New York City's labor force was unemployed.[109] Those lucky enough to keep their jobs saw their wages significantly reduced. Many workers went on strikes to demand higher salaries and better working conditions (and sometimes, those strikes became very violent). In the meantime, native-born workers saw immigrants as unwanted competition for limited employment opportunities. Labor unions became the leading anti-immigrant forces in the U.S.

In 1877, the Workingman's Union was established in San Francisco, and Denis Kearney, a leading anti-Chinese union member, was elected secretary. The initial objective of the Workingman's Union was to support a railroad workers' strike. But the union members quickly turned their hostility against Chinese immigrants. They

> Went on a rampage that lasted three nights, killing several Chinese, destroying Chinese laundries, and raiding the wharves of the Pacific Mail Steamship Company, which transported Chinese immigrants to America. The rioters burned adjacent lumberyards and hay barns, but were unable to burn the company's steamships.[110]

The Workingman's Union later formed the Workingman's Party and became a powerful political force in California. The party supported legislators who drafted many discriminatory bills against Chinese immigrants.

Rather than prosecuting discriminatory acts and upholding our nation's founding principle of "all men are created equal," politicians supported the popular anti-Chinese sentiment by passing the Page Act of 1875, the first immigration law in U.S. history that excluded a specific group of people from the United States. The law was based on false assumptions that all Chinese men were forced into working as "coolies," they depressed wages for white men, and that all Chinese women were prostitutes and "caused disease and immorality among white men."[111] As we discussed earlier, most Chinese men came to the U.S. voluntarily. Like earlier German and Irish immigrants, it is typical for new immigrants to concentrate on lower-paying occupations until they gain the language skills and education to move up the economic ladder. The assumption about all Chinese women being prostitutes is so absurd that it doesn't even warrant a rebuttal.

Nonetheless, it was based on these false assumptions that the Page Act included the following main provisions:[112]

- Prohibition of contracted labor from "China, Japan, or any Oriental country" that was not "free and voluntary."

- Prohibition of the immigration of Chinese prostitutes.

- Exclusion of two classes of potential immigrants from all countries: convicts, and women "imported for the purposes of prostitution."

As a result of the Page Act, U.S. officials so rigorously screened Chinese women in China that most wives and other non-prostitutes were prohibited from coming to the U.S. It's laughable that the law aimed at preventing Chinese prostitutes from entering the U.S. ended up allowing only prostitutes to enter the country. Among the 40,000 Chinese immigrants who came to the U.S. that year, only 136 were women.[113] The Page Law exacerbated the problem of life without families among Chinese immigrants and effectively made Chinese immigrants a declining population.

But for the anti-Chinese immigrant crowd, especially the labor unions, the Page Act of 1875 didn't go far enough. The Knights of Labor led the cry: "The Chinese must go!" Samuel Gompers, president of the American Federation of Labor, claimed "the superior whites had to exclude the inferior Asiatics, by law, or if necessary, by force of arms."[114] The labor unions pushed the U.S. government to do more. Since the U.S. economy during the second half of the 19th century was dominated by manufacturers and railroads, organized laborers from these industries were powerful political forces that many politicians were only too happy to appease.

So, just a few years after the Page Act, the U.S. Congress passed the Chinese Exclusion Act in 1882. The Act suspended immigration for Chinese laborers (skilled or unskilled) for a period of 10 years. The law didn't expel Chinese immigrants who were already in the U.S., but it did prevent them from receiving U.S. citizenship unless they were born here. The Exclusion Act also required every Chinese person traveling in or out of the country to carry a certificate identifying his or her status as a laborer, scholar, diplomat, or merchant.[115]

The 1882 Act was the first immigration law that prevented immigration and naturalization based on race and nationality. It practically gave radical labor union members carte blanche to deal with the "Yellow Perils" with their own hands. The worst act against Chinese immigrants occurred on September 2, 1885, at Rock Springs, Wyoming. Rioters robbed Chinese workers of their valuables, burned down 75 Chinese homes, murdered 28 Chinese miners, and injured a dozen more. This is known as the Rock Springs Massacre. The first Wyoming official to arrive in Rock Springs described the horrible scene:

> Not a living Chinaman — man, woman or child — was left in the town, where 700 to 900 had lived the day before, and not a single house, shanty, or structure of any kind, that had ever been inhabited by a Chinaman was left unburned. The smell of burning human flesh was sickening and almost unendurable, and was plainly discernible for more than a mile along the railroad both east and west.[116]

The survivors of the massacre followed railroad tracks and walked 15 miles to the next town. President Grover Cleveland was so horrified by the incident that he deployed federal troops to Wyoming to restore law and order. But the rioters were not punished because no eyewitnesses were willing to testify against them. Later, president Cleveland recommended that the U.S. Congress approve financial compensation to the Chinese government, "in aid of innocent and peaceful strangers whose maltreatment has brought discredit upon the country."[117]

Unfortunately, many communities followed the Rock Springs terror with more violence against Chinese immigrants. On February 7, 1885, the Seattle police, along with an armed mob, went into Chinatown and deported the Chinese immigrants by forcing them onto a steamboat at gunpoint.[118] It's almost ironic that four years after the passage of the Chinese Exclusion Act, Americans dedicated the Statue of Liberty at New York Harbor. Serving as master of ceremonies, president Cleveland remarked: "We will not forget that Liberty has here made her home; nor shall her chosen altar be neglected . . . a stream of light shall pierce the darkness of ignorance and man's oppression, until Liberty enlightens the world." [119]

In 1888, Pennsylvania Representative William Scott, a Democrat, introduced legislation to extend restrictions embodied by the Chinese Exclusion Act of 1882. The Scott Act excluded immigration of "all persons of the Chinese race" except "Chinese officials, teachers, students, merchants, or travelers for pleasure or curiosity." A Chinese laborer who had come to the United States prior to 1882 was permitted to leave and return only if he had "a lawful wife, child, or parent in the United States, or property therein of the value of one thousand dollars, or debts of like amount due him and pending settlement." Further, all Chinese who qualified for entry, except "diplomatic or consular officers and their attendants," were required to obtain certificates of clearance in advance from U.S. representatives in China.[120] President Cleveland signed the Scott Act into law about six weeks before the presidential election, probably hoping that attaching his name to a populist legislation would enhance his chance of re-election.* Maybe it was karma that he lost his re-election to Republican Benjamin Harrison.

The Scott Act prevented an estimated 20,000 Chinese immigrants who were abroad at the time from returning to the U.S. One of those immigrants impacted by the Scott Act was Yung Ming. While working in China in 1902, he received a letter from Secretary of State John Sherman informing him that his citizenship had been revoked and that he would not be allowed to return. Yung had to sneak back into the U.S. to see his son graduate from Yale.[121]

---

* Although Cleveland lost his re-election bid to Harrison in 1889, he won the presidential election again in 1893. Cleveland was the only U.S. president ever to serve two discontinuous terms. His records on immigration were complicated. Although he insisted on restricting immigration from China, he voted a bill prohibiting immigration by the illiterate.

Similar to the Page Act, the Chinese Exclusion Act and the Scott Act were triggered by some Americans' fear of unemployment and racial bigotry. These laws marked a significant departure from our nation's founding principles. Not surprisingly, the Chinese Exclusion Act was soon challenged in court, and the most famous case was the *United States v. Wong Kim Ark*.

Figure 3.5. Wong Kim Ark

Wong was born in 1873 in San Francisco, and his parents were legally domiciled and residents of the U.S. In 1894, he left the U.S. to visit China and returned in August of the same year. He was denied reentry based on the Chinese Exclusion Act of 1882, which wouldn't grant Chinese immigrants naturalized U.S. citizenship. Wong challenged the government that he was a natural-born U.S. citizen per the 14th Amendment to the Constitution, which declares that "all persons born or naturalized in the United States, and *subject to the jurisdiction thereof*, are citizens of the United States." The Supreme Court ruled in Wong's favor based on their interpretation of the critical phrase "*subject to the jurisdiction thereof*," which they believed referred to being required to obey U.S. law. On this basis, the majority of the Supreme Court interpreted the language of the 14th Amendment in a way that granted U.S. citizenship to at least some children born to foreigners because they were born on American soil (a concept known as *jus soli*). Until recently, this landmark decision and the parameters of the *jus soli* principle haven't been seriously challenged.

Not all Americans harbored hostility toward Chinese immigrants. In April of 1881, Julian Carr, a devout Southern Methodist from Durham, North Carolina, welcomed an 18-year-old Chinese, Charlie Soong, at the Durham train station.[122] With Carr's help, Charlie enrolled in Trinity College (today's Duke University) to study Christianity. When Charlie returned to China in 1886, he carried a beautiful Bible, a gift from Julian, and church offerings to help him spread the gospel in China. Charlie Soong became a key figure in China. He was an early supporter of Sun Yat-sen's revolutionary movement to overthrow the feudal Manchu government and establish democracy in

China. Sun himself studied in Hawaii and was baptized by an American missionary.

In 1905, Soong returned to the U.S. to raise funds for Sun's revolution. Soong purchased a Portuguese passport in Macao to avoid detention at U.S. customs due to the Chinese Exclusion Act and came through U.S. customs in San Francisco as a Portuguese citizen. Soong's American patrons, especially those from Southern Methodist churches, contributed two million U.S. dollars to help fund Sun's revolution. China's modern history could have been very different without these generous American donations.

Soong extended his political influence through his children: he had three daughters and one son. They were all educated in America and played critical roles in China's history in the 20th century.* His oldest daughter, Ailing, married a descendant of Confucius. His second daughter, Chingling, became Sun's second wife and later the Vice-chairwoman of Communist China. His third daughter, Mayling, married Generalissimo Chiang Kai-shek, the leader of the Nationalist Party and the ruler of China from the 1920s till 1949. Chiang fled to Taiwan after losing in a civil war with Mao's communist army.

The American-educated and supported Soong family was the most influential family in modern China's history.

3.4 Summary

Loads of immigrants from many parts of the world came to the United States during the same period. It is possible to cover only some of their histories and contributions to America here. But one thing is clear: the 19th century wouldn't be the Gilded Age if not for the contributions made by all immigrants — whether settling the frontier, providing laborers in mining, building canals and roads, or fighting for America. "Immigrants and their children were the majority of workers in the garment sweatshops of New York, the coal fields of Pennsylvania, and

---

* All of Soong's daughters attended either Wellesley or Wesleyan, while his son went to Harvard.

the stockyards of Chicago. The cities of America during the age of industrialization were primarily immigrant cities."[123] The open-door immigration policy and the laissez-faire economic policy helped turn the 19th century into a Gilded Age for America. The economy boomed, and real wages grew 60% between 1860 and 1890.[124]

Despite immigrant groups' different cultural backgrounds, their American journey shared some striking similarities. Each group began their American journey at the bottom of the economic ladder by taking unwanted jobs as unskilled laborers. They all suffered discrimination from some Americans (descendants of earlier immigrants) who regarded themselves as natives, despite the fact that their ancestors being discriminated against merely one or two generations ago. As Frederick Douglass pointed out in 1869, "Repugnance to the presence and influence of foreigners is an ancient feeling among men. It is peculiar to no particular race or nation."

The accusations against new immigrants were strikingly similar: their cultures and customs were "incompatible" with American culture; their native languages were "funny" or "incomprehensible," and they didn't speak English well; they were often seen as unwanted competition for jobs; they were especially accused of taking lower-paying jobs from "natives." Is it any a surprise that the "No Irish Wanted" sign is similar to the "No Chinese Wanted" sign?

Some immigrant groups gained acceptance and became an integrated part of society sooner than others, but all made great contributions to American history. Their cultural influences, once considered alien, are now the norm. Today's Americans don't think twice when hanging gifts on Christmas trees (a German tradition), or participating in a St. Patrick's Day parade (an Irish tradition), or ordering Chinese takeout.

The last piece of significant immigration legislation in the 19th century was the Immigration Act of 1891. Before this Act, the administration of U.S. immigration rested with each state. The Immigration Act of 1891 centralized the enforcement of immigration law in the executive branch of the federal government. According to the 1891 Act, the Secretary of the Treasury was responsible for laying down rules for the inspection of the nation's coastal ports and its borders with Canada and Mexico. The Act also created the first federal bureaucracy, the

Office of Superintendent of Immigration, to oversee immigration-related matters. The superintendent, appointed by the President of the United States, reported to the Secretary of the Treasury. By 1894, the Office of the Superintendent of Immigration had become the Bureau of Immigration.

The 1891 Act strengthened the inspection and deportation of immigrants. Prior to this act, immigrants who crossed the Canadian or Mexican borders were not inspected. For example, it was reported that "six months before the passage of the Immigration Act of 1891, as many as fifty thousand immigrants entered the United States from Canada without inspection."[125] But after the passage of the 1891 Act, the federal government enacted inspection of immigrants at border crossings. Immigrant inspectors were stationed at ports of entry. They collected passenger lists and questioned each new arrival to determine his or her admissibility. These inspectors had the authority to deport immigrants. The 1891 Act expanded the categories of deportable immigrants to include "idiots, the insane, paupers, and polygamists; persons liable to become a public charge; people convicted of a felony or other crime or misdemeanor involving moral turpitude; and sufferers 'from a loathsome or dangerous contagious disease.'"[126]

Towards the end of the 19th century, the U.S. suffered several economic recessions, including the panic of 1893, which saw a stock market and banking collapse caused by the failure of the U.S. Reading Railroad and the withdrawal of European investment. Some anti-immigration groups blamed the influx of immigrants for exacerbating the severe consequences of the economic recession. Consequently, anti-immigrant groups, such as the American Protective Association (established in 1887) and the Immigration Restriction League (founded in Boston by a group of Harvard graduates in 1894), advocated for the restriction of immigrants from poor and "backward" regions of Europe because these immigrants were "racially inferior" to the Anglo-Saxons and they were believed to threaten the American way of life by bringing poverty and organized crime.[127]

To help push the immigration restriction agenda, the Immigration Restriction League joined with labor unions. To restrict poorly educated immigrants, they advocated for an immigrant literacy test. At the time, illiterate or poor immigrants comprised more than 25 percent of the immigrant population. Congress passed a literacy bill in 1896, but President Grover Cleveland vetoed it in 1897. Explaining his reason for the veto, President Cleveland called this bill "a radical departure from our national policy relating to immigration." Regarding the bill's argument that the quality of recent immigrants was "undesirable," Cleveland pointed out:

> In my opinion, it is infinitely safer to admit a hundred thousand immigrants who, though unable to read and write, seek among us only a home and opportunity to work than to admit one of those unruly agitators and enemies of governmental control who can not only read and write, but delights in arousing by inflammatory speech the illiterate and peacefully inclined to discontent and tumult. Violence and disorder do not originate with illiterate laborers. They are, rather, the victims of the educated agitator.[128]

He further attested:

> A century's stupendous growth, largely due to the assimilation and thrift of millions of sturdy and patriotic adopted citizens, attests the success of this generous and freehanded policy which, while guarding the people's interests, exacts from our immigrants only physical and moral soundness and a willingness and ability to work.[129]

Anti-immigrant groups tried to pass similar bills many times. Still, throughout the 19th century, from Jefferson's Immigration Act of 1802 to the Immigration Act of 1891, U.S. policy largely followed the open-border principle—except for the restrictions on Chinese immigrants—with few restrictions on legal immigration, other than setting rules on the naturalization of citizenship). The U.S. didn't face any illegal immigration issues in the 19th century because people who wanted to become legal residents of the U.S. could easily do so unless they were Chinese.

CHAPTER 4

The Push and Pull of the 20ᵗʰ Century

4.1 The First Half of the 20ᵗʰ Century: "Let Us Shut the Door"

Between 1880 and 1920, America received more than 20 million immigrants, mainly from Central, Eastern, and Southern Europe, including four million Italian immigrants. On October 5, 1909, Israel Zangwill's play *The Melting Pot* opened on Broadway, and the phrase "melting pot" has since become a perfect metaphor for our nation of immigrants. 1913 was a remarkable year for the U.S. Not only did the country receive nearly 1.2 million new immigrants, but for the first time, the GDP per capita in the U.S. ($5,301) was higher than that of the U.K. ($4,921).[130]

Figure 4.1. Theater Program of *The Melting Pot*

Many famous entrepreneurs who powered America's economic engine during this period were immigrants, including Scottish-born Alexander Graham Bell, one of the primary inventors of the telephone, and Swiss-born Louis

Chevrolet, co-founder of the Chevrolet Motor Car Company. The large influx of immigrants provided labor and talent to help accelerate America's economic growth and served as an ever-expanding consumer market.

But economic growth is never a straight line. Since Andrew Jackson had withdrawn the charter for the Bank of the United States in 1837, the federal government had promoted a financial system consisting of small banks. From the mid-19th century to the early 20th century, America had thousands of small banks, including many run by immigrants out of grocery stores. Besides normal banking operations — such as savings and lending — these immigrant banks "transferred money abroad, sold steamship and train tickets, read and wrote letters for illiterate or non-English-speaking customers, and helped people find jobs."[131] Still, they were vulnerable to the financial crisis, and they helped make the financial system volatile. Between 1814 and 1914, the U.S. experienced 13 economic recessions caused by banking panics. The worst occurred in 1907, and its fallout led Congress to establish the Federal Reserve System.

With every economic recession, the anti-immigration sentiment got louder. Soon, anti-immigration groups found sympathetic ears with some members of Congress and, ultimately, President Theodore Roosevelt. President Roosevelt signed the Naturalization Act of 1906, which required immigrants to learn English in order to become naturalized citizens.* The law also limited naturalization to someone who was a "white person" or had African nativity and descent. The Act created the Bureau of Immigration and Naturalization and established a uniform procedure for U.S. naturalization.

The anti-immigrant sentiment didn't go away when the 1906 Act was passed. "On October 11, 1906, the San Francisco school board arranged for all Asian children to be placed in a segregated school."[132] Many Asian children were of Japanese descent. Between 1907 and 1908, President Teddy Roosevelt intervened by reaching several

---

* As I mentioned before, in 1897, President Cleveland voted on a bill prohibiting the illiterate from migrating to the U.S. He saw the bill as an anti-immigration bill because about a quarter of immigrants were illiterate at the time. Therefore, requiring immigrants to pass the English language test was also a covert way to restrict immigration.

agreements with the government of Japan to curb Japanese immigration to the U.S. The Japanese government agreed to "deny passports to laborers intending to enter the United States and recognize the U.S. right to exclude Japanese immigrants holding passports originally issued for other countries."[133] Historians refer to these agreements as gentlemen's agreements because none were official treaties. Thus, the U.S. Congress didn't ratify them.

The anti-immigrant sentiment wasn't solely aimed at Asian immigrants. In 1907, the House and Senate established the United States Immigration Commission, led by Senator William P. Dillingham. This commission issued a report recommending restrictions on immigration from certain parts of Europe. The commission claimed that immigrants from Central and Eastern Europe were "racially inferior," lacked intelligence, and were poor.[134] Woodrow Wilson*, who was later elected President of the United States, remarked:

Now there come multitudes of men of lowest class from the south of Italy and men of the meanest sort out of Hungary and Poland, men out of the ranks where there was neither skill nor energy nor any initiative of quick intelligence; and they came in numbers which increased from year to year, as if the countries of the south of Europe were disburdening themselves of the more sordid and hapless elements of their population.[135]

Congress passed the literacy test bill again in 1912, but President William Howard Taft vetoed it. Even though he agreed that the literacy test would have reduced the number of undesirable immigrants, he argued it would have excluded a large number of desirable immigrants. He explained that, "Frequently the attempt to learn to read and write the language of the particular people is discouraged by the government and these immigrants in coming to our shores are really

---

* Woodrow Wilson, a Democrat, was the president of the United States between 1913 and 1921. Born in the South, he defended the Confederacy when he was young and maintained his racial prejudices towards blacks and other minorities throughout his life. He was one of the leading figures on the left who transformed the Democratic Party into one that advocates for the big government and excessive spending we know today.

striving to free themselves from the conditions under which they have been compelled to live."[136] Therefore, Taft contended, America would never have attained the greatness it did if it had excluded such people.

The anti-immigration groups didn't give up easily, and they were able to influence policies at the state level. The state of California enacted some of the worst anti-immigration policies. An immigration station was established near San Francisco Bay on Angel Island to process incoming Asian immigrants. Many Chinese immigrants were stuck on the island, waiting months or even years to enter the U.S.

In 1913, the California legislature passed the Alien Land Law (a.k.a. the Webb-Haney Act), which prohibited "aliens ineligible for citizenship" from owning agricultural land or possessing long-term leases over it, but permitted leases lasting up to three years. This unfair law greatly affected the economic survival of immigrants from China, Japan, India, and Korea.[137] After the passing of the Alien Land Law, becoming a naturalized citizen was a life-or-death issue for many Asian immigrants. Some resorted to litigation since they were keenly aware that public opinion was not on their side.

There were two famous court cases during this period. The first one was *Takao Ozawa v. United States*. Ozawa, born in Japan but had lived in the United States for 20 years, filed for United States citizenship in 1915 under the Naturalization Act of 1906, which allowed only "free white persons" and "persons of African nativity or persons of African descent" to naturalize. He argued in his legal brief, "My

honesty and industriousness are well known among my Japanese and American friends. In name, Benedict Arnold was an American, but at heart, he was a traitor. In name, I am not an American, but at heart I am a true American."[138] His case reached the Supreme Court, and in 1922, Justice George Sutherland deemed Ozawa racially "ineligible for citizenship" because Justice Sutherland believed the word "white" was synonymous with "what is popularly known as the Caucasian race."

Figure 4.2. Bhagat Thind in U.S. Army Uniform

Justice Sutherland seemed to change his understanding of "white" when he ruled in another case, *United States v. Bhagat Singh Thind*. Thind, an immigrant from India and a U.S. Army veteran from World War I, argued that he was Caucasian because he was a "high caste Hindu." While conceding that people of Hindu descent were part of the Caucasian race (per anthropology), Justice Sutherland still deemed Thind ineligible for naturalization. In his opinion, Justice Sutherland reasoned that the phrase "white person" in the Naturalization Act was "synonymous with the word 'Caucasian' only as that word is popularly understood." Thus, a "white person" means one has to be of the Caucasian race and have a white complexion.

The rulings in these two landmark cases became the legal foundation for Congress to pass immigration laws that prevented many Asian immigrants from becoming U.S. citizens for decades to come—until 1965.

Anti-immigration groups continued to push their agendas at the federal level. They tried to pass the same literacy test bill through Congress again in 1915. President Woodrow Wilson vetoed it and condemned it as a "negation of America's moral value of an open door." However, his opponents argued that they were following the science by pointing to findings from the eugenics movement. Francis Galton, a Victorian British scientist, was the founding father of eugenics. He believed that it was beneficial for the greater good of society if the supposedly undesirable human traits were eliminated from the population. Galton and his followers advocated for higher birth rates among people with desirable genetic traits (positive eugenics) and encouraged sterilization of people with less-desirable or undesirable traits (negative eugenics).[139] The eugenics movement reached the peak of its popularity in the early 20th century and became a discipline for many universities and academics.*

One notable eugenicist who offered anti-immigration groups a scientific cover was Madison Grant (1865-1937), an American lawyer and amateur anthropologist. In 1916, Grant published his influential book *The Passing of The Great Race or, The Racial Basis of European History*, considered one of the main works of scientific racism in the 20th century. Adolf Hitler, a devoted fan, called this book "my bible." In

---

* The eugenics movement was responsible for some of the worst horrors in human history, including Nazi Germany's mass murder of Jews in WWII.

this book, Grant argued that people from Northern Europe, the Nordics, were "rulers and organizers," racially superior to all other races. Therefore, Grant advocated that the U.S. restrict immigration from East Asia and Southern Europe. He also believed

> A rigid system of selection through the elimination of those who are weak or unfit — in other words social failures — would solve the whole question in one hundred years, as well as enable us to get rid of the undesirables who crowd our jails, hospitals, and insane asylums.[140]

Grant's book captured the national mood and made possible the passage of a series of immigration restriction measures in the early 20th century. Grant himself became the vice president of the Immigration Restriction League and held the position until his death.

Many states adopted the eugenics theory and implemented policies to sterilize citizens who were deemed mentally ill or deficient. Indiana was the first state in the U.S. to pass a sterilization law that prevented people with disabilities from having children. In *Buck v. Bell* (1927), Supreme Court Justice Oliver Wendell Holmes declared, "Three generations of imbeciles is enough,"[141] and ruled in favor of government-mandated sterilization.* Even labor unions adopted eugenics theories to their advantage. In the early 20th century, labor unions, such as the American Federation of Labor, tried to increase their membership by promising higher wages for "high quality" (read: skilled Northern European) workers. In contrast, the workers not of Northern European descent were deemed "unemployable." Unions successfully lobbied politicians to pass the minimum wage law that made it illegal for employers to pay wages below a certain level, which deprived employers of their right to hire whomever they wanted and deprived immigrants of employment opportunities.

Along with the eugenics movement, the Prohibition movement (also known as the dry crusade) was a veiled attack against the mass influx of immigrants. Supporters of Prohibition — mainly select Protestant groups that considered alcohol consumption a personal

---

* In total, about 70,000 people in the United States were forcibly sterilized. This inhumane practice was finally outlawed in the 1970s.

sin—subscribed to the eugenics view and nativism. They believed America was made remarkable only by people with white Anglo-Saxon ancestry. They blamed mass immigration in the early 20th century for crime, disease, poverty, and moral decay. Saloons in big cities, where immigrants liked to gather and where booze was sold, were believed to be breeding grounds for political corruption because politicians who sought immigrants' votes often frequented them and were thought to exchange favors for votes. Prohibition supporters were also suspicious of the loyalty of the German-dominated American brewery industry.[142] Thus, to make America great again, Prohibition supporters believed it was necessary to ban the sale, production, importation, and transportation of alcohol. Not surprisingly, German Lutherans joined Irish Roman Catholics to oppose Prohibition. Unfortunately, the Prohibition supporters won, and Congress passed Prohibition as a constitutional amendment in December of 1917.

1917 was a productive year for Congress. In addition to adding the 18th Amendment (Prohibition) to the U.S. Constitution, Congress passed the Immigration Act of 1917, also known as the Asiatic Barred Zone Act. Its main goal was to restrict immigration, particularly immigrants from Asia, through four key provisions:[143]

- People from the Asiatic Barred Zone were restricted from entering the country. This restriction included "any country not owned by the U.S. adjacent to the continent of Asia" along specified longitudes and latitudes.

- The immigration of "undesirables" from other countries* was restricted.

---

* The immigration law defines "undesirables" as "idiots, imbeciles, epileptics, alcoholics, poor, criminals, beggars, any person suffering attacks of insanity, those with tuberculosis, and those who have any form of dangerous contagious disease, aliens who have a physical disability that will restrict them from earning a living in the United States . . . polygamists and anarchists, those who were against the organized government or those who advocated the unlawful destruction of property and those who advocated the unlawful assault of killing of any officer." Prostitutes and others involved in or with prostitution were also barred from entering the United States.

- An $8 head tax was imposed on immigrants, except children under 16 accompanied by a parent. Those over 16 had not paid for their own tickets were prohibited from entering the country.

- A literacy test was imposed on immigrants. Those over the age of 16 who could read some English had to read 30 to 40 words to show they were capable of reading. Those entering the U.S. to avoid religious persecution in their country of origin did not have to pass this test.

The Immigration Act of 1917 successfully limited immigration from Asia except for the Philippines and Japan,* but it didn't slow down immigrants from Central, Eastern, and Southern Europe. The literacy test was elementary between 1918 and 1920, so 99% of new immigrants passed it. Still, like the Chinese Exclusion Act of 1882, the Immigration Act of 1917 marked a significant departure from our founding ideology that "all men are created equal."

Around this time, the eugenics movement was at its height. Its supporters included the Surgeon General, some senior officials from the Public Health Service (PHS), and powerful labor unions, who wanted the government to keep immigrants out in order to maintain high wages for native-born American workers. In 1920, Harry Laughlin of the Eugenics Record Office testified before the U.S. Congress Committee on Immigration and Naturalization. He argued that "the 'American' gene pool was being polluted by a rising tide of intellectually and morally defective immigrants — primarily from eastern and southern Europe."[144]

The eugenicists' fear-mongering tactics worked particularly well when the economic recession of 1920-1921 hit the U.S. The recession was characterized by extreme deflation and an unemployment rate of 11.7%. The main cause of this recession was the Federal Reserve's interest rate policy, as Milton Friedman and Anna Schwartz explained

---

* The Philippines was a U.S. colony, and Japan agreed to deny issuing passports to Japanese laborers intending to enter the U.S. as part of the gentlemen's agreements of 1908 between the Japanese government and President Theodore Roosevelt.

in their book *A Monetary History of the United States*. Yet, labor unions and eugenicists blamed the recession on immigrants. Albert Johnson, chair of the House Committee on Immigration, tried to suspend all immigration.

Congress didn't support a complete ban on immigration after businesses let their representatives know they needed laborers. Still, Congress did pass the 1921 Emergency Quota Act to impose immigration quotas based on country of birth, and President Warren G. Harding signed it into law. The quota law exempted immigrants from Western Europe. For everyone else, the law capped the number of total annual immigrants at 350,000. The yearly allowable quota for each country was 3% of the total number of foreign-born persons of that country of origin recorded in the 1910 United States Census. This law drastically reduced the number of new immigrants from everywhere else except Western Europe. It was the first time U.S. immigration law adopted a quota system, which has remained a part of that policy until the present day. In 1922, the U.S. received only 309,556 new immigrants, compared with 805,228 the prior year.[145]

Thanks to President Harding's and his successor Calvin Coolidge's general hands-off economic policies, the U.S. economy recovered handsomely in 1922. "By 1923, it was hard to find an unemployed man."[146] The Emergency Quota Law was supposed to be a temporary measure. But when the U.S. Congress began working on a more permanent immigration bill in 1924, the quota system seemed to work so well at restricting the number of newcomers that no one wanted to get rid of it, so the debate focused on how to adjust it. The anti-immigration voices triumphed again. Standing on the U.S. Senate floor, Senator Ellison DuRant Smith of South Carolina declared, "Let us shut the door and assimilate what we have, and let us breed pure American citizens and develop our own American resources." To Senator Smith, "pure American citizens" were made up of Anglo-Saxons, as he cried out:

Thank God we have in America perhaps the largest percentage of any country in the world of the pure, unadulterated Anglo-Saxon stock; certainly the greatest of any nation in the Nordic breed. It is for the preservation of that splendid stock that has characterized us that I would make this not an asylum for the oppressed of all countries, but a country to assimilate and perfect that splendid type of manhood that has made America the foremost Nation in her progress and in her power, and yet the youngest of all the nations.[147]

Not all members of Congress shared Senator Smith's view. Robert H. Clancy, a Republican congressman from Detroit, which had a large immigrant constituency, defended immigrants by counting their contributions to the U.S.:

Italians formed about 4 percent of the population of the United States and they formed 10 percent of the American military force. The Polish-Americans are as industrious and as frugal and as loyal to our institutions as any class of people who have come to the shores of this country in the past 300 years.[148]

Unfortunately, his plea failed to persuade the majority of lawmakers, who voted for a new bill to restrict immigration.

President Calvin Coolidge signed the Immigration Act of 1924 into law, further limiting immigration by lowering the annual total quota from 350,000 to 165,000. The law reduced the allowable percentage for each country of origin from 3% to 2% of the foreign-born population. It pushed the base year for the quota calculation back to the 1890 census (a deliberate effort to limit immigration from Southern and Eastern Europe, which mainly occurred after 1890). The new law also changed the base number of the quota formula, from the number of people *born outside* the U.S., to the entire U.S. population, including native-born American citizens. Consequently, the percentage of visas allocated to immigrants from Britain and Western Europe increased while drastically reducing immigration from everywhere else. For example, prior to the 1924 Act, an average of 200,000 Italians immigrated to America each year. The annual quota established by the 1924 Act limited Italian immigrants to fewer than 4,000.[149] (See Appendix 1 for immigration quotas allocated by country from 1925 to 1927.)

In the late 19th century, immigrants from Asian countries, such as Japan and the Philippines (except China), could still get legal residency but were excluded from becoming naturalized citizens. The 1924 Immigration Act reaffirmed the race-based naturalization policy by making only white people or people of African nativity or descent eligible for naturalization. Therefore, this law barred immigration from all Asian countries, including Japan and the Philippines. The 1924 Act suspended the Gentlemen's Agreement between President Teddy Roosevelt and the government of Japan.

In addition, the 1924 Immigration Act sharply lowered the number of new immigrants from Southern and Eastern Europe. As President John F. Kennedy remarked decades later in his book *A Nation of Immigrants*, the 1924 Immigration Act changed what our nation once stood for. Instead of being a sanctuary for all who are "yearning to breathe free," now we only welcome immigrants "as long as they come from Northern Europe, are not too tired or too poor or slightly ill, never stole a loaf of bread, never joined any questionable organization, and can document their activities for the past two years."[150]

Naturally, after the passage of this Act, overall immigration plummeted (see Figure 4.3 below). From 1910 to 1919, 6.3 million immigrants arrived in the U.S. But between 1920 and 1929, only 4.5 million new immigrants, 75% of whom entered before 1925. Between 1930 and 1950, America's foreign-born population decreased from 11.6% to 6.9% of the total population.[151] Immigration fell to its lowest point in 1933: only 23,048 immigrants came to the U.S. that year.

Our nation had changed from one that opened its arms to one oppressed into one that was dominated by an isolationist policy and an anti-immigration attitude. The Immigration Law of 1924 "violated the basic principle of American democracy — the principle that values and rewards each man on the basis of his merit as a man."[152]

The isolationist policy and anti-immigration attitude achieved a significant reduction in immigration. Still, it didn't generate an immediate economic benefit to the nation or produce the American workers the isolationists had imagined. In 1929, the U.S. was hit by the Great Depression. By 1933, the unemployment rate had reached 25%.[153] The Great Depression severely affected the Americans psyche. "There was a new sense of permanence about the Depression. Being poor was no longer a passing event — it was beginning to seem like a way of life."[154] The financial struggles of many ordinary Americans evoked images of

Charles Dickens' Victorian London. Deep in their financial woes, few Americans wanted anything to do with the outside world or outsiders.

The one good thing that came out of the 1930s occurred on December 5, 1933, when the ratification of the 21st Amendment repealed the 18th Amendment. President Franklin Roosevelt remarked, "I think this would be a good time for a beer." To celebrate the end of Prohibition, the Busch family, owner of the Budweiser Brewery Company, sent a six-horse hitch across the East Coast to deliver beers. That's how the tradition of the Budweiser Clydesdales started.

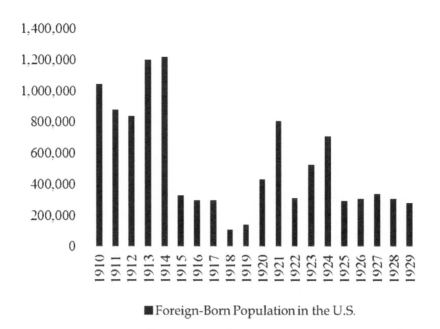

■Foreign-Born Population in the U.S.

Figure 4.3.[155] Foreign-Born Population in the U.S. from 1910 to 1929.

The start of World War II gave rise to anxiety over enemy espionage and radical ideologies such as Bolshevism, which reignited public fears and mistrust of immigrants. In 1940, the U.S. Congress passed the Alien Registration Act, also known as the Smith Act (its chief author was Howard Smith, a Democrat from Virginia, and President Franklin Roosevelt signed it into law. President Roosevelt also moved the Immigration and Naturalization Service from the Department of Labor to the Department of Justice, reflecting the popular sentiment that the immigrant population was a national security issue.

The stated objectives of the Alien Registration Act were "to prohibit certain subversive activities; to amend certain provisions of law with respect to the admission and deportation of aliens; to require the fingerprinting and registration of aliens."[156] One provision of the law required all immigrants who were 14 and older to be fingerprinted and registered. Between August 1, 1940, and March 31, 1944, the Immigration and Naturalization Service collected fingerprints of 5.6 million immigrants. Since then, fingerprinting has remained part of the naturalization process.

When the U.S. officially entered World War II, the data the U.S. government had collected through the Alien Registration Program allowed it to identify immigrants from enemy nations such as Germany and Japan and impose different treatment upon them. Japanese Americans received the harshest treatment. After the attack on Pearl Harbor and the U.S. went to war with Japan, President Roosevelt signed Executive Order 9066, ordering Japanese Americans to evacuate into concentration camps* located inland in states such as Colorado, Wyoming, and Montana. Many families were forced to quickly sell their assets for a fraction of their actual value. Congressman Norman Mineta, the 14th U.S. Secretary of Transportation under President George W. Bush, was only 10 years old when he and his family were forced to relocate to concentration camps. In an interview, he recalled:

> I remember my dad had just purchased a 1941 Packard in November of '40, and he, I believe, paid about $1,100 for the car, and he sold it in March for about $400, just to get rid of the car. A lot of people . . . there were stories of people who would come along and say, "Well, that refrigerator, Mr. Suzuki, you can't take with you. I'll buy it for $5.00," or $10.00, whatever, and I remember there was a story about a woman who had her things for sale. Someone came to buy her good china, and they

---

* I chose to use the phrase "concentration camp" because internment is about the confinement of enemy aliens. Yet, most incarcerated Japanese Americans were U.S. citizens. A concentration camp is "where persons are confined, usually without hearings and typically under harsh conditions, often as a result of their membership in a group the government has identified as a suspect." Therefore, it's more accurate to call the camps Japanese Americans were forced to relocate to concentration camps.

said, "Well, we'll pay you $5.00." So she took them and just threw them to the floor and said, "I am not going to sell them for five and you are not going to get it," and had just, in anger, broken all of her dishes. There were many, many examples of that.*

Mr. Mineta and his family were first sent to Santa Anita Racetrack and later moved to Heart Mountain, Wyoming. The influx of Japanese Americans instantly turned Heart Mountain into the third largest city in Wyoming. Overall, about 127,000 Japanese Americans were impacted, including some veterans from World War I.[157] They were forced to live in concentration camps solely because of their ancestry. No comparable harsh treatment was imposed on any Italian Americans or German Americans.

Two Japanese Americans challenged the legality of the government's incarceration of Japanese Americans without due process of law. One of them was Gordon Hirabayashi, a student at the University of Washington and a Quaker. Gordon refused to register for the forced "relocation." Instead, he turned himself in and filed a legal challenge. His case went all the way to the U.S. Supreme Court. Rather than ruling on the constitutionality of President Roosevelt's Executive Order, the court convicted Gordon of disobeying the war-time curfew and sentenced him to 90 days in jail.

Fred Korematsu challenged the constitutionality of Roosevelt's executive order in the landmark case *Korematsu v. United States*. Unfortunately, the Supreme Court sided with the government in a 6-3 decision. In his dissent, Justice Frank Murphy rightly called the incarceration of Japanese Americans the "legalization of racism," and declared that

Racial discrimination in any form and in any degree has no justifiable part whatever in our democratic way of life. It is unattractive in any setting, but it is utterly revolting among a

---

* *Interview of Norman Mineta and Alan Simpson by the Academy of Achievement.* (June 3, 2006). Retrieved from:
http://www.achievement.org/autodoc/printmember/min0int-1.

free people who have embraced the principles set forth in the Constitution of the United States. All residents of this nation are kin in some way by blood or culture to a foreign land. Yet they are primarily and necessarily a part of the new and distinct civilization of the United States. They must, accordingly, be treated at all times as the heirs of the American experiment, and as entitled to all the rights and freedoms guaranteed by the Constitution.[158]

A lesser-known lawsuit took place in Cheyenne, Wyoming. As the United States expanded its involvement in WWII, the U.S. Army need-ed all the men it could get. So, it asked young Japanese Americans, nicknamed "Nisei," first to volunteer and later to answer the draft to join the U.S. Army. According to former Wyoming Senator Alan Simp-son, a friend of Congressman Mineta, 19 Nisei from the concentration camp at Heart Mountain, Wyoming, were drafted into the U.S. Army during World War II:

> They refused to go until their people were turned loose from Heart Mountain. They went to the Federal District Court in Cheyenne . . . They lost of course, and they all were drafted. They said, "Okay, we love America, we don't even know Japan, but let my mother and my little brother out of Heart Mountain."[159]

History is often more complicated than it appears. Not all Japanese Americans opposed the U.S. government's mass exclusion and incar-ceration of Japanese Americans. The Japanese American Citizen League (JACL), one of the most influential organizations in the United States, chose to cooperate with the federal government and criticized those Nisei who resisted the draft.*

---

* "After the war, the JACL became active in turning back discriminatory legislation through the courts, lobbied for legislation that would allow greater rights for Japanese immigrants and subsequent generations of American citizens of various ethnic and racial backgrounds, and was a key player in the redress movement." Retrieved from
https://encyclopedia.densho.org/Japanese_American_Citizens_League/

Although a small number of young Nisei refused to serve in the U.S. military, the majority of them chose to answer the call. They

wanted to prove their loyalty and regain the trust of the American government and the general public. The Nisei formed an all-Japanese American unit, the 442nd Regimental Combat Team (RCT), almost exactly a year after President Roosevelt signed EO 9066. They were deployed to Europe mainly because military brass and civilian leaders still doubted these

Figure 4.4. Members of the Mochida family awaiting an evacuation bus. Identification tags were used to aid in keeping the family unit intact during all phases of evacuation (1942).

Americans' loyalty and weren't comfortable sending Nisei soldiers into the Pacific theater. The 442nd RCT, with 18,000 Nisei men, became the most decorated unit in the U.S. Army. Although the 442nd represented just 0.11 percent of the U.S. military, they earned "over 4,000 Purple Hearts, 4,000 Bronze Stars, 560 Silver Star Medals, 21 Medals of Honor, and seven Presidential Unit Citations," and more. Texas Gov. John Connally made the entire 442nd RCT honorary Texans on October 21, 1963. [160]

About 3,600 Japanese Americans from the internment camps, along with 22,000 others living outside of those camps (i.e., Hawaii), joined the U.S. armed forces during World War II. After the U.S. victory, Japanese Americans were allowed to leave the camps and return to their original homes, but many found nothing to return to. The last Japanese concentration camp was closed in 1946.

Even a great nation can commit horrible mistakes. What truly makes a country great is when its leaders admit those mistakes and take action to correct them. It was only fitting on August 10, 1988: President Reagan signed into law a bill to award restitution payments of $20,000 to Japanese-American survivors of World War II civilian concentration camps.* In his remarks upon signing the bill, President Reagan explained, "What is most important in this bill has less to do with property than with honor. For here we admit a wrong; here we reaffirm our commitment as a nation to equal justice under the law."[161]

A great nation strives to live up to its lofty ideals by correcting past mistakes, learning from them, and never repeating them again. Let's remember these words from President Reagan:

> Blood that has soaked into the sands of a beach is all of one color. America stands unique in the world: the only country not founded on race but on a way, an ideal. Not in spite of but because of our polyglot background, we have had all the strength in the world. That is the American way.[162]

Since China and the U.S. were allies during World War II, Americans' attitudes towards the Chinese changed from antagonism to friendship. This attitude shift was partially assisted by Pearl Buck's novel *The Good Earth*, which depicts Chinese farmers' strong work ethic and devotion to their land. For many Americans, who had never known much about China or its people before, this book cast the Chinese positively and helped Americans see that they shared many of the same values, such as love for their families. American public sentiment towards China reached its height when Madame Mayling Soong, wife of Generalissimo Chiang Kai-shek, visited the United States in 1943 and delivered a speech to a joint session of the U.S. Congress in fluent English with a slight Southern accent. Not only did Americans offer China financial aid and military assistance to fight the war against Japan, but the American government also reversed the discriminatory immigration law against the Chinese by repealing the 1882 Chinese Exclusion Act through the 1943 Magnuson Act.

The Magnuson Act established an annual quota of 105 immigration visas for Chinese immigrants. On January 18, 1994, Edward Bing Kan, the son of a Chinese vegetable peddler and an interpreter who

---

* The bill President Reagan signed is H.R. 442, or "An Act to Implement Recommendations of the Commission on Wartime Relocation and Internment of Civilians." It provides for a restitution payment to each of the 60,000 surviving Japanese Americans of the 120,000 who were relocated or detained.

worked for the Immigration and Naturalization Service's (INS) Chicago office for 35 years, became the first Chinese American to take the oath and become a U.S. citizen after the repeal of the Chinese Exclusion Act.[163]

The repeal of the Chinese Exclusion Act was a welcome sign, but it only opened a very narrow door for would-be Chinese immigrants to America because:

> Unlike European quotas based on country of citizenship, the Chinese quota would be based on ethnicity. Chinese immigrating to the United States from anywhere in the world would be counted against the Chinese quota, even if they had never been to China or had never held Chinese nationality.[164]

The refugee issue was the final legacy of World War II that impacted the U.S. immigration system. American immigration law didn't single out "refugee" as a separate category. So, the strict quotas set by the Immigration Act based on country of origin presented a challenge for war refugees, especially Jewish refugees from Europe. The demand for immigration visas from many war-torn European countries far exceeded the annual immigration quotas set by the Immigration Act of 1924. Yet, the U.S. government didn't want to increase the annual quota, fearing it would not be popular. Gallup's American Institute of Public Opinion surveyed in 1939, asking Americans whether the U.S. government should accept 10,000 Jewish children from Germany. A whopping 61% responded "no."[165] A few months later, a bill to admit 20,000 German Jewish children into the U.S. failed in a congressional committee.

Jewish leaders pointed out an alternative that would help admit more Jewish refugees without a sweeping change to the immigration law. According to Jewish scholar Dr. Rafael Medoff, "Nearly 190,000 quota places from

Figure 4.5. The most famous refugee: Albert Einstein's Declaration of Intention card. (1936)

Germany and Axis-controlled countries sat unused."[166] The Roosevelt administration could have allocated these unused visa quotas to refugees. Unfortunately, that didn't happen. Instead, the Roosevelt administration established a War Refugee Board (WRB) in 1944, two years after the Nazis declared the "Final Solution" on Jews. The WRB was tasked with the "immediate rescue and relief of the Jews of Europe and other victims of enemy persecution." Although the WRB was able to rescue 200,000 people, it was too little, too late. By then, more than one million Jews had already perished in Auschwitz. The U.S. didn't amend its immigration policy for refugees until the Immigration Act of 1952, which addressed refugee applications on a case-by-case basis. Only after the passage of the United States Refugee Act of 1980 did the U.S. establish a permanent and systematic procedure for immigration based on refugee status.

4.2 The Immigration Acts of 1952 and 1965

The U.S. Congress didn't ease immigration significantly after World War II. The Cold War that followed had some politicians paranoid of any real or imagined Communist infiltration through immigration. Under this kind of political atmosphere, Congress passed the Immigration Act of 1952, also known as the McCarran-Walter Act, named after its co-sponsors, Senator Pat McCarran (D-Nevada) and Congressman Francis Walter (D-Pennsylvania). This law was controversial because it was a mixed bag of progress and setbacks.

The new law repealed the 1924 Immigration Act's ban on Asian immigrants by allotting 100 immigration visas to each Asian nation. But the quota for Asians was based on race, not nationality. So, when an Indian who resided in the U.K. applied for immigration to the U.S., he used one of the 100 visas allocated to India. The quotas for immigrants from Central, Southern, and Eastern Europe were slightly higher than for Asians. At the same time, there were no quota restrictions for Western European nationals. The whole system was still designed to encourage immigration from "desirable" countries, such as England

and Ireland,* while limiting immigration from "places like Asia or the rest of Europe.

The 1952 Immigration Act also made progress by abolishing a restriction in the U.S. immigration laws since 1792: the limitation of granting naturalization to only "free white person" with "good moral character." Removing the racial barrier from the naturalization process meant an eligible Asian immigrant could become a naturalized U.S. citizen.

Despite this progress, the 1952 Act also had setbacks. It established a preferential system to prioritize immigration applications for those with families already residing in the U.S. By prioritizing blood relations and family connections, the system discriminated against people who didn't have any familial bonds, even though they might have possessed knowledge, skills, and experience that could contribute to our economy as productive citizens. Even though the 1952 Act gave second preference to applicants who had arranged employment in the U.S., the employment-based immigration category received fewer visa quotas.

To make matters worse, the 1952 Act also established a complicated labor certification process to ensure immigrants wouldn't compete against native-born Americans for employment. The complexity of the process discouraged potential applicants from seeking employment-based immigration. Despite these flaws, once the preference system was enshrined in the law, politicians had no political will to remove it. Thus, we are still using it today.

One provision of the 1952 Act that reflected lawmakers' Cold War mentality was the section that prohibited any current or former Communist Party member from entering the U.S. The law granted the Attorney General the power to deport any alien who had engaged in or had any purpose of engaging in activities "prejudicial to the public interest" or "subversive to national security."

President Harry Truman vetoed the 1952 Act as he believed it "discriminates, deliberately and intentionally, against many of the peoples of the world." He felt he couldn't support a law based on the same theory that enabled the Immigration Act of 1924, driven by the

---

* Keep in mind that not so long ago, Irish immigrants were considered "undesirable" by earlier immigrants and their native-born descendants.

eugenicist thought that immigrants from Western Europe made better U.S. citizens than immigrants from Eastern, Southern, and Central Europe. Truman decried it by saying,

> Such a concept is utterly unworthy of our traditions and our ideals. It violates the great political doctrine of the Declaration of Independence that "all men are created equal."[167] It denies the humanitarian creed inscribed beneath the Statue of Liberty proclaiming to all nations, "Give me your tired, your poor, your huddled masses yearning to breathe free."

Truman also took issue with the law's deportation provision because "no standards or definitions are provided to guide discretion in the exercise of powers so sweeping." He further declared: "To punish undefined 'activities' departs from traditional American insistence on established standards of guilt. To punish an undefined 'purpose' is a thought control."

Unfortunately, the U.S. Congress had enough votes to override Truman's veto, and the Immigration Act of 1952 became the law of the land.

By the early 1960s, calls for immigration reform had gained broad support from the rebellious social culture as well as the success of the Civil Rights movement. President Kennedy lent his support by stating that the "national origins quota system has strong overtones of an indefensible racial preference."[168]

After JFK's assassination, the U.S. Congress took up the call for immigration reform by passing the Immigration and Nationality Act of 1965, also known as the Hart–Celler Act—named after its two key sponsors, Senator Philip Hart of Michigan and Representative Emanuel Celler of New York. Senator Ted Kennedy also played a vital role. Without his support, this bill wouldn't have passed. The most notable achievement of this law was that it abolished the National Origins Formula, which had been in place since 1921 and restricted immigration on the basis of proportion to the existing U.S. population.

The 1965 Act kept the preference system introduced in the Immigration Act of 1952, prioritizing family reunion for relatives of U.S. citizens and permanent residents (a.k.a., green card holders) over employment and humanitarian needs. The order of priority is the following:[169]

1. Unmarried children under 21 years of age of U.S. citizens
2. Spouses and unmarried children of permanent residents
3. Professionals, scientists, and artists "of exceptional ability"
4. Married children over 21 years of age and their spouses and children of U.S. citizens
5. Siblings and their spouses and children of U.S. citizens
6. Workers in occupations with labor shortages
7. Political refugees

Our nation's immigration system continues to rely on this preference system today, with family-based immigration utilizing 70% of the annual visa quota and employment-based immigrants using another 20%.

The 1965 Act imposed a numeric cap on the number of immigration visas to be issued every year: 170,000, exempting immediate relatives of U.S. citizens and "special immigrants."* When President Lyndon Johnson signed the Immigration Act of 1965 into law on October 3, with the Statue of Liberty in the background, he applauded the new immigration law: "For it does repair a very deep and painful flaw in the fabric of American justice. It corrects a cruel and enduring wrong in the conduct of the American Nation."[170]

President Johnson also recognized that a welcoming immigration policy was an effective tool against communism when he singled out the special treatment of political refugees from Cuba in his speech at the foot of the Statue of Liberty. He proclaimed that "it stamps the mark of failure on a regime when many of its citizens voluntarily choose to leave the land of their birth for a more hopeful home in America."[171]

---

* Special immigrants refer to "those born in 'independent' nations in the Western hemisphere; former citizens; ministers; employees of the U.S. government abroad."
Retrieved from
http://library.uwb.edu/guides/usimmigration/1965_immigration_and_natio nality_act.html.

Neither President Johnson nor the other proponents of the 1965 Immigration Act could have foreseen what a watershed moment it would be when the law went into effect. In 1965, the U.S. population was 194 million, with 6% of its population (a little less than 10 million people) being foreign-born immigrants. Among these immigrants, 84% were born in Europe or Canada.[172] So politicians from both parties were confident that the new law wouldn't change the racial and ethnic composition of the United States. U.S. Senator Ted Kennedy of Massachusetts declared on the Senate floor that "Our cities will not be flooded with a million immigrants annually . . . Secondly, the ethnic mix of this country will not be upset."[173] President Johnson also noted in his speech upon signing the new immigration law that "This bill that we will sign today is not a revolutionary bill. It does not affect the lives of millions. It will not reshape the structure of our daily lives, or really add importantly to either our wealth or our power."[174] The reality proved that neither of their predictions was accurate.

By the 1960s, the influx of new immigrants from Europe had slowed down due to the post-war economic boom in Europe. Many Americans with European ancestry had already been in the U.S. for several generations, so there wasn't a great need for family-reunion-based immigration. However, that was not the case for many people from Asia and Latin America. Until 1965, immigration from these regions had been restricted for more than a century. The new immigration law opened the door for immigrants from these regions for the first time by removing the national origin quota system. Many immigrants took advantage of the family-reunion preference and sponsored their families to become legal immigrants in the United States. Thus began the "chain immigration" cycle. As the following table shows, between 1960 and 1980, the percentage of total immigrants from Asia and Latin America increased from 13.3% to 47.4%.

Figure 4.6.[175] Origins of the U.S. Immigrant Population, 1960-1980

Year	Europe/Canada	South and East Asia	Other Latin America	Mexico
1960	84.0	3.8	3.5	6.0
1970	67.8	6.8	10.8	8.1
1980	42.4	15.3	15.5	15.6

4.3 The Immigration Act of 1990

Between 1970 and 1990, the number of immigrants in the U.S. more than doubled, growing from 9.6 million (4.7% of the total U.S. population) in 1970 to 19.8 million (7.9% of the total U.S. population) in 1990.[176] This growth was driven primarily by immigrants from Latin America and Asia.

Senator Ted Kennedy led the push to pass the Immigration Act of 1990. When President George H. W. Bush signed it into law, he declared that the 1990 Act was "the most comprehensive reform of our immigration laws in 66 years" because it was "a complementary blending of our tradition of family reunification with increased immigration of skilled individuals to meet our economic needs."[177]

The 1990 Act included changes to immigration and non-immigration categories. The main components of the immigration section were:[178]

- Increased total worldwide immigration visa cap from 530,000 per year under the Immigration Act of 1965 to 700,000 per year for fiscal years 1992-1994, and 675,000 per year thereafter.

- Family reunification continued to be our immigration policy priority; 465,000 visas were reserved for family-based immigration for fiscal years 1992-1994 and 480,000 per year thereafter. There are four family-based preferences:

  o **F1**: Unmarried Sons and Daughters of U.S. citizens: 23,400 plus any numbers not required for fourth preference.

  o **F2**: Spouses and Children, and Unmarried Sons and Daughters of Permanent Residents.

  o **F3**: Married Sons and Daughters of U.S. citizens.

  o **F4**: Brothers and Sisters of Adult U.S. citizens.

- Expanded employment-based visa cap and categories. An annual cap for employment-based visas was set at 140,000 and was divided among five preference categories:

    o **EB1**: Priority Workers including: (a) aliens with extraordinary ability in the arts, sciences, education, business, or athletics, (b) outstanding professors and researchers, and (c) certain multinational executives and managers.

    o **EB2**: Members of the Professions Holding Advanced Degrees or Persons of Exceptional Ability.

    o **EB3**: Skilled Workers, Professionals, and Other Workers.

    o **EB4**: Certain Special Immigrants, such as ministers and religious workers, can immigrate to the U.S. based on established religious affiliation and the continuation of their profession in the United States.

    o **EB5**: Investors. Entrepreneurs who invest $1 million or at least $500,000 in a targeted employment area and who plan to create or preserve 10 permanent full-time jobs will be granted a conditional green card. On an annual basis, up to 10,000 visas may be authorized in this particular category.

    o Only EB2 and EB3 applicants are subject to the Labor Certification process, which requires employers to prove that no American workers are to be harmed by hiring foreign workers and foreign workers are paid prevailing wages so they won't depress wages for American workers.

- The law introduced a "Diversity Program," commonly known as the "visa lottery" program. The program allots an annual quota of 50,000 green cards randomly to nationals from countries historically with low levels of immigration to the U.S. Nationals from mainland China, India, Mexico, and a few other countries are not eligible to participate. The 50,000 lottery winners will become legal permanent residents based on pure luck as long as they meet the minimum requirements of having a high school education or two years' work experience. There is no minimum English language skill requirement. It is a popular but controversial program and has been riddled with fraud and scandals since its inception in 1995.

Another channel to become a legal U.S. resident is through Asylum/Refugee visas:

  o **Asylum seekers:** Persons already in the United States who were persecuted or fear persecution upon returning to their home country may apply for asylum within the United States or at a port of entry when they seek admission. There is no limit to the number of individuals who may be granted asylum in a given year, and there is no clear definition of what constitutes persecution.

  o **Refugees:** People who are fleeing persecution or are unable to return to their homelands due to life-threatening or extraordinary conditions. Unlike asylum seekers, there is a yearly quota for refugee admissions determined by the president. President Joseph Biden set the refugee cap for the fiscal year 2022 at 125,000, a 733% increase from the 15,000-person ceiling set by former President Donald Trump.

- On the non-immigration side, the 1990 Act modified existing visa categories and greatly expanded the number of new visa categories. For example, it made it easier for tourists to visit the U.S. for up to 90 days without first obtaining visas. The Act dramatically expands the H working visa categories. It capped H1B non-immigration working visas for highly skilled workers at 65,000 per year anH2B working visas for lesser-skilled workers at 66,000. In addition, the Act created many new visa categories, such as the O visa for aliens of "extraordinary ability" in science, education, and business; and the P visa for foreign athletes and entertainers. There are over twenty nonimmigrant working visa categories (see Appendix 4).

The complexity of the law helped turn the Immigration and Naturalization Service (INS) into an enormous bureaucracy. In 2003, "the INS was abolished and its functions placed under three agencies — U.S. Citizenship and Immigration Services (USCIS), Immigration and Customs Enforcement (ICE), and Customs and Border Patrol (CBP) — within the newly created Department of Homeland Security."[179] The USCIS alone has over 19,000 employees.

Like previous immigration laws, the 1990 Act was a mix of successes and failures. For example, President Bush declared that the 1990 Act would "improve this Administration's ability to secure the U.S. border." Yet, the number of illegal immigrants has increased annually since, except during the 2008-2009 economic recession and again during the 2020-2021 COVID pandemic. We will discuss these immigration issues in more detail in Chapter 5.

Our nation's immigration law hasn't changed much since the 1990s. Thus, today we live with the legacy of the Immigration Acts of 1965 and 1990, which have profoundly impacted our nation's demographics, culture, and politics. The Pew Research Center estimates that if we factor in the second-and third-generation offspring of immigrants, the post-1965 immigration wave has added 72 million people to the U.S. population, which is a little more than the population of France (67 million).

In addition to the population increase, we have seen a change in the ethnic-racial composition of the U.S. population. From 1900 to 1965, most immigrants came from Europe (see Figure 4.7) due to a quota system favoring European immigrants. In 1965, the ethnic-racial composition of the U.S. population was 84% white, 11% black, 4% Hispanic, and 1% Asian. The Immigration Acts of 1965 and 1990 opened doors for immigrants from Asia, Africa, and Latin America. "By 2000, almost half of newly arrived immigrants were from Central and South America (including 34% from Mexico alone)."[180] Starting as early as 2010, more Asian immigrants than Hispanic immigrants have arrived annually in the U.S., and the trend is expected to continue. As of 2020, the ethnic-racial composition of the U.S. population is 61.6% white, 18% Hispanic, 12.4% black, and 6% Asian.[181] By 2050, the U.S. will likely have no racial or ethnic majority.

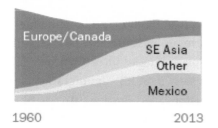

Figure 4.7. Sources of Immigrants from 1960-2013

Like previous generations, today's native-born Americans have mixed feelings about the arrival of immigrants and changing demographics. Based on anthropological theory, it's been human nature that we want to bond with our kinsmen against outsiders since the time of the cavemen. Throughout human history, the demagogues amongst us have exploited this "tribal propensity" by blaming our sufferings on outsiders to "deflect internal scrutiny and impeding reform" (William Saletan).[182]

Descendants of immigrants are often the most vocal critics of new immigrants, using arguments similar to those used against their own ancestors. Therefore, all Americans need to get educated on the immigration history of our nation. As President John F. Kennedy eloquently summarized:

> Perhaps our brightest hope for the future lies in the lessons of the past. As each new wave of immigration has reached America it has been faced with problems, not only the problems that come with making new homes and new jobs, but, more important, the problems of getting along with

people of different backgrounds and habits. Somehow, the difficult adjustments are made and people get down to the tasks of earning a living, raising a family, living with their neighbors, and, in the process, building a nation.[183]

CHAPTER 5

Issues and Challenges with Current Immigration Laws

The path to becoming a legal immigrant to the U.S. is narrow. There are only a few channels. As dictated by the Immigration Act of 1990, an aspiring immigrant can be sponsored by an employer or a family member, such as a parent, spouse, or sibling who has permanent status in the United States; or enter the country as a refugee or asylum seeker; or be lucky enough to be a visa lottery winner. The annual quota for green cards issued per channel for the fiscal year 2022 was as follows:

- Family-sponsored: 480,000

- Employer-sponsored: 140,000

- Refugees:* 125,000 (FY 2022)

---

* The quota for refugee-based green cards is set by the president on annual basis.

- Political asylum: unlimited

- Visa lottery: 55,000

The 1990 immigration law also prescribes a per-country limit of 7% of the total number of visas that can be issued via family-sponsored and employer-sponsored channels*.

My interest in immigration reform results from my experience as a legal immigrant. I came to the United States on a student visa in 1996 and didn't become a U.S. citizen until 2013. I had never imagined my citizenship quest would turn into a 17-year-long march. During this long journey, I shifted from an employment-based to a family-based application and experienced high financial costs coupled with long delays, typical experiences for legal immigrants. The U.S. legal immigration process is notorious for its long delays, huge backlogs, strict quotas, complexity, high costs, and inconsistent messages. I'll examine these issues, their causes, and their impacts in greater detail in this chapter.

5.1 Long Delays and Huge Backlogs

Currently, more than 5.2 million legal immigration applications stuck in the bureaucratic backlog. Most Americans outside of immigrant communities have no idea about the excruciating wait times many legal immigrants must endure. Also, it is politically expedient for many on the left and the right to focus on illegal immigration. Therefore, most media, think tanks, and policymakers rarely pay attention to the enormous backlogs in our legal immigration system. The most thorough analysis of it that I can find is a 2019 study by David J. Bier of the Cato Institute, a libertarian think tank based in Washington, D.C. His key findings included[184]:

- "More than 100,000 legal immigrants—28 percent of the family-sponsored and employment-based lines with

---

* If the limits are 480,000 and 140,000, respectively, the per-country limit will be 43,400, which is 7% of (480,000 + 140,000). Furthermore, the per-country cap of 43,400 is divided into a family-based limit (33,600) and an employment-based limit (9,800).

quotas—waited a decade or more to apply for a green card in 2018, up from 3 percent in 1991. By contrast, 31 percent had no wait at all from the quotas in 1991, while just two percent had no wait in 2018.

- Nearly five million people are waiting in the applicant backlog. Without significant reforms, wait times will become impossibly long for these immigrants ... **about 675,000 would-be legal immigrants—14 percent of those waiting in 2018—would die without seeing a green card if they refused to give up and stayed in the line indefinitely** [highlighted by me]. It will take decades and—in some categories—a half-century or more to process everyone else waiting now."

The long waits and backlogs have only gotten worse since the 2019 study. All you have to do is to look at the latest visa bulletin board, published by the U.S. State Department, to see the problem.

To understand the visa bulletin, one must first grasp the concept of a "priority date." The 1990 Immigration Act dictates that an applicant must have a visa number before he or she can apply for permanent residency (a.k.a. a green card). When intended legal immigration applicants submit their applications for green cards, they are given priority dates based on when their applications were received. These priority dates determine when those immigration visas will be available.

The State Department's website publishes a visa bulletin monthly. The visa bulletin shows current priority dates for different visa types of applicants (Appendix 6 shows the visa bulletin for December 2022).

Here is an example of how to interpret the bulletin: I am a naturalized U.S. citizen from China. Hypothetically speaking, to sponsor my brother and sister to immigrate to the U.S. legally, I would have to file a petition for family-based visas, Category 4 for siblings, on their behalf.

According to the visa bulletin (Appendix 6), the priority date for Category 4 of the family-based visa petitions of immigrants from mainland China is December 15, 2007, which means that the U.S. Citizenship and Immigration Services (USCIS) is currently processing applications they received on or before December 15, 2007. Given this backlog, if I were to start applying for family-based legal immigration for my brother and sister in December 2022, they would have to wait for at least 15 years before USCIS began to process their applications.

My siblings speak English, are college-educated, and are at the most productive time of their lives. Suppose they waited 15 years to become legal immigrants after their applications were approved in 2037 or later. They would already have passed their prime. The same visa bulletin shows that someone emigrating from the Philippines has to wait 18 years to bring his siblings over, and for someone from Mexico, the wait is even longer — 21 years.

It's a sad irony that an immigration system ostensibly keyed to family reunification ends up causing so much pain for many families due to its long delays. Without justifying the illegality, one can understand why many people become illegal immigrants instead. Few will put their lives on hold for a decade or longer.

The wait time for an employment-based visa is even more ridiculous. On December 17, 2022, a group of Indian tech workers from Silicon Valley marched in San Jose, California, demanding immigration reform because some of them had waited for decades for their green cards. But according to the Cato Institute's David Bier, some immigrants from India with advanced degrees may have to wait 151 years before receiving their green cards.[185]

Essentially, the long delays in the U.S. immigration system have hindered our nation's ability from attract top talent. One study found, "The stay rate of Chinese graduates [from U.S. universities] declines by 2.4 percentage points for each year of delay, while Indian graduates facing delays of at least five and a half years have a stay rate that is 8.9 percentage points lower."[186]

Sometimes the long delays in the U.S. immigration system mean life or death for certain applicants. For example, when the U.S. military pulled out of Afghanistan in August 2021, it left behind about 78,000 Afghan allies eligible for the Special Immigrant Visa (SIV). The Afghan SIV program was created in 2009 to give Afghans who served as interpreters for the U.S. military and their family members a path to escape Taliban threats to their lives and resettle in the United States. But as of May 2022, "the National Visa Center's Afghan SIV email account had more than 325,000 unread messages," and "staff were still opening unread emails from August 2021 -- the month of the U.S. withdrawal from Afghanistan."[187] The snail pace of the SIV process means Afghan allies and their families continue to face the Taliban's threat to their lives daily.

Why does the legal immigration process take so long? Here are four of the primary reasons.

First, it is a simple mismatch between supply and demand. There are a limited number of visas available. The Immigration and Nationality Act sets an annual limit of all legal immigration at 675,000 (not including visas for refugees and political asylum seekers). This annual quota hasn't changed much since 1990, and the demand far exceeds the outdated quotas.

Second, the long wait is worse for immigrants from certain countries due to the per-country limit. The 1990 Act sets a per-country limit of 7% of the total of the family-based and employment-based categories, no matter the size of the population of the country of origin. The dependent visa limit is set at 2% of the total number of family-sponsored and employment-based visas. The per-country limit skews the supply and demand of visas for nations that traditionally send us the most immigrants. For example, 1,316,118 Mexican citizens applied for permanent residency in 2012, but that year's cap was 47,250. The four countries with the most extended wait times for family- and employer-sponsored visa applications are Mexico, India, China, and the Philippines.

Third, emphasizing on family reunion results in chain immigration, exacerbating the long waits and backlogs. Close to 70% of our annual visa quota is allocated to family-based immigrants. Every legal resident or U.S. citizen can not only sponsor his or her nuclear relatives, such as spouses and children, but also non-nuclear relatives, such as parents, adult children, and siblings. The more family-based visas we hand out, the higher the demand will be because everyone has some family members he or she wants to bring over, and those family members have their own family members, and so on. Chain immigration has been the main driver behind immigration population growth since the Immigration Act of 1965. Although it is understandable that immigrants want to reunite with their extended families, they chose to leave those families behind when they emigrated to another country. Demanding family reunions from the host country on human-itarian grounds makes the situation worse — and waiting for a decade or more for that reunion is far from humane.

Fourth, some delays are caused by U.S. government priorities out-side of existing immigration law. For example, on January 28, 2015, the U.S. Justice Department notified to thousands of immigrants awaiting hearings that their cases would be delayed for five years until the day after Thanksgiving in 2019. The reason for the delay? To make room for higher-priority cases caused by the summer surge in unaccom-panied minors and families crossing the U.S. border from Mexico.

There are other causes for the long delays and backlogs. For exam-ple, the complexity of the law spreads USCIS resources thin. Also, outdated systems and a lack of efficiency within the USCIS system contribute to those delays. We will discuss these factors in more detail in the following several sections.

5.2 Complexity

U.S. immigration laws are known for their complexity, and some people consider these laws even more complex than our tax code. The majority of applicants cannot navigate the U.S. immigration process without legal counsel. As one federal judge put it:

> The statutory scheme defining and delimiting the rights of aliens is exceedingly complex. Courts and commentators have stated that the Immigration and Nationality Act resembles "King Minos' labyrinth in ancient Crete," and is "second only to the Internal Revenue Code in complexity." (*Chan v. Reno*, 1997 U.S. Dist. Lexis 3016, *5 [S.D.N.Y. 1997].)

Most legal immigrants come to the U.S. through one of these four primary channels: family-based, employment-based, political asylum/refugees, or the diversity lottery program. But within each channel, many sub-categories cater to specific groups, each subject to different rules. Besides the normal immigration channels, politicians have piled on many special immigration programs. Currently, there are over two dozen immigration visa categories through which people outside the U.S. can obtain green cards without going through the normal legal immigration channels. For example, according to the United States Citizenship and Immigration Services (USCIS), there is a unique program for "a person who was born in Korea, Vietnam, Laos, Kampuchea (Cambodia), or Thailand between January 1, 1951, and October 21, 1982, and fathered by a U.S. citizen to get a green card." Another unique program is for "certain individuals from Guatemala, El Salvador, and the former Soviet bloc countries who entered the United States and applied for asylum."

Some of these unique programs were created to serve a political purpose at one point in time, such as the special treatment of citizens from Cuba or South Vietnam. In these cases, a special immigration program became a foreign policy tool to combat the Cold War against communism. Although historical justifications for such programs are long gone, "Government programs, once launched, never disappear" (President Reagan).

Other notable programs were created to get around the long delays and backlogs of normal immigration channels. For example, the USCIS explains on its website: "Due to a backlog of immigrant visa petitions at that time, a long separation could occur between the overseas fiancé(e) and their intended U.S. citizen spouse." Thus, the K-visa category, including the K-3 fiancée visa and the K-4 stepchildren visa, was created as part of the Legal Immigration and Family Equity (LIFE) Act amendments of 2000 to expedite the immigration process. Yet the very existence of these programs not only makes the immigration laws more complex than ever, but it further exacerbates the long delays and backlogs for all immigrants.

In fiscal year 2021, over 13,000 immigration visas were issued under these special visa programs,[188] but this list is not all-inclusive. For example, it doesn't list a particular program for Cuban citizens. The Cuban Adjustment Act of 1966 gave migrants from Cuba special treatment by allowing them to become permanent residents if they had been in the United States for at least two years. The Immigration and Nationality Act Amendments of 1976 reduced it to one year. Today, there are several special immigration programs for people from Cuba and annual visa quota caps on immigration that do not apply to Cuban migrants. In addition, any Cuban citizen can also migrate through general channels such as the visa lottery program and family-based or employment-based immigration.

Each of the two dozen special visa programs has rules, eligibility requirements, and screening processes. In addition to immigration visas, the USCIS administers over two dozen non-immigration visa programs for visitors, students, and others. The complexity of our immigration system stretches federal resources thin and creates insane backlogs.

5.3 A Costly Endeavor

Becoming a legal immigrant to the U.S. is a costly endeavor. There are several categories of expenses:

Filing fees. These are fees charged by the U.S. government for various forms. Some forms do not require a fee, but many do. Filing fees vary by the type of form and range from $10 to $17,795 per person. Whether your immigration petition is approved or denied, these fees are non-refundable. Fees cover more than 90% of USCIS operating costs.

Attorney fees. Since the U.S. legal immigration system is so complex and the process is so time-consuming, many legal immigrants have to hire lawyers to help them navigate the system and file additional paperwork to remain legal while waiting. Depending on the visa category, some immigrants will pay thousands of dollars for immigration lawyers. A *Washington Post* article reported one immigrant going through the investor channel paid upwards of $84,000 in attorney fees.[189]

Other expenses. Some legal immigrants must take medical exams and pay for the expenses. Some have travel expenses to USCIS branch offices for interviews. The USCIS schedules interviews only via regular mail, and the interview schedule doesn't take into consideration applicants' availability or circumstances. Rescheduling sometimes takes a year if an applicant cannot make the initial interview appointment. Therefore, most applicants have no choice but to take time off from work to try to be at the interview, no matter what they're doing or how far they have to travel.

Expenses as a result of long delays. The long waits and backlogs in our immigration system sometimes force applicants to repeat the same steps and complete the same forms more than once. For example, almost all legal immigrants are required to go through medical exams, and the results are valid only for one year.* The U.S. government covers medical exam costs for refugees. Everyone else has to pay for his or her own medical exam, which typically costs several hundred dollars. Suppose there is little or no progress in the immigration process within that year. In this case, the applicant has to redo the medical exam and provide new results to ensure his or her medical record is up to date, which means additional costs. The long wait some immigrants must endure means they will wait longer and spend more money on repetitive medical exams.

Non-financial cost. Some costs are qualitative, such as the emotional toll on applicants due to the uncertainty of the process. During the seemingly endless wait, many legal immigrants are afraid to travel abroad, change jobs, and buy a home because they are uncertain if they can stay legally or not. Puneet Chowdhary came to the U.S. from India in 2001 and had been waiting for her green card ever since, as she told National Public Radio in 2020[190]

> "I haven't been back to India in the last eight years because I'm scared I won't be able to come back into the U.S. I lost my father this year and I could not go home to pay my respects to him. "

For applicants residing outside of the United States, some postpone marriage or delay having kids, worrying that such a life-changing event may increase the probability of their applications being denied.

---

* Some immigrants are exempt from the medical exam. For example, immigrants with specific disabilities are exempt. For more information, please check the USCIS website: www.USCIS.gov.

5.4 Refugees and Asylum Seekers: What's the Difference?

Historically, no other country has done more for refugees than the United States. Most countries have just one immigration program on a humanitarian basis, which allows legal immigration based on refugee status or political asylum. The United States is one of the few countries that provides two annual programs and many one-off special programs for humanitarian causes.

The first annual program is the refugee program. The U.S. Citizenship and Immigration Services (USCIS) defines refugees as people who live outside of their home countries, "were persecuted or fear persecution due to race, religion, nationality, political opinion, or membership in a particular social group," and are "not firmly resettled in another country." The president of the United States determines the annual visa quota for refugee admissions in consultation with Congress. In 2021, President Biden raised the visa cap for refugees for fiscal year 2022 from the low 15,000-person ceiling set by former President Donald Trump to 125,000, representing a 733% increase.

In addition, since 2012, the USCIS has reinstated a family reunion program to allow refugees to bring their family members to the U.S. on refugee status (the program had been halted for four years due to widespread fraud). Upon arrival, refugees can legally work in the U.S.

The second annual program is the asylum program. People already in the United States who were persecuted or fear persecution upon returning to their home country may apply for asylum within the United States or at a port of entry when they seek admission. In the past, asylum petitions were mostly based on political and/or religious persecution concerns. In recent years, the State Department has changed its asylum policy by calling sexual orientation a basic human right. This change has caused a surge of successful asylum petitions from gays and lesbians from Central America. *The Wall Street Journal* reported that one New York advocacy group, Immigration Equity, saw its caseload for LGBTQ asylum seekers jump 250% from 2009 to 2014, and it has a success rate of 98% — whereas Latin Americans who file asylum claims based on generalized violence are routinely denied.[191]

Since the federal law on asylum doesn't define how someone gets into the United States, even someone already in the country illegally is still eligible to seek asylum. An asylum-seeker can get approval and become a permanent U.S. resident after one interview or one appearance in an immigration court. They are eligible to work in the U.S. even before their court appearances as long as they have filed their petitions. Once their petitions are approved, many asylees are eligible for federal welfare benefits and can apply for permanent residency after one year. So, asylum is the quickest way for someone illegally in the U.S. to start working and to become a legal resident. Thus, in recent years, asylum applications from those who entered the U.S. illegally have spiked, rising to 191,367 in fiscal year 2020, more than doubling from the year before. Most of them were migrants who sought employment opportunities in the U.S. rather than escaping persecution back home.

The surge in asylum applications has worsened the wait times in the immigration process because there are only 66 immigration courts and about 350 immigration judges available who handle all immigration-related cases, including asylum petitions. I will discuss asylum more in Chapter seven.

Although the refugee and asylum programs both fall under humanitarian-based immigration, the operation of these two programs couldn't be more different.

Figure 5.1. United States Asylum Applications Summary[*][192]

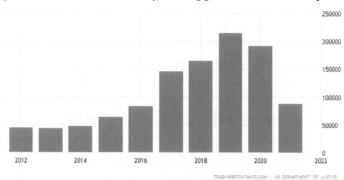

TRADINGECONOMICS.COM | US DEPARTMENT OF JUSTICE

Quotas. The refugee program has an annual visa quota, but the asylum program doesn't, so its number fluctuates yearly. According to the

---

[*] Due to reporting delay, fiscal year 2020 was the most recent data available.

USCIS 2022 annual report, the U.S. admitted 11,840 refugees and their families in the fiscal year 2020. Meanwhile, 31,429 individuals were granted asylum.

Source of applicants. The U.S. works closely with UN agencies on the refugee program. The United Nations High Commissioner for Refugees (UNHCR) typically determines if an individual qualifies as a refugee. The UNHCR, or occasionally another nongovernment agency, will refer a refugee applicant to the United States for resettlement. In 2020, the leading countries of nationality for individuals admitted as refugees were Congo (24 percent), Burma (18 percent), and Ukraine (16 percent).

An asylum seeker doesn't need a UN referral, so that anyone can claim such status. For the fiscal year 2020, Central America's Northern Triangle countries (El Salvador, Guatemala, and Honduras) and Mexico comprised 63 percent of all asylum seekers. Unaccompanied children from Central America's Northern Triangle accounted for 91 percent of all unaccompanied child asylum applications in 2020.

Screening. Each refugee applicant will undergo a background check and multiple in-person interviews by federal agents from the Department of Homeland Security's U.S. Citizenship and Immigration Services (USCIS). The entire process can take 18 months or longer. The screening for asylum is much less stringent because the definition of what constitutes persecution has become very broad and is not evidence-based. Immigration officers rely solely on their intuition and the applicant's words. Before the recent surge in asylum applications, an asylum seeker could get approval and become a permanent U.S. resident in just a few months. The simple screening process, and the short timeframe to get a green card turn the asylum program into a fraud heaven. Even the liberal media agrees. *The New Yorker* profiled how some asylum seekers either fabricated horror stories on their own or were coached by lawyers or advocates based on previously approved asylum cases. "The immigration people know the stories. There's one for each country. There's the Colombian rape story—they all say they were raped by the FARC. There's the Rwandan rape story, the Tibetan refugee story. The details for each are the same."[193]

Welfare benefits. The U.S. Department of State works with nine domestic agencies to resettle refugees inside the U.S. Its Reception and Placement program pays each agency a sum of cash to resettle each refugee for the first three months after arrival. Then,

> The Department of Health and Human Services' Office of Refugee Resettlement works through the states and other nongovernmental organizations to provide longer-term cash and medical assistance, as well as language, employment, and social services.[194]

Asylees do not get direct financial assistance from the Department of State. Still, they are eligible for federal government welfare benefits immediately, including welfare (Temporary Aid to Needy Families and Safety Net); Supplemental Security Income (SSI); Medicaid; and food stamps. Meanwhile, some other legal immigrants (family-based or employment-based) must wait five years before they are eligible for such benefits.

I couldn't find any reasonable explanation for why the U.S. operates two humanitarian-based immigration programs and why they work so differently. These programs represent significant portions of our annual legal immigrant inflow. For example, for the fiscal year 2020, we as a nation granted close to 120,000 green cards to immigrants on an asylum/refugee basis (not including one-off special programs for humanitarian causes). In addition to these programs, the United States government awards immigration visas to immigrants under the Cuban Adjustment Act of 1966, the Nicaraguan Adjustment and Central American Relief Act (NACARA), the Haitian Refugee Immigration Fairness Act (HRIFA), and a Special Visa Program (SIV) for Afghanistan or Iraqi nationals who supported the U.S. Armed Forces as translators). Overall, a quarter of our annual immigration visa quota goes to immigrants on a humanitarian basis.

5.5 A Program That Shouldn't Ever Have Existed

The Immigration Act of 1990, Section 131, established the Diversity Visa (DV) program, also known as the Visa Lottery program. The program's stated goal was to bring individuals to the U.S. from nations that had been sending few immigrants in the past. The word "diversity" here refers to the country of origin. The law set the annual quota for DV visas at 55,000. But the U.S. Congress later reduced the quota to 50,000 in 2000*. The U.S. is the only country gives foreign nationals permanent residency based on pure luck.

There are many problems with this program, including but not limited to the following:

It serves no national interests. Anyone can apply if his/her home country is not on the exclusion list. There is no cost to register. The admission criteria are shallow. The program requires the principal DV applicant to have only a high school education or equivalent or two years of work experience. Applicants are admitted based on luck, not humanitarian needs or skills. Applicants also do not have to show any familial ties to the U.S.

The program is heaven for fraudsters. Since there is no limit to how many times a person can enter the lottery, many foreign nationals apply for the program multiple times and use different aliases and other false personal information. Illegal immigrants are eligible to apply as well. The State Department has issued fraud warnings due to an increasing number of fraudulent emails and letters sent to applicants that falsely promise success in exchange for large sums of money.

The program is an administrative nightmare. Since 2005, more than 200 million people have participated in the DV program. It drew more than 13 million applicants in 2020 alone.[195] Some countries that

---

* During the COVID-19 pandemic in 2020, President Donald Trump stopped all Diversity Vsia applicants from entering the United States. Between the executive order and the processing time, the U.S. issued only 19,125 DVs in fiscal year 2020, well below the typical 50,000. Retrieved from https://www.forbes.com/sites/stuartanderson/2022/01/31/state-dept-continues-to-fight-diversity-visa-immigrants-in-court/?sh=1e8c4104480e

consistently produce over a million lottery entries year after year are Ghana, Nigeria, Uzbekistan, and Ukraine. Even a tiny country like Nepal (population 28 million) submitted more than one million lottery entries in 2016.

In the past, applicants didn't even have to present a passport or other legal document to prove that they lived in the country from which they were applying. Therefore, many people participated in DV pools in multiple countries, hoping to increase their odds. The U.S. Department of State finally began to require foreign nationals who enter the DV program to have valid and unexpired passports. The State Department said, "The new requirement was necessitated by the significant number of fraudulent entries for the Diversity Visa program each year, noting that sometimes criminal enterprises submit entries for individuals without their knowledge . . . and hold the entry information from the named petitioner in exchange for payment."[196]

It is a considerable burden for the U.S. government to process millions of applications and verify applicants' information. Although the annual number of visas allocated to this program is 50,000, the State Department typically selects about 100,000 applicants randomly in the first round. These applicants are then interviewed and undergo background checks and medical exams. The first 50,000 deemed eligible will receive visas. Since applicants do not pay any fees to enter the lottery, all the costs of time and personnel are borne by the State Department and the Department of Homeland Security. These agencies are already overwhelmed and have difficulties handling existing immigration backlogs.

National security threats. This program encourages immigration from some countries or regions where fraud is common and where terrorist groups are active. It allows people to become legal U.S. residents through random selection without any family or other ties to the U.S. Once applicants have become legal U.S. residents, they can move freely around the country and take any jobs they like. It is an almost perfect program for terrorists to take advantage of, and several known terrorists came to the U.S. as lottery winners. The most notorious one is Hesham Mohamed Hedayet, who shot several people at the LAX airport in 2002. According to testimony from the State Department's

Inspector General during the 109th Congress, "The Diversity Visa program contains significant risks to national security from hostile intelligence officers, criminals, and terrorists attempting to use the program for entry into the United States as permanent residents."

Failed to achieve its original goal. The goal of this program was to bring in immigrants from countries with historically low rates of immigration to the United States, so the pool of immigrants wouldn't be dominated by migrants from a few countries. The program failed to achieve this goal on several fronts.

First, the top immigrant-sending countries haven't changed much. The countries contributing the most immigrants have become *more concentrated* and *less diverse*. For example, in 2012, the top five countries of origin for the U.S. were Mexico, India, the Philippines, China, and Vietnam. In 2020, the top five countries of origin to the U.S. were Mexico, India, China, the Dominican Republic, and Vietnam.[197]

Second, even though the program selects applicants randomly, historically, the winners have primarily come from the same few countries, such as Congo and Egypt in Africa. Over 60% of the lottery winners from Asia were from Iran and Nepal, and citizens from Uzbekistan and Ukraine have consistently claimed the most lottery winners from Europe.

Third, according to analysis provided by blackimmigration.net, the government's emphasis on the lottery program as one of the most coveted avenues for immigration from Africa is factually wrong,[198]

> Most black immigrants—especially those from the Caribbean—arrive as legal permanent residents based on their family ties. Refugees from Ethiopia, Somalia, Liberia, Sudan, and Eritrea accounted for 30 percent of all black African immigrants in 2009, while around **one-fifth** of black African immigrants entered the United States through the diversity visa lottery program.

While many legal immigrants have waited for years to be admitted into the U.S., the DV program randomly gives 50,000 visas away with little language or work experience requirements and without a strict vetting process. It doesn't strengthen family ties nor promote diversity or our nation's economic interests. Congress should abolish the DV program and allocate that 50,000 quotas to employment-based immigration applicants.

5.6 Unequal Treatment and Mixed Messages

The United States was founded upon the principle that "all men are created equal," but there are various examples of inequality in our immigration policies, processes, and enforcement.

Not all visa categories have quotas. There are annual quotas on the number of employment-based, family-based, and investment-based immigrants, but there is no limit on political asylum seekers. Some special immigration programs, like those set up for Cuban citizens, also operate outside the annual visa quota. This mixed bag sends the wrong message that the U.S. values some groups more than others.

Not all visa categories are subject to country-of-origin limitations. The Immigration Act of 1990 set a per-country limit of 7% of total family-ly-based and employment-based immigrants, no matter the size of the population of the country of origin. But anyone can apply for an asylum-based visa, "regardless of your country of origin or your current immigration status" (USCIS website).[199] Some countries, i.e., China and India, are completely excluded from participating in the visa lottery program. For those countries and regions that are allowed to participate, there is no country-of-origin limit, resulting in Africans and Europeans making up 75-80% of all visa lottery winners from 2010-2014. The data also showed that many lottery winners were concentrated in only a few countries. Again, the per-country limit gives the impression that the U.S. discriminates against immigrants based on their origins and has worsened the wait time for immigrants from other countries.

Not all visa applicants have to wait a long time. Lots of family-based and employment-based immigrants have been waiting for their petitions to be processed for several decades. Yet, winners of the visa lottery program generally get their green card within a year. The significant difference in wait time suggests that the U.S. believes one group of people is more desirable than another, so it deserves to jump to the head of the line.

The minimum eligibility requirements are vastly different for different visa applicants. Some visa categories, such as the asylum and lottery programs, need more precise definitions for qualifications. Some visa categories require few qualifications, while others set the bar extremely high. For example, the visa lottery program allows people with no ties to America to become legal residents overnight based on luck, as long as they meet the minimum requirement of having a high school education or two years' work experience. On the other hand, to qualify for an employment-based, 2nd preference category visa (see Appendix 6), an applicant must hold an advanced degree, have exceptional abilities, and have at least five years of professional work experience. The requirement for investment-based immigration is even more rigid. Entrepreneurs who invest $1 million or at least $500,000 in a targeted employment area and plan to create or preserve ten permanent full-time jobs will be granted a conditional green card. Such different requirements suggest that our country cares little about the knowledge, skills, and contributions some immigrants can bring.

Illegal immigrants are treated better than legal immigrants in some states. As of 2022, 20 states* offer in-state tuition to illegal immigrant children, and five states even allow these children to receive state financial aid. Yet, the children of those who are here legally and waiting in line for years to get their applications processed have to pay out-of-state tuition rates and are not eligible for state financial aid. The Department of Homeland Security (DHS) worked tirelessly to improve

---

* About 16 state legislative actions and four by state university systems offer in-state tuition to illegal immigrant children. Sixteen state legislatures — California, Colorado, Connecticut, Florida, Illinois, Kansas, Maryland, Minnesota, Nebraska, New Jersey, New Mexico, New York, Oregon, Texas, Utah and Washington.

Retrieved from https://www.ncsl.org/research/immigration/in-state-tuition-and-unauthorized-immigrants.aspx

immigration detention centers to house illegal immigrants, "including female hormone treatments for transgender men, abortions for women and 'ethnically diverse' diet options."[200] Legal immigrants, however, mostly have to pay for their own immigration-related expenses. No wonder many legal immigrants feel frustration and betrayal at the attention and preferential treatment conferred upon illegal immigrants.

A garden variety of state laws and resolutions create further confusion. Since the United States hasn't enacted any new or comprehensive federal immigration laws for decades, many states have taken it upon themselves to pass state-level laws to tackle immigration-related issues. As of 2021, lawmakers in 49 states enacted 206 laws and 263 resolutions related to immigration.[201] That means an immigrant can be treated very differently depending on where they live.

For instance, in January 2022, New York City passed a new law that would allow more than 800,000 non-citizens, including those who only have work authorizations in the U.S. and "Dreamers" — people brought to the U.S. illegally when they were children, to vote in municipal elections.[202] As of February 2022, illegal immigrants can get driver's licenses in 16 states and in the District of Columbia. Another example is that 11 states and many of their cities became sanctuary jurisdictions as of October 2022, enacting laws, regulations, and policies that shield illegal immigrants from U.S. Immigration and Customs Enforcement (ICE) and refuse to cooperate with ICE's enforcement. Rules become mere suggestions when there is such variety, and trying to follow them is a joke.

5.7 The Least Efficient and Most Technically Challenged Bureaucracy

The Department of Homeland Security (DHS) was created after the 9/11 attacks with the goal of "transforming and realigning the current confusing patchwork of government activities into a single department whose primary mission is to protect our homeland."[203] Instead, the DHS, with a $38-billion budget and 240,000 employees, became the worst patchwork ever. Rather than streamlining anything, it has become our nation's least efficient and most technically challenged bureaucracy.

Most native-born Americans consider spending time at the Department of Motor Vehicles offices the ultimate test of patience. There is no shortage of jokes about how inefficient most DMV offices are. However, compared to the United States Citizenship and Immigration Services (USCIS), one of the dozen sub-organizations under DHS, employees of DMV have nothing to be ashamed of. With 19,000 employees and 223 offices worldwide, the USCIS is one of the most inefficiently run organizations on the planet.

DHS's operation remains in the technical Stone Age. Once you submit your application, it falls into a black hole. The USCIS only communicates with applicants via first-class mail. Yes, there is a USCIS website where you can supposedly check your case status, but the site takes so long to process a case that it often remains in the same status for months and years. If you try to call USCIS customer service, be ready for an endurance test because the wait is often longer than 30 minutes. The recorded message and any customer service representative you are lucky enough to speak to will tell you the same thing: check the website. They can't give you any information unless it already appears on the website. It's no use relating to them that the website is not updated.

Let me share with you some of my own experiences dealing with USCIS. Below is an excerpt from my autobiography, *Confucius Never Said*:

Several months after I submitted my citizenship application, I received a letter from the immigration office that asked me to appear on X day at X time in X location to have my fingerprints taken. I am used to the fingerprinting process. It has always been the first step whenever I change my visa type and legal status: from a student visa to H1B visa to a green card. Additionally, whenever I came back from China, U.S. customs agents at the airport recorded my fingerprints. Therefore, the government already had at least a dozen records of my fingerprints. I didn't mind doing it again, but the appointment date on the letter turned out to be a date on which I had a business trip, for which I had already booked my hotel and airplane. Therefore, I had to request a reschedule. According to the letter, I could send my request only in writing. Thus, I wrote a letter stating my request and mailed it out immediately.

A month later, I still hadn't received any letter about rescheduling. I wrote another letter, including a copy of my first letter. After another month went by, I wrote the third letter, including copies of my two previous letters. Three months passed, and three letters later, I hadn't received reply. I called the immigration office's customer service number. After several attempts, I finally got through the annoying automated system and talked to a customer service agent, a real human being. Once I explained my situation, he told me that he could do nothing. He had no access to the scheduling system. All I could do was wait. The immigration office only communicated with applicants via letters. According to him, I should drop everything the next time the letter asks me to be at X location on X day at X time.

We live in the Amazon, Twitter, and Facebook age, but I couldn't make a fingerprinting appointment online and choose a time when I would be available. My only option was to wait for a letter from the federal government. Something is seriously wrong with this picture.

I'm sure USCIS has dedicated and responsible employees who are customer friendly and stay on top of the cases; unfortunately, that wasn't my experience. Here is another incident from *Confucius Never Said*:

Right after Mike and I married, we submitted a green card application since Mike is a U.S. citizen. I waited for six months without receiving my green card. We were planning to spend our honeymoon in China. Still, I needed a legal status to return to the U.S. When we called the immigration office's 1-800 customer service number, we only got a recording that asked us to check for updates on the web. But the status on the web never changed. So Mike and I each took another half day off and went to the immigration office in Centennial. We were escorted into a room on the first floor. A couple of agents were sitting behind several windows. We went to sit in front of one of them and explained our situation to him. After we presented our paperwork and ID, he checked his computer for a while. Then he and I had the following conversation:

"Ma'am, your case is in transit."

"What do you mean? Is it in the mail?"

"No. It says here that it is between the second and third floors of the building, and we do not know where it is."

Mike became upset, and I started to cry. The agent behind the window showed no emotion. Mike wanted to argue with him, but I pulled him away because I knew that arguing with the front office agent was no use.

Since we had already booked our trip to China, we asked our lawyer to get me a piece of paper saying my green card application was pending. That paper cost me more than our airline tickets. Once again, I carried a suitcase full of legal documents starting from 1996, when I was a student, and we went on our trip to China.

5.8 Are We Willing and Capable of Enforcing Immigration Laws?

The Department of Homeland Security (DHS) proclaims on its website that its mission includes "preventing terrorism and enhancing security; managing our borders; facilitating legal immigration and enforcing laws."[204] On any one of these measures, the DHS deserves a grade of "F."

Not "preventing terrorism and enhancing security." The DHS doesn't adequately screen dangerous visa applicants. On December 2, 2015, a radicalized couple opened fire at a company holiday party in San Bernardino, California. They killed 14 people and injured many more. This event brought terrorist attacks close to home like never before. One of the San Bernardino shooters, Tashfeen Malik, came to the U.S. originally on a K-1 fiancée visa. She didn't encrypt her radical thoughts and ideas on Facebook before her visa application; they were posted for anyone to read. But our immigration officials were prevented from viewing her easily accessible social media postings due to an internal secret policy that prohibits immigration officials from reviewing foreign visa applicants' social media. Why does this policy exist? Because the Secretary of Homeland Security fears a civil liberty backlash and bad PR. The DHS failed to stop criminals and protect Americans letting political correctness dictate its policies.

Not "managing our border." The Biden administration claimed that there was no border crisis. But for the Fiscal Year 2022, border agents encountered nearly 2.4 million illegal immigrants crossing the U.S.-Mexico border, not including the getaways. Agents made 98 terror watch list arrests, four times the arrests from the previous five years combined. The Biden administration has claimed that there is no border crisis.[205] In addition to the endless inflow of people, about 95 percent of all fentanyl, the drug that is now the leading cause of death for Americans between the ages of 18 and 45, flows into our nation across the southern border. If we, as a sovereign nation, can't even secure our borders, how can we effectively protect our people?

Not "enforcing immigration laws." The DHS exacerbates the illegal immigration problem by failing to address visa overstays. An estimated 40-60 percent of overstays come to the U.S. on legal non-immigration visas and then stay after those visas have expired. Unfortunately, visa overstays have never been an enforcement priority for the Department of Homeland Security. A foreigner can come to the U.S. legally on a non-immigration visa and continue to roam around the country after visa expiration with little consequence.

For instance, Mariya Chernykh came to the U.S. from Russia in 2009 on a three-month educational-exchange visa. She didn't return to Russia after her visa expired. Instead, she remained in the U.S. illegally until she married a citizen, Enrique Marquez Jr., who bought rifles and sold them to the San Bernardino shooters. Her marriage qualified her to become a legal immigrant and a green card holder. The day after the San Bernardino shooting, she took her green card interview. Even though Mariya Chernykh is not implicated in the San Bernardino shooting case, the fact that she overstayed in the U.S. for six years with no consequences and is eligible to become a green card holder says a lot about DHS's failure to enforce the law. In a country that has sent people to the moon, we have embarrassingly few means of identifying and tracking visa overstayers.

Summary

Our nation's existing immigration system is unmistakably broken and no longer serves our national interests. It makes life difficult for America-loving and hard-working immigrants who want to become Americans, and it doesn't do enough to keep out those who intend us harm.

There has been an increasing call for a moratorium on immigration based on perceived economic and security concerns. Thus, before I go into immigration reform proposals, I want to dive into this question:

Is immigration good for America?

CHAPTER 6

Is Immigration Good for America?

As of the beginning of 2022, some 46.6 million immigrants live in the U.S. Among them, an estimated 11-12 million are illegal immigrants.[206] The total number of immigrants is 14.2% of the total population of the United States (332 million). For perspective, the foreign-born population in the U.S. was at 14.8% in 1890 and 14.7 in 1910.[207] Therefore, today's immigration inflow is approaching historical highs.

As our nation's history has shown, we generally welcome immigrants, even though, from time to time, anti-immigrant sentiment takes hold of our politicians and specific segments of the public, triggering actions and policies that don't reflect our founding principles and values. Many Americans not only recognize that immigrants strengthen our economy and enrich our culture, but they also accept the moral argument that "American exceptionalism is rooted in its powerful belief that all people are created equal, and that America is the land of equal opportunity where all could thrive."[208] Today, however, immigration has become a front and divisive issue in America like never before. What has changed? The economy, national security, and the Covid-19 pandemic.

Economy. For immigrants, the incentives to come to the U.S. have been mostly the same for more than 200 hundred years: escaping poverty and political turmoil and seeking better-paid work and a better future in the US. For native-born Americans, how secure they feel about their economic situations primarily drives their attitudes toward immigrants.

The U.S. economic recovery since the 2008 financial crisis has been sluggish, with GDP growth at a tepid pace compared to the strong growth in the late 1980s and mid-1990s (see Figure 6.1). After-tax income expanded at an annual rate of 1.8%, much slower than in previous economic recoveries. Under the first two years of the Trump presidency, his business-friendly policies and tax cuts (which reduced both personal income tax and business tax rates)* gave the U.S. economy a badly-need boost. The U.S. GDP growth rates were 2.92 percent (2018) and 2.29 percent (2019), inflation rates were well below the Federal Reserve's target rate of 2 percent, and the unemployment rate fell to 3.5 percent in September of 2019, the lowest it had been since May of 1969.

Unfortunately, the 2020 Covid-19 pandemic and the lockdowns imposed by governments worldwide wiped out these economic gains and then some. In the early days of the pandemic, the unemployment rate spiked to 14.7 percent, the highest in the post-WWII era. Although that rate has fallen due to some people permanently leaving the labor force, U.S. employers reported at least 11 million open positions as of early 2022.

According to the latest Pew Research, the American middle class† has shrunk and is no longer the economic majority. Middle-class people made up 42% of the U.S. adult population in 2021, down from 61% in 1971.[209] The number of lowest-income Americans has also grown by more than five times. There are now 48.9 million adults in

---

* IRS income tax data show that while all income brackets benefited from the Republicans' 2017 tax reform law, the biggest beneficiaries were working and middle-income filers, not the top 1 percent, as many Democrats have argued. Retrieved from https://news.yahoo.com/irs-data-prove-trump-tax-130007569.html

† Pew Research Center defines "middle-income" Americans as adults whose annual household income is about $42,000 to $126,000 in 2020 dollars for a household of three.

this category, up from 21.6 million in 1971, representing 30 percent of the U.S. population.*

Government stimulus packages and massive spending under President Biden caused the U.S. inflation rate to soar to 9.1 percent in June 2022, the highest in four decades. The inflation rate has come down slightly since then. Still, as of December 2022, four in 10 Americans reported struggling financially due to inflation and rising energy costs.

When Americans feel anxious about their financial security or give up hope that their children will have better lives than theirs, attitudes toward immigrants also change.

Figure 6.1.† U.S. GDP Growth Rate per Year from 2012 to 2021

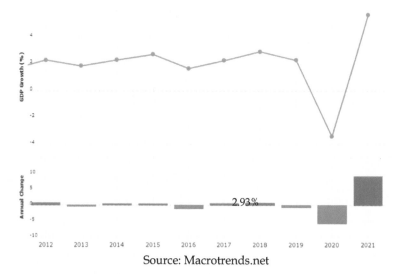

Source: Macrotrends.net

National security. After 9/11, many Americans believed "another terrorist attack causing large numbers of Americans to be lost" was likely. We suddenly realized that we were vulnerable even in our homeland. Our fears of another attack only heightened when we watched in shock the multiple mass shootings in Paris in 2015. After it

---

* Pew Research Center defines "low-income" Americans as adults whose annual household income is less than $31,402 annually in 2020 dollars for a household of three.

† Source: https://www.macrotrends.net/countries/USA/united-states/gdp-growth-rate

was reported that one of the terrorists who carried out the November Paris attack had pretended to be a Syrian refugee, some Americans and politicians called for measures to stop President Obama's commitment to resettle 10,000 Syrian refugees in the U.S. It didn't help when people were reminded that the Boston Marathon bombing on April 15, 2013, was perpetrated by the Tsarnaev brothers, who came to the U.S. from the former Soviet Republic of Kyrgyzstan on refugee status. But the mass shooting in San Bernardino, California, on December 2, 2015, really put our nation on edge. When it was revealed that one of the attackers came to the U.S. legally on a K-1 fiancée visa, there was a growing demand to scrutinize our legal immigration system.

Tapping into people's fears and anxieties, the U.S. House of Representatives passed a bill in December of 2015 imposing new restrictions on the Visa Waiver Program, which was created in 1986 to encourage business travel and tourism. The Visa Waiver Program allows citizens of 38 countries to visit the U.S. for a short duration (up to 90 days) without a visa, and some 20 million foreigners enter the U.S. through this program every year. There have been several efforts to restrict this program since its inception because it makes it too easy for a would-be terrorist to enter the U.S. In the past, such action received very little support from lawmakers. Still, after the San Bernardino attack, Congress voted for restrictions on the program with an overwhelming majority and without a committee debate. Under the new rule, people who have traveled to countries such as Syria, Iran, Iraq, or Sudan in the last five years or hold citizenship in one of those countries can no longer enter the U.S. through an expedited screening process. They have to obtain a visa.

The increasing number of terrorist attacks globally and their threats to our homeland enabled national security concerns to overtake the economy as the number one issue on American voters' minds in late 2015. About 70% of Americans believed the country was on the wrong track, and 6 in 10 adults disapproved of President Obama's handling of the war on terror and his foreign policy.[210]

Covid-19 pandemic. In early 2020, a mysterious virus outbreak in Wuhan, China, spread globally like wildfire. Many countries responded with travel restrictions and lockdowns. On January 31st, 2020, the Trump administration announced that it would temporarily bar foreign nationals who had traveled in China within the last 14 days from entering the U.S. The only exceptions were immediate family members of U.S. citizens and permanent residents. In the following months, President Trump issued several executive orders that restricted legal and illegal immigration.[211] He temporarily halted the issuance of certain green cards, saying it was necessary to "preserve jobs for American workers in an economy ravaged by the coronavirus." He issued Title 42, a public health order that enabled U.S. immigration enforcement agencies to turn back most migrants who tried to cross the U.S.-Mexico border legally and illegally or to seek asylum in the U.S. Within U.S. borders, fears of the virus sparked rising waves of verbal harassment and physical assaults against Asian Americans.

One repeated lesson throughout the history of immigration is that when Americans feel anxious about their financial well-being and fear for their physical safety, nationalism, and anti-immigration sentiments run high. Never underestimate the power of fear.

At this juncture, objectively answer this question is more important than ever: Is immigration good for America? I will try to address this question by answering four frequently asked questions:

- Are immigrants hurting American workers?

- Do immigrants use more welfare?

- Do immigrants commit more crimes?

- Do immigrants assimilate?

Hopefully, answers to these questions will help clear up misperceptions about immigrants and provide support for meaningful legal immigration reform.

6.1 Are Immigrants Hurting American Workers?

The argument blaming immigrants for "stealing" jobs away from native-born Americans is as old as our republic. Every generation of new immigrants, whether German, Irish, Chinese, Italian, or Latino, has been the target of this rhetoric. Before addressing this topic, I'd like to review how a foreign worker can legally work in the U.S. There are two ways: to become a legal immigrant and to obtain a temporary work visa.

Technically, anyone who has obtained permanent U.S. residency (a.k.a. green card) can legally work in the U.S. at any job as long as he or she is qualified and an employer is willing to hire them. But depending on which channel of immigration you used to become a green card holder, some restrictions and requirements apply. For example, suppose you apply for employment-based immigration. In that case, you first have a job offer from a U.S. employer, and your employer must obtain approval from the U.S. Department of Labor (DOL) through a process called "labor certification." The DOL labor certification verifies the following:

- There are insufficient available, qualified, and willing U.S. workers to fill the position being offered at the prevailing wage.

- Hiring a foreign worker will not adversely affect the wages and working conditions of similarly employed U.S. workers.

Only upon receiving approval from DOL can the employer submit an immigration petition on your behalf to the United States Citizenship and Immigration Services (USCIS). There are five classifications (preferences) of employment-based immigration:[212]

- First Preference (EB-1): for persons of extraordinary ability in the sciences, arts, education, business, or athletics; outstanding professors or researchers; and multinational executives and managers.

- Second Preference (EB-2): for persons who are members of professions holding advanced degrees or for persons with exceptional ability in the arts, sciences, or business.

- Third Preference (EB-3): for professionals, skilled workers, and other workers.

- Fourth Preference (EB-4): for "special immigrants," which includes certain religious workers, employees of the U.S. Foreign Service posts, retired employees of international organizations, alien minors who are wards of courts in the United States, and other classes of aliens.

- Fifth Preference (EB-5): for business investors who invest $1 million or $500,000 (if the investment is made in a targeted employment area) in a new commercial enterprise that employs at least 10 full-time U.S. workers.

Labor certification is not required for EB-1, EB-4, and EB-5 applicants, but it is for EB-2 and EB-3 applicants. Annually, approximately 140,000 foreigners immigrate to the U.S. through employment visas. Immigrants who obtain green cards through family, refugee/asylum, and other channels don't need to undergo the labor certification process. They can start working as soon as they want to, assuming an employer is ready to hire them.

As discussed in Chapter 5, there is a considerable backlog in our legal immigration system, and the wait is sometimes decades-long. Over two dozen working visas are available for foreign workers who can't wait long, especially those who want to work in the U.S. but do not intent to become permanent residents. These work visas enable foreign workers to legally come to the U.S. and work temporarily (see Appendix 4), including the H-1B visa for skilled workers, the H-2A for seasonal farm workers, and the H-2B for seasonal non-farm workers. Most of these visas require the foreign worker first to have a job offer from a U.S. employer. Before the foreign worker can legally work in the U.S., the prospective employer must apply for a labor certification at the Department of Labor (DOL). Only upon receiving approval from DOL can the employer file a nonimmigrant petition with the United

States Citizenship and Immigration Services (USCIS) to get a temporary work visa for the prospective foreign worker. The U.S. annually gives out approximately 600,000 temporary work visas to foreign workers.

Whether a foreign worker comes to the U.S. through a temporary work visa or any other legal immigration channel, the question remains: Are immigrants hurting American workers by driving down wages and taking jobs away? This question is probably the most contentious subject related to immigration. Most immigration advocates say "no," while people who advocate for limiting immigration or who are outright anti-immigration not only say "yes," but also use this issue as a linchpin for their anti-immigration movement. In truth, the answer to this question depends on the long-term or short-term effects and whether we are talking about the overall job market or specific occupations.

First, immigrants do lower the wages of competing American workers on a short-term basis, but the impact on occupations is unevenly distributed. Famed economist Ludwig Von Misses acknowledged:

> [I]n territories of immigration, immigration depresses the wage rate. That is a necessary side effect of migration of workers and not, say, as Social Democratic doctrine wants to have believed, an accidental consequence of the fact that the emigrants stem from territories of low culture and low wages.[213]

There are many contributing factors as to why new immigrants' wages are lower than those of the native-born. New immigrants often face language and cultural challenges, and U.S. employers often do not recognize their educations and professional licenses. Many new immigrants are also unfamiliar with American labor practices. Thus, they have little leverage to negotiate a better salary—one that is more reflective of their experiences and skills. To survive, they will do just about anything at any wage. In addition, many foreigners migrate from developing countries, and even a low salary by American standards is considerably higher than what they could get back home.

So, the influx of immigrants who compete for work will no doubt drive down pay for everyone else in the short term. It's Economics 101: an increase in supply (labor) drives down the price (wages).

Analysis from Harvard labor economist George Borjas shows that immigrants (both legal and illegal) from 1990 to 2010 reduced the average annual earnings of American workers by $1,396 in the short run. The same analysis concluded that "a 10-percent increase in the size of an education/age group due to the entry of immigrants (both legal and illegal) reduces the wages of native-born men in that group by 3.7 percent and the wage of all native-born workers by 2.5 percent."[214]

However, the downward pressure on wages caused by new immigrants doesn't impact the entire American workforce in the same way. Some American populations get hit worse than others, depending on the type of work and the requirements for education, skills, and experience. Professor Borjas's analysis shows that the less-educated and least-skilled Americans suffer the most negative impact on their wages in the short term (See Figure 6.2) when competing against immigrants for low-paying, least-skilled occupations—such as fruit pickers and restaurant dishwashers. These jobs have high turnover, low barriers to entry, and are less dependent on education and work experience. At the same time, the employers of these occupations are cost-conscious because any slight increase or decrease in labor costs will significantly impact their bottom line. Immigrants who are willing to work at any wage help keep operational costs down so these businesses can become profitable. The Americans who used to supply labor for these businesses are often poor, and without many employment alternatives, so they are particularly vulnerable.

Prevalent bias claims that all immigrants are poor and uneducated, which couldn't be further from the truth. About 46% of immigrant workers are in white-collar occupations, including 22% of dental, nursing, and health aides and 31% of computer software developers—well above immigrants' 16% share of the labor force.[215] Pew research shows 54% of Asian immigrants have a bachelor's degree or higher, compared to 33% of the general population in the U.S. The median Asian household had a higher income ($85,800) than the median of all U.S. households ($61,800).[216]

Second, immigration increases the wages of complementary workers. This is one aspect that anti-immigration groups refuse to talk about. For businesses that employ both immigrants and native-born American workers, having more immigrants in one skill group—for example, computer programmers—will not only help improve business profitability but will also allow the firm to expand employment opportunities for complementary workers in fields such as accounting, sales, and human resources. When the population of immigrants increases, the native-born switch to occupations requiring higher language skills.

David Frum, a senior edit at *The Atlantic*, proposed an interesting immigration reform idea based on the concept that immigration in one skill group can improve the wages and quality of life for workers in other skill groups:

> If we admit a lot of foreign-born surgeons, we could hugely drive down the cost of major medical operations. American-born doctors would shift their labor to fields where their language facility gave them a competitive advantage: away from surgery to general practice. This policy would hugely enhance the relative purchasing power of plumbers and mechanics, enabling them to eat out more often and buy more American-made entertainment, increasing GDP and creating jobs.[217]

Third, in the long run, the net negative wage impact on American workers is very small. Although it's evident that the influx of immigrants has a negative impact on the wages of native-born workers in the short run, studies have shown such impact becomes statistically negligible in the long run. Giovanni Peri, an economics professor at the University of California-Davis, found:

> Little evidence of a wage-depressing effect of immigration because immigrants are absorbed into the receiving economy through a series of adjustments by firms and other workers. Once these adjustments are accounted for, the wages of native

workers, even workers with skills similar to those of immigrants, do not change much in response to immigration.[218]

Harvard professor Borjas's study on immigration and American workers (which is often cited by anti-immigration groups) drew the same conclusion (see Figure 6.2).

Figure 6.2.[219] Wage Impact of 1990-2010 Immigrant Influx on Pre-Existing Workers (by percent)

			High School Dropouts	College Graduates	Post College	All Workers
All Immigration	Percentage Supply Increase		25.9	10.9	15.0	10.6
	Wage Effects	Short Run	-6.2	-3.2	-4.1	-3.2
		Long Run	-3.1	-0.1	-0.9	0.0
Legal Immigration Only	Percentage Supply Increase		4.4	9.8	13.3	8.0
	Wage Effects	Short Run	1.7	-2.8	-3.5	-2.4
		Long Run	0.7	-0.4	-1.1	0.0
Native-born Workers	Average Annual Salary		$ 20,865	$ 60,765	$ 88,555	$ 43,612

In addition, let's not forget that immigrants have their own desires and aspirations. They didn't leave everything they were familiar with and their loved ones behind so they could stay at the bottom of the economic ladder in a new country. Once they obtain the language skills, credentials, education, and work experience they need, or once they understand the culture of their new homeland and what a good wage is, they will demand better pay and move from lower-paying to higher-paying occupations. The better they assimilate, the faster they move up the economic ladder. That is another reason why the net negative wage impact on American workers is insignificant in the long run.

Some research even shows increased household and disposable income in areas with a significant influx of immigrants. In a 2008 study on immigration and the wealth of states, Richard Nadler identified 19 high-immigration jurisdictions (HIJ) in the U.S. that account for 83.8% of the resident immigration population in the U.S. He compared the economic data from these HIJs to the rest of the country and found that:[220]

- In 2006, the Per Capita Disposable Personal Income in the 19 HIJs exceeded that of the 32 other states, $33,957 to $32,111.

- From 1999 to 2006, the Per Capita Disposable Personal Income grew $8,739 in the 19 HIJs, compared to $7,247 in the 32 other states.

- In 2006, the Median Income in the 19 HIJs exceeded that of the 32 other states, $52,689 to $44,220. From 1999 to 2006, Median Household Income grew 16.49% in the 19 HIJs, compared to 12.36% in the 32 other states.

He concluded that

High resident population and/or inflow of immigrants is associated with elevated levels and growth rates in Gross State Product, Personal Income, Per Capita Personal Income, Disposable Income, Per Capita Disposable Income, Median Household Income, and Median Per Capita Income.[221]

Fourth, American businesses and consumers benefit from immigrant workers. Immigrants are consumers. An influx of immigrants increases demand for housing, food, education, and healthcare, spurs demand for American businesses, increasing demand for American workers. This benefit to businesses improves their bottom lines and enables American companies to provide goods and services at competitive prices. American workers, who are also consumers, can thus enjoy these goods and services at lower prices, which means more disposable income.

In addition, immigrants help American businesses ease the pains of labor shortages in both high-skilled and low-skilled fields. A National Federation of Independent Businesses survey reported that 44% of companies could find "few or no qualified applicants for positions they were trying to fill." The Covid-19 pandemic is the most critical event that has changed how Americans work and how they think of their relationships with their employers. Several factors, including the ability to work remotely, the fear of Covid-19, the desire for work-life balance, and the government's generous unemployment benefits during the pandemic, drove many Americans to quit their jobs as part of the movement known as "The Great Resignation." In 2021 alone, more than 47 million Americans quit their jobs. As of 2022, U.S. employers reported 11 million job openings.[222] While Americans leave work, immigration provides American businesses with the younger workers they need to maintain and expand operations, hire more American workers, and better serve American consumers.

More importantly, some immigrants are job creators. Legal immigrants have a higher propensity to start businesses than native-born Americans. That shouldn't come as any surprise because people who are also risk-takers will pick themselves up and move to another country. Immigrants are 13% of the U.S. population but own 20% of all small businesses. About 40% of Fortune 500 companies were founded by either immigrants or the children of immigrants. In Silicon Valley, 44% of high-tech companies have at least one immigrant founder. Some well-known American companies founded by immigrants include Google, Tesla, Intel, and Pfizer. Immigrant-owned companies have become the engine of growth in the U.S. economy and provided ample employment opportunities for American workers.

The EB-5 visa is a unique program to bring immigrant entrepreneurs to the United States to create jobs and stimulate the American economy. A foreign national who invests $1 million or at least $500,000 in a targeted employment area and plans to create or preserve ten permanent full-time jobs will be granted a conditional green card. Annually, up to 10,000 visas may be authorized in this particular category. The EB-5 is a highly successful program for American workers and the economy. According to Invest-in-USA.org, "Between 2008 and 2015, the EB-5 Program helped generate $20.6 billion in foreign direct investment to create and retain U.S. jobs for Americans, all at no cost to the taxpayer."[223]

Last but not least, all immigrants, including illegal immigrants, are taxpayers.* Taxes from immigrants help fund local and federal government operations and contribute to our social welfare system.

Overall, Professor Borjas's research concluded that all immigrant workers (legal and illegal) enlarged the U.S. economy by 11%, or $1.6 trillion annually. Even though 97.8% of this $1.6 trillion goes back to the immigrants themselves in the form of wages and benefits, the remainder constitutes the "immigration surplus," which equals $35 billion a year net benefit to American businesses and workers.[224]

6.2 A Discussion on H-1B Visa Program

The H-1B visa is one of over two dozen work visa categories and, unfortunately, has become a target of anti-immigration groups as a "job-stealing" program. Since I was once an H-1B visa holder, I'd like to share my experience to clarify some common misconceptions.

H1-B visa holders are not immigrants. The H-1B visa is a non-immigrant **visa** under the Immigration and Nationality Act, Section 101(a)(15)(H). This program allows U.S. employers to temporarily hire foreign workers, usually for up to three years. The federal government sets an annual cap of 65,000 H-1B visas, with an additional 20,000 visas for people with master's degrees or higher. An H-1B visa holder can extend the visa once at the end of the three-year term for another three years. So, an H-1B visa holder can legally work and stay in the U.S. for six years. At the end of the sixth year, the visa holder has to leave the U.S. unless he or she becomes an immigrant through other channels, i.e., marriage, employment, etc. I was an H-1B visa holder for six years and became a U.S. citizen through marriage.

---

* A 50-state analysis by the Taxation and Economic Policy found illegal immigrants paid more than $11.74 billion in state and local taxes in 2017. The majority of that comes from sales and excise taxes, and the second-highest category is property taxes, while income tax makes up the rest.
    Retrieved from https://marketrealist.com/p/do-illegal-immigrants-pay-taxes/.

H-1B visa holders have to meet very high qualification standards. Not everyone can apply for an H-1B visa because the bar is set very high. Analysis performed by the Heritage Foundation shows that all H-1B visa holders have at least a bachelor's degree, 31% have master's degrees, and 12% have doctorate degrees.[225] When I was offered a job at Citibank through the H-1B program, I earned two master's degrees from two accredited U.S. universities. Most H-1B holders have at least one master's degree from an accredited U.S. university. In addition to a master's degree, many H-1B visa holders, including me, have professional licenses or certifications in our fields of specialization.

However, more than a good education is required. The United States Customs and Immigration Services (USCIS) requires that an H-1B visa holder can only be hired to fill occupations where "the specific duties are so specialized and complex that the knowledge required to perform the duties is usually associated with the attainment of a bachelor's or higher degree." USCIS requires both the employer and employee to give a very detailed description[226] of the job duties entail and how the prospective employee's field of study relates to the specific occupation he or she intends to perform. Here is an excerpt from the USCIS on what constitutes a detailed description:

- A detailed explanation of the specific duties of the position, the product or service your company provides, or the complex nature of the role you will perform, and how your degree relates to the role.

- Written opinions from experts in the field explaining how the degree is related to the role you will perform.

H-1B visa holders are not cheap laborers. Unlike the popular misapprehension, an employer cannot pay a foreign worker as little as possible. The Immigration and Nationality Act (INA) requires that hiring foreign workers can't harm American workers' wages and working conditions. To comply with this statute, the Department of Labor (DOL) requires that "the wages offered to a foreign worker must be the prevailing wage rate for the occupational classification in the area of employment." The DOL website defines the "prevailing wage rate" as "the average wage paid to similarly employed workers in a specific occupation in the area of intended employment." An employer can't just claim the salary it is going to pay the prevailing wage rate; it has to submit a request to the National Prevailing Wage Center (NPWC) to obtain the prevailing wage for the position or get it from an independent authoritative source.

Since most H-1B visa holders are well educated and highly skilled, it is a no-brainer that they are well compensated. In fact, H1-B visa holders are among the highest-paid workers in the United States, and their wages are in the top ten percent of what the U.S workforce typically earns in a year. The median salary for H1-B visa holders in 2021 was $108,000, which is twice the median wage earned by U.S workers ($45,000). Additionally, the wage growth for H1B visa holders "has surpassed all U.S workers' average increase by 52% since 2003."[227]

H-1B visa holders are often a costly and risky option for employers. Hiring a foreign worker on an H-1B visa is not a cheap alternative.

First, hiring is much longer and more costly than hiring an American worker. After a job is posted, every applicant, foreign or not, must undergo the same screening and interviewing process. I went through five interviews. When Citibank made me an offer, it was contingent upon approval from the Department of Labor. This approval process is commonly called "labor certification," which is a complicated, time-consuming, and costly process. Part of the process was for Citibank to continue advertising the position it offered me for three additional months in national media. Citibank also had to disclose my salary in the advertisement. Any American could contact Citibank to object to my hiring and apply for the same position. Citibank had to go through the entire hiring process until it could prove I was more qualified.

Second, once a foreign worker is identified, an employer usually bears all the filing and legal fees for the H-1B visa, which usually include the following (as of 2022):

- **Standard H-1B filing fee**. $460 per person.

- **ACWIA (Training) H-1B Fee***. Employer must pay $750 if fewer than 25 employees and $1,500 if more than 25 employees.

- **Public Law 114-113 Fee†**. Employer pays $4,000.

- **H-1B fraud fee**. Employer is required to pay a $500 fraud-prevention fee per application.

- **Premium processing fee**. A normal H-1B application process takes 2-6 months. The premium processing can shorten the process to 15 business days if the employer is willing to pay an additional $2,500.

- **Legal fee**. Employers usually hire immigration lawyers to handle the entire process. The cost of the lawyer is usually several thousand dollars.[228]

The total cost of hiring a foreign worker on an H-1B visa could be as much as $10,000. As mentioned earlier, employers must also pay H-1B visa holders the prevailing wage. Therefore, getting a skilled foreign worker is not exactly cheap for employers.

In addition to cost and time, employers who hire H-1B visa holders may encounter other risks because H-1B visa holders are not immigrants. For instance, when I was working for Citibank, our corporate lawyers and HR representative warned against my traveling internationally because I had to apply for a visa with the local U.S. consulate to return to the U.S. There was no guarantee that the local U.S. consulate would grant me a visa even if I provided evidence of employment in the U.S. Each of my overseas trips became a headache for my boss

---

* ACWIA stands for American Competitiveness and Workforce Improvement Act of 1998. The ACWIA fee varies depending on the size of the sponsoring company. Source: https://www.nnuimmigration.com/h1b-visa-cost/

† This fee is paid by companies with more than 50 employees, where over half of those is employed through the H1B or L1 visa routes.

because he had to be ready for the possibility that I wouldn't be able to return.

So why do employers go through so much trouble to hire H-1B visa holders? They don't do it out of the kindness of their hearts, but out of necessity. The U.S. needs more skilled workers since about 11 million job openings still need to be filled. The National Federation of Independent Businesses' latest survey reported 44% of companies could find "few or no qualified applicants for positions they were trying to fill." Highly educated and highly skilled foreign workers, capped at 65,000 per year, are not the cause but rather a tiny remedy to fill this skill gap. "In economic terms, [skilled workers] represent a transfer of skills to the receiving country without cost to the recipient but at the expense of the immigrant's country of origin, which developed the immigrant's mind and muscle." American businesses are willing to go through all the trouble to get this talent to help them compete in the global economy.

Critics of the H-1B program accuse it of hurting American workers by substituting them with cheap foreign workers. To support their argument, they focus on: which employers benefit most from the H-1B program and how much the H-1B workers are paid compared to their American counterparts in similar occupations, not to average Americans.

So which employers benefit most from the H-1B program? *The New York Times* reported that "the top 20 companies took about 40 percent of the visas available—about 32,000—while more than 10,000 other employers received far fewer visas each."[229] These top American companies include Apple, Amazon, and Google. The demand for H-1B visas far exceeds the annual quota of 85,000. For instance, the USCIS received more than 300,000 H-1B visa applications in fiscal year 2022.

Two Indian outsourcing firms, Tata Consultancy Services (TCS) and Infosys, topped the list of companies applying for H-1B visas on behalf of foreign workers (in this case, mainly from India). Thus, many critics of the H-1B program conclude that the visa gives outsourcing firms an unfair advantage. But the truth is that for each foreign worker, only one application can be submitted by the employer. Since a global outsourcing firm that relies mainly on foreign workers tends to submit more H-1B visa applications, the probability of its applications being selected is higher. But no official bias that favors global outsourcing firms over other businesses because U.S. immigration officials use a lottery system to randomly choose H-1B visa recipients.

The second criticism against the H-1B program is that top outsourcing firms pay the H-1B visa holders much less than experienced technology workers. Visa Explorer, a database of tech workers, reported that "the two companies [Tata and Infosys] appear to be paying well below their Silicon Valley counterparts. Among the 9,300 jobs Tata has filed LCAs [Labor Certification Applications] for in 2015, the median salary is just over $66,000, while at Infosys, the median is $76,000."[230]

This criticism ignores two essential facts. First, it ignores the additional legal costs an employer has to bear for each H-1B application. As mentioned earlier, hiring a foreign worker on an H-1B visa can cost an employer as much as $10,000. In addition, all these costs will recur in three years if the employer wants to file an extension for the same foreign worker. Second, the criticism neglects to mention that most H-1B visa holders are 35 years of age or younger.[231] They may be well educated. Still, they are young and likely have less experience than older and more experienced American workers in similar occupations. Remember that a young American worker would be paid less than an older and more experienced American counterpart.

6.3 Other Factors Holding American Workers Back

Rather than blaming immigrants, we as a nation need to honestly examine the inner factors that hold American workers back: education, culture, and welfare.

First, our education system fails to produce a sufficiently educated workforce. There is no other country in the world that spends the kind of money we do on education with the kind of poor results we receive in return. Today, the U.S. spends an average of $15,000 per pupil per year in K-12, one of the highest amounts in the world. Between 1960 and 2020, inflation-adjusted K-12 education spending per student increased by 280 percent. Yet such investments have failed to improve American students' learning outcomes. For example, Baltimore City

Public High Schools (BCPS) had a budget of $1.4 billion in 2021, which was about $18,000 per student. Yet, about 41 percent of its students earned a GPA below 1.0 during the 2020-2021 school year. Only 21 percent of their students earned a GPA of 3.0, equivalent to a B average. The cost-benefit of our K-12 public education delivery system has failed. A private business with such a dismal return on investment would have gone out of business.

Unfortunately, extended school closures and ineffective remote learning during the Covid-19 pandemic have only exasperated our nation's poor learning outcomes, despite the federal government providing an additional $190 billion of stimulus funds to schools during the pandemic. According to the Wall Street Journal, the 2022 National Assessment of Educational Progress (NAEP) report for fourth graders showed "the largest drop in reading scores since 1990 and the first statistically significant decline in math scores since the math portion of the test began in 1973. Math and reading scores for the exam are now at their lowest levels since the 1990s." Not surprisingly, "learning loss generally is worse in districts that kept classes remote longer, with the effects most pronounced in high-poverty districts."[232] Without reform, our current K-12 public education system is perpetuating the sad outcome and condemning the most vulnerable children to lifelong poverty. David Steiner, executive director of the Johns Hopkins Institute for Education Policy, said, "As a nation, a lower level of cognitive skills in math and science is very serious. Ultimately this will impact our GDP and our well-being as a nation and that's not a good thing."

Our higher education system doesn't fare any better.

For those students who managed to earn a college degree, the Federal Reserve Bank of New York's analysis shows that since 2001, underemployment among recent college graduates has increased. About 45% of recent college graduates are "underemployed," holding jobs that typically do not require a bachelor's degree.[233] There are 11 million job openings in the U.S., and employers are struggling to find workers. There is a mismatch between what students learn in school and the skills and knowledge businesses need.

We all know that a good education greatly impacts someone's future happiness and prosperity. Anyone serious about helping American workers should support effective education reform to give young people more choices and teach them knowledge and skills that will lead to success and prosperity.

The second factor holding America back is our culture. We as a nation, have experienced a cultural shift into one that doesn't appreciate physical work. Low-paying, labor-intensive jobs such as picking fruit, slaughtering chickens, and housekeeping are not desirable to even many of the poorest Americans. In the summer of 2015, *The Wall Street Journal* reported a persistent farm labor shortage due to the decline of illegal immigrants. Despite farmers raising some wages by more than 20%, the youth unemployment rate was 12.2% in July 2015[234] — few Americans flock to farms. At $11.20 an hour, back-breaking work is not attractive to even the least skilled American workers. Consequently, "a years-long decline in farmhands is reducing annual fruit and vegetable production by 9.5%, or $3.1 billion, in the U.S."[235] Besides farming, the construction industry heavily depends on immigrant workers because it cannot entice sufficient Americans to perform the physical and sometimes dangerous work.

Mike Rowe, host of the popular TV show *Dirty Jobs*, criticized this cultural phenomenon of looking down on physical or labor-intensive work. He said, "Dirt used to be a badge of honor. Dirt used to look like work. But we've scrubbed the dirt off the face of work, and consequently we've created this suspicion of anything that's too dirty." By doing so, according to Rowe, "we waged a war on work," and the American working-age population suffers the most.

Research shows that only 3% of Americans who work full time, year-round, are in poverty. So, no weapon is more powerful to fight the war on poverty than work — any work. As a nation, we need to re-emphasize the honor and dignity of work. No matter what you do, all work is valuable because "work allows you to renew your life, which is part of the renewing of civilization. Work gives us purpose, stability, integration, shared mission" (Peggy Noonan).

Another aspect of our culture that hurts American workers is the war on merit. The advocates for equity, or equal outcomes, claim anything that results in unequal outcomes among different racial groups is racist. They've already deemed math, science, proper English grammar, and standardized testing "culturally biased" and racist. There is a national push to "decolonize" curriculums, eliminating standardized tests, gifted programs, and challenging entrance exams to elite high schools, all in the name of "racial equity." Many colleges have eliminated standardized tests such as the SATs from their college admission criteria. The elimination of objective measures doesn't eliminate mediocre learning outcomes and achievement gaps across racial groups and social and economic status, but only temporarily disguises them.

When inadequately prepared students go to college, they're not academically ready. Not surprisingly, college remediation rates have spiked. An estimated 60% of community college students and 33% of students at 4-year public colleges have taken at least one remediation course. According to the Center for American Progress and the National Bureau of Economic Research, remedial education is not cheap. It costs students $1.3 billion and $7 billion in federal financial aid annually. Remedial courses are not as effective either, as research shows that less than 25% of students in remediation earn a college degree within eight years.[236]

There is no denying that a culture that despises physical labor and merit holds its people back from achieving economic prosperity.

The third factor that holds American workers back is our welfare system. Our generous welfare benefits are disincentives to work. A study by the Cato Institute shows that "in nine states—Hawaii, Massachusetts, Connecticut, New Jersey, Rhode Island, New York, Vermont, New Hampshire, and Maryland—as well as Washington, D.C., annual benefits were worth more than $35,000 a year." Keep in mind that these benefits are not taxed. So the study shows that $35,000 worth of annual benefits for a welfare recipient is equivalent to earning $60,590 in pretax income. This study concludes that,

> In fact, welfare currently pays more than a minimum-wage job in 34 states and the District of Columbia. In Hawaii, Massachusetts, Connecticut, New York, New Jersey, Rhode Island, Vermont, and Washington, D.C., welfare pays more

than a $20-an-hour job, and in five additional states it yields
more than a $15-per-hour job.

Since the 2008 economic recession, the U.S. government has made it
even easier for Americans to sign up for welfare benefits. For example,
eligibility rules for food stamps were relaxed, and work requirements
were waived. University of Chicago economist Casey Mulligan
concluded in his research that "the American stimulus reduced
average incentives to be employed."[237] In 2013, there were 48 million
Americans on food stamps, representing a 16-million increase since
2008.

Yet, politicians have refused to learn from their past mistakes. In
the early days of the Covid-19 pandemic, the U.S. government
increased unemployment benefits through the CARES Act in March
2020. Americans received approximately $794 billion in combined state
and federal unemployment benefits from March 2020 through July
2021. This financial stimulus not only helped fuel inflation but also
contributed to a persistent labor shortage. A survey conducted in April
2021 found that more than 1.8 million unemployed Americans have
turned down job offers since March 2020 because of the generous
unemployment insurance benefits. Employers struggled to find workers and had to cut back on services and raise prices.

Our nation's generous welfare system and its relative ease of
accessibility have incentivized workers not to work, and created an
unofficial minimum wage. Since welfare benefits equate to $20 an
hour, welfare recipients have no incentive to take any job that pays
less. Thus, if anti-immigration advocates demand American businesses
hire only American workers, especially for entry-level positions, that's
essentially imposing a drastic minimum wage hike—of at least $20 an
hour—for these companies. At this rate, the cost of doing business
would have skyrocketed, forcing firms to choose between passing the
higher prices on to consumers (which companies have limited power
to do) or cutting back hiring. A minimum wage hike of this magnitude
would hurt the employment of the most vulnerable American
workers. Economists William Wascher and David Neumark found "a
1% or 2% reduction for teenage or very low-skill employment for each
10% minimum-wage increase."[238] It's Economics 101: when you raise

the price of something (labor), demand for it will decrease (fewer people will be hired). A mandatory wage increase is meaningless when one can't find a job. Additionally, some firms might have been forced out of business if they couldn't find a financially viable way to survive the higher cost.

These outcomes will harm consumers, especially low-income families, who rely on businesses like Walmart and McDonald's to provide goods and services at affordable prices. Americans, even people with low incomes, enjoy a very high standard of living compared to the rest of the world. If American businesses can hire only American workers, ask yourself: Do you want to pay $30 for a pound of chicken or $25 for a pound of apples?

Education, culture, and welfare are not the only factors holding American workers back. Other factors — including ruinous regulations, such as occupational licensing requirements — harm employment opportunities of American workers too. These factors have nothing to do with immigration but have contributed to our nation's low labor participation rates and the bleak employment picture in America.

In summary: immigration doesn't take jobs away from American workers and doesn't drive down wages in the long term. To help American workers, the United States must address education reform, culture change, welfare reform, and ruinous anti-work regulations.

6.4 Do Immigrants Use More Welfare?

Immigrants and their use of welfare are another hotly debated topic. Anti-immigration groups argue that most immigrants are on welfare, and pro-immigration groups dispute this and present much data to argue the contrary. There are merits and flaws on both sides. Most studies lump all immigrants together, but through which immigration channel someone became a resident and where that immigrant lives make a big difference in welfare usage.

Before August 22, 1996, legal immigrants (green card holders) could access federal welfare programs just like any U.S. citizen, thanks to the Social Security Act of 1935. That changed in 1996. The Personal Responsibility and Work Opportunity Reconciliation Act of 1996 (PRWORA), signed by President Clinton on August 22, 1996, profoundly changed legal immigrants' eligibility for welfare benefits run by the federal government. PRWORA stipulates the following:[239]

- Legal immigrants (except refugees, asylees, veterans, and active-duty personnel) are ineligible for federal means-tested public benefits for the first five years after U.S. entry, or until they obtain their U.S. citizenship or have a 10-year work history in the U.S.* This restriction doesn't apply to certain immigrants from Cuba and Haiti. Nonimmigrants and illegal immigrants are not eligible for public benefits.

- The prohibition applies to these federal means-tested public benefits: (1) Supplemental Security Income (SSI), (2) food stamps, (3) Temporary Assistance for Needy Families (TANF), (4) Social Services Block Grants (SSBG), and (5) Medicaid.

- The prohibition doesn't apply to: (1) emergency medical services, (2) certain emergency disaster relief, (3) public health immunizations and treatment of communicable diseases, (4) housing assistance, (5) certain in-kind community services, and (6) Social Security Act benefits under specified circumstances.

PRWORA might have barred legal immigrants from accessing federal means-tested public benefits programs, but gave states' great leeway to determine their eligibility requirement for legal immigrants to access state benefit programs. Prohibitions on legal immigrants defined by PRWORA do not apply to naturalized U.S. citizens and the children of legal and illegal immigrants born in the U.S. (and are thus U.S. citizens through "birthright citizenship").

---

* A legal immigrant (green card holder) typically has to wait for five years before applying for naturalization of U.S. citizenship. The only exception is if the person became a legal immigrant through marriage to a U.S. citizen. In that case, the wait is three years before applying for naturalization.

About 935,000 noncitizens lost benefits due to the passage of PRWORA. Between 1994 and 1999, all major federal public benefit programs saw a decline in usage by legal immigrants: TANF (-60%), food stamps (-48%), SSI (-32%), and Medicaid (-15%).[240] The law was effective for a short while. What PRWORA didn't do was deny legal immigrants state-run welfare programs. Consequently, all states except Alabama chose to provide Temporary Assistance to Needy Families of legal immigrants. Several states also provided Medicaid. "In 1997, states have been mandated to provide State Children's Health Insurance Program (SCHIP) coverage to immigrant children legally in the U.S. before August 22, 1996."[241]

Subsequent revisions to PRWORA gradually chipped away at its effectiveness. For example, the Balanced Budget Act of 1997 reinstated Supplemental Security Income benefits for elderly or disabled legal immigrants receiving such benefits on or before August 22, 1996. The Farm Security and Rural Investment Act of 2002 restored immigrants' access to food stamps. The Children's Health Insurance Program Reauthorization Act of 2009 (CHIPRA) granted states the option to provide Medicaid and CHIP coverage to all children and pregnant women who resided in the U.S. lawfully.

So, have immigrants been using more welfare benefits than native-born Americans? The Center for Immigration Studies (CIS), a group that advocates immigration restrictions, says "yes." The most recent study by CIS shows welfare usage by immigrant households was higher than by households headed by native-born Americans. Major findings of this study included the following:[242]

- In 2012, 51% of households headed by an immigrant (legal or illegal) reported using at least one welfare program during the year, compared to 30% of native-born households. Welfare in this study includes Medicaid, cash, food, and housing programs.

- Immigrant households have much higher use of food programs (40% vs. 22% for native-born) and Medicaid (42% vs. 23%). Immigrant use of cash programs is somewhat higher than native-born (12% vs. 10%), and use of housing programs is similar in both groups.

- Welfare use varies among immigrant groups. Households headed by immigrants from Central America and Mexico (73%), the Caribbean (51%), and Africa (48%) have the highest overall welfare use. Those from East Asia (32%), Europe (26%), and South Asia (17%) have the lowest.

Anti-immigration groups and politicians have widely cited this study as evidence that immigrants are here to take advantage of our nation's generous welfare system. Like all studies, this CIS study has several caveats.

First, the study measured welfare usage by household, not by individuals. Immigrants tend to have larger families, and children in immigrant household born in the U.S. are U.S. citizens and therefore have U.S. citizen access to public benefits. Even CIS admitted in its study that "immigrants often receive benefits on behalf of their US-born children." But these immigrant children's welfare usage should have been counted as part of native-born usage, not an immigrant.

Second, this study didn't separate naturalized citizens and refugees/asylum seekers from other legal immigrants. The PRWORA law clearly states that naturalized citizens and refugees/asylum seekers are eligible for all public benefits, just like U.S. citizens. They don't have to wait for five years like other legal immigrants do. So measuring welfare usage by households headed by legal immigrants against households headed by native-born Americans may inflate the numbers in CIS's analysis. Thus, the CIS conclusion that immigrants use more welfare than the native-born may not be accurate.

Leighton Ku and Brian Bruen of the Cato Institute conducted a study comparing *individual* welfare usage between poor immigrants and poor native-born American citizens and drew different conclusions than the CIS. The analysis by Ku and Bruen shows that poor immigrants use public benefits at lower rates than the native-born. Some of their key findings include:

- More than one-quarter of native-born and naturalized citizens in poverty receive Medicaid, but only about one in five non-citizens do.

- About two-thirds of low-income citizen children receive health insurance through Medicaid or CHIP, compared to nearly half of non-citizen children.

- Among low-income adults, 33% of native-born citizens, 25% of naturalized citizens, and 29% of non-citizens received SNAP benefits in 2011.

- About half of poor citizen children in citizen households receive SNAP, compared to about one-third of non-citizen children and two-fifths of citizen children in non-citizen-headed families.

- SSI receipts were used more for native-born and naturalized citizens than non-citizen immigrants.

- Besides the Cato study, research done by the Policy Institute for Family Impact at Purdue University concluded that "receipt of public benefits by non-refugees and working-age immigrants is roughly the same as for citizens— 5.1 % for immigrants compared to 5.3% for citizens."[243]

Why the discrepancy between these analyses? Our nation's welfare system is highly complicated. Michael Tanner and Charles Hughes of Cato counted 126 separate federal anti-poverty programs, including 72 that provide "cash or in-kind benefits to individuals." In addition, there are numerous welfare programs at the state level. Truth be told, our nation's overly generous welfare system is unsustainable, whether for immigrants or the native-born, and it is in dire need of reforms. Based on the 2022 budget, all federal welfare programs total roughly $1.3 trillion.

An entire book could be written on welfare reform, but that's not what I want to focus on here. Regarding immigrants, we want to attract people willing to work and contribute, not live off the welfare system. PRWORA was a step in the right direction, and we need to update it to continue holding down welfare costs and encouraging able-bodied benefits recipients to work.

6.5 Do Immigrants Commit More Crimes?

On July 19, 2017, the United States Department of Justice indicted 17 MS-13 gang members and associates for the murders of four young men in Long Island, New York. The gang, which takes its name from the Salvadoran peasants who fought in the country's civil war, first emerged in impoverished Los Angeles neighborhoods among refugees fleeing the conflict and has since become the most dangerous criminal group in the United States. Some quickly pointed to these indictments as evidence that immigrants commit more crimes than native-born Americans.

Despite such widespread misperceptions, the actual data tells a different story. Scores of studies of immigrants and crime rates, some going as far back as a century, show that regardless of nationality, ethnicity, education level, or legal status, immigrants are not more likely to commit violent crimes than native-born Americans. Increasing numbers of immigrants are not associated with higher rates of crimes—quite the opposite. Below are some of the results from studies conducted by well-respected economists over the years:

- A 2008 study by Richard Nadler of the America Majority Foundation shows that high immigration areas may actually be correlated with lower crime rates: "From 1999 to 2006, violent crime decreased 15.0% in high immigration jurisdictions, compared to a 1.2% decrease in 32 'other states.'"[244] He concluded that high levels of immigration aren't correlated with elevated levels of crime at the state level. Graham C. Ousey and Charis E. Kubrin investigated data from 159 cities between 1980 and 2000 and drew the same conclusion.[245]

- A recent American Immigration Council[246] study also correlates increased immigration with lower crime rates:

- Between 1990 and 2013, the foreign-born share of the U.S. population grew from 7.9% to 13.1%, and the number of unauthorized immigrants more than tripled from 3.5 million to 11.2 million.

- During the same period, FBI data indicate violent crime rates declined by 48%, including falling rates in aggravated assault, robbery, rape, and murder. Likewise, the property crime rate fell by 41%, including declining rates in motor vehicle theft, larceny/robbery, and burglary.

While all the data on the subject of immigration and crime shows that immigrants are less likely to commit violent crimes than native-born, it's important to remember that:

- No studies claim that immigration is responsible for reducing crime rates because crime rates are sensitive to criminal justice policies unrelated to immigration (Richard Nadler, 2008).

- No studies excused illegal immigrants who broke our immigration law. However, just because someone broke our immigration law doesn't mean he or she is more likely to commit other crimes.

So why are immigrants less likely to commit violent crimes than native-born Americans? Alex Nowrasteh from the Cato Institute offered two explanations.[247] One is that immigrants caught committing a crime will be subject to deportation, which acts as a disincentive to breaking the law. The second is the self-selection factor: immigrants come to the U.S. to better their lives, making them less likely to ruin their economic opportunities by committing crimes.

Interestingly, some of the same studies I cited here show an increased risk of incarceration among immigrants' children and immigrants who have lived in the U.S. for a long time. This phenomenon is called "the paradox of assimilation," and it holds across all ethnic groups and nationalities. The study done by Ruben G. Rumbaut and Walter Ewing shows:

- Among foreign-born men from Mexico, El Salvador, Guatemala, and Cuba, the chance of being in prison was more than twice as great for those in the country for 16 years or longer than for those in the country five years or less.

- The incarceration rate of native-born Hispanic men without a high-school diploma in 2000 (12.4%) was more than 11 times higher than the 1.1% rate of foreign-born Hispanic high-school dropouts.

- The incarceration rate of foreign-born Laotian and Cambodian men (0.9%) was the highest among Asian immigrant groups in 2000 but was more than eight times lower than that of native-born men of Laotian and Cambodian descent (7.3%).[248]

- No one so far can offer a clear explanation of why this is happening.

Immigrants are less likely to commit violent crimes, but that doesn't mean we should dismiss crime data associated with immigrants. Some of the crimes committed by immigrants were preventable, such as the shooting on San Francisco's Pier 14 on July 1, 2015. Francisco Sanchez, who shot Kate Steinle, is an illegal immigrant from Mexico, a repeat felon who was deported five times but kept sneaking back into the U.S. through the unsecured U.S.-Mexico border. In March 2015, after being apprehended again by federal authorities, he was handed over to authorities in San Francisco on outdated drug-related charges. The U.S. Immigration and Customs Enforcement (ICE) requested an immigration detainer,* asking that the agency be notified before Sanchez was released. But San Francisco is a so-called "sanctuary city"[249] that doesn't honor such requests. So, Sanchez walked out of jail as a free man after the drug-related charge was dismissed.

The shooting of Steinle should have never happened, and it exposed our nation's vulnerability when our borders are unsecured and local authorities refuse to enforce existing laws. Although I'm

---

* An immigration detainer is an official request from Immigration and Customs Enforcement (ICE) to another law enforcement agency (LEA) — such as a state or local jail — that the LEA notify ICE prior to releasing an individual from local custody so that ICE can arrange to take over custody.
Retrieved from http://www.immigrationpolicy.org/just-facts/immigration-detainers-comprehensive-look.

afraid I have to disagree with anti-immigrant activists and politicians' generalizations of immigration and crime, I believe they have a valid point: we must secure our borders. Had we secured borders, repeat felons like Sanchez would never have been allowed to walk freely around the U.S. He should have been stopped and sent back to his country of origin.

Even though I support immigration, I find the idea of sanctuary cities troubling. The sanctuary movement started in the 1980s, when about a million Central Americans, mainly from El Salvador and Guatemala, crossed the U.S. border seeking asylum from their repressive governments and seemingly never-ending civil wars. But the Reagan administration supported these governments' (especially the governments of El Salvador and Guatemala) attempts to fight communist rebels. Therefore, the administration would only characterize Salvadorans and Guatemalans as "economic migrants, not eligible for political asylum." Hundreds of churches in the U.S. openly defied immigration policy by providing safe havens for Central Americans. The movement later turned into an indictment of the Reagan administration's Central America policy. Eventually, in 1990, Congress passed legislation allowing the president to grant Temporary Protected Status (TPS) to specific groups in need of a temporary haven, including explicitly designating Salvadorans for TPS.[250]

Influenced by the sanctuary movement, San Francisco passed the "City and County of Refuge" Ordinance in 1989, which barred city money from being used to enforce immigration laws. Hundreds of U.S. cities and counties have followed suit and adopted similar "sanctuary" rules or policies. While San Francisco barred city money from being used to enforce immigration laws, it didn't hesitate to use the city's money (really, taxpayers' money) to shield "convicted juvenile offenders who were in the country illegally from federal authorities, either escorting them to their home countries at city expense or transporting them to group homes, often outside the city."[251] This sends the wrong message. When lawless behavior goes unpunished, it only encourages more lawlessness. It turns out that advocates for "sanctuary" jurisdictions don't really have tolerance for illegal immigrants. Frustrated by increasing inflows of illegal immigrants due to the Biden Administration's hands-off approach at the U.S.-Mexico border, the governors of Florida and Texas have sent illegal immigrants in their states to sanctuary cities such as New York and Washington D.C. When Florida Governor Ron DeSantis sent a plane of 50 illegal immigrants to Martha's Vineyard, one of the wealthiest communities and a self-proclaimed sanctuary city, the city's affluent residents declared a humanitarian crisis. Within 48 hours, the city shipped all illegal immigrants out of their community with the assistance of the National Guard. Liberals accused Governor DeSantis of using immigrants in a political stunt, which was probably true. But we couldn't deny that the stunt exposed the hypocrisy of the "sanctuary" jurisdiction movement. Comedian Dave Smith wrote on Twitter,

> The Martha's Vineyard thing might be the best and clearest example of what so many of us have been talking about for years. The progressive elites advocate for policies that they never have to suffer the consequences of. And the one time they do, it ends quickly. They are against building a wall but they live in gated communities. They are for gun control but they have armed security. They destroy public education but send their kids to elite private schools. They support mask mandates but only their servants wear them at their parties.[252]

His words spoke of how many Americans feel. We believe in the entire United States as a sanctuary for people seeking better lives by working hard and abiding by the laws of the land. The idea of establishing sanctuary jurisdictions in the U.S. that operate outside of specific laws of the land does a disservice to all American people, and governments at both the local and federal levels need to gain more credibility on their abilities to protect lawful citizens. When we cease to uphold the rule of law, our nation will cease to be a sanctuary for anyone.

6.6 Do Immigrants Assimilate?

Our nation's founding has long been regarded as the "American experiment." One of the key factors in making this experiment successful is the assimilation of new immigrants. George Washington believed it was good for America for new immigrants and their descendants "get assimilated to our customs, measures and laws: in a word, soon become one people."[253] For more than 240 years, we have proudly proclaimed our nation to be a melting pot: no matter who you are, where you came from, your skin color, or your native language, when you immigrate to America and embrace American ideas, you become an American.

Much data shows the majority of immigrants do assimilate well. For example, a study shows that 88% of second-generation and 94% of third-generation Hispanics speak fluent English.[254] Such assimilation occurs not only in a cultural and economic sense but also in a civic sense. Many immigrants gave their lives to defend American ideals in combat, from the Civil War to the war in Iraq and Afghanistan.

However, anti-immigration groups allege that newer immigrants haven't been doing as good of a job assimilating as their predecessors, especially in a civic sense. Research seems to support their claims.

According to the Pew Research Center, in the 1970s, 67% of legal immigrants became naturalized U.S. citizens. In the 1990s, that number fell to 38%, although it has gradually climbed since then. In 2011, 56% of legal immigrants in the U.S. became naturalized citizens, but the remaining 44% (9.7 million legal immigrants) chose not to pursue citizenship even though they were eligible. Hispanics made up the largest immigrant group, but their naturalization rate was only 46%, compared to 71% for all other legal immigrants. Legal immigrants from Mexico have the lowest naturalization rate at 36%.[255] The 2016 presidential election motivated more legal immigrants to apply for U.S. citizenship so they could vote. The number of citizenship applications has been rising ever since. Over a million legal immigrants became U.S. citizens in 2021, the third-highest number in U.S. history.[*]

It is concerning that large numbers of eligible legal immigrants choose not to become U.S. citizens because obtaining citizenship is essential to civic assimilation. Some immigration advocates blame the costs of naturalization for preventing most legal immigrants from

---

[*]About 1.4 million legal immigrants became U.S. citizens in 2007, the highest number in U.S. history.
Retrieved from https://www.pewresearch.org/fact-tank/2020/08/20/key-findings-about-u-s-immigrants/

obtaining citizenship. I don't buy that argument because immigrants have already spent tens and thousands of dollars to come to the U.S. legally or illegally. I suspect that 56% of legal immigrants chose not to become naturalized citizens for other reasons.

All they want is to live, work, send their kids to school, move, and travel without any constraints and without having to carry their paperwork everywhere. A green card is sufficient for all these purposes. Thus, they don't see value in pursuing citizenship, which grants one the right not to be deported, the right to vote, and the duty to serve on juries. Thus, immigrants who want to assimilate economically but not civically choose not to apply for U.S. citizenship.

In 2013, John Fonte, a senior fellow at the Hudson Institute, and Althea Nagai, a statistician, published a study on civic assimilation based on a Harris Interactive survey of 2,421 American citizens, compared native-born to naturalized citizens. Some of their major findings include:[256]

- By 21 percentage points (65% to 44%), native-born citizens are more likely than naturalized immigrants to view America as "better" than other countries as opposed to "no better, no worse."

- By about 30 points (85% to 54%), native-born citizens are more likely to consider themselves American citizens rather than "citizens of the world."

- By 30 points (67% to 37%), native-born citizens are more likely to believe that the U.S. Constitution is a higher legal authority for Americans than international law.

Fonte believes that multiculturalism is responsible for this civic assimilation gap between native-born and immigrant citizens. The Stanford Encyclopedia of Philosophy defines multiculturalism as,

A body of thought in political philosophy about the proper way to respond to cultural and religious diversity. Multiculturalism demands that people be treated as groups. Mere toleration of group differences is said to fall short of treating members of minority groups as equal citizens; recognition and positive accommodation of group differences are required through "group-differentiated rights," a term coined by Will Kymlicka (1995).

Multiculturalism is closely associated with identity politics, endorsed by many U.S. government policies and promoted by left-leaning media, corporations, and the education system. Supporters of multiculturalism treat assimilation as a dirty word, a social construct based on colonial racism.

Discouraging immigrants from cultural and civil assimilation in the name of multiculturalism harms immigrants and America. For one, some cultural beliefs and practices are incompatible with the principles America was founded upon and values we Americans hold dear. For example, some cultures glorify female genital mutilation (FGM), also known as female genital cutting (FGC). FGM/FGC is a procedure that "involves partial or total removal of the external *female* genitalia, or other injury to the female genital organs for non-medical reasons"* for girls as soon as they reach puberty. It's demeaning and inhuman, and it has brought generations of women nothing but pain, infection, infertility, and sometimes even death. Even the United Nations and the World Health Organization have called for the abolition of FGM, as it violates human rights.

Yet, supporters of multiculturalism want Americans to accept FGM as a cultural norm that immigrants should keep practicing in the United States. More than 500,000 women and girls (most are immigrants or the children of immigrants) in the U.S. have already undergone this procedure or are at risk of being forced to undergo the procedure, either in the U.S. or abroad. FGM is rising in the U.S. due to immigration from African and Middle Eastern countries. According to a *Newsweek* report, "California is the state with the largest number of at-risk women and girls, with 56,872, followed by New York, with 48,418, and Minnesota, with 44,293."[257] How could we tell these women and girls that they can be anything they want to be because

---

* As defined by the World Health Organization (WHO). Retrieved from https://www.who.int/news-room/fact-sheets/detail/female-genital-mutilation

they live in a free country while turning a blind eye to their inhuman suffering, choosing to do nothing about it because multiculturalism demands that all cultural practices and beliefs be accepted and endorsed?

History of U.S. immigration has shown that assimilation is essential for immigrants to become full members of society and to obtain all the benefits that society offers. Multiculturalism divides people rather than unites them. It isolates immigrants in their cultural bubbles and makes it difficult to realize their full potential in society. Thus, we as a nation need to reject multiculturalism and return to policies and activities that help immigrants assimilate socially and civically.

As an immigrant and an American by choice, I believe every immigrant ought to ask him or herself this question: "What is my responsibility to the host country, and what do I need to do to be part of this new home of my choice?" The keywords here are "responsibility" and "choice."

Let's face it. Very few countries have immigration policies that actively recruit immigrants. For whatever reasons, whether to escape war or to seek a better life, an immigrant voluntarily makes a conscious choice of which country he or she wants to move to. Immigration is not for everyone. The immigration process generally exacts substantial financial and emotional tolls. Some immigrants are even subjected to life-threatening dangers, like the Syrian refugees who drowned while trying to reach Greece. Immigration is not for the faint of heart. Who would uproot themselves and their families and move to an unfamiliar place unless they believed the move would be worth the trouble because life in their birth country was unbearable, and the prospect of life in another country is much better?

Since every immigrant decides to move to another country and live in a different culture, it is an immigrant's responsibility to strive to be part of the new homeland of his/her choice. The assimilation process is not about what our new homeland can do for us; but about our effort to be part of it. Based on my own experience, there are at least three things each immigrant can do:

First, respect and obey the law. Many immigrants migrate to Western countries because they are tired of the chaos and lawlessness in their birth countries. They voted with their feet for a more peaceful and prosperous life, made possible only by the rule of law. Therefore, every immigrant needs to respect and obey the laws of their new homeland, including immigration laws.

If we believe a particular law is unjust and should be changed, let's do it by participating in the civic process and advocating changes through the existing legal and democratic framework. Simply ignoring the law will bring chaos and lawlessness to our adopted country, which defeats why we chose to move here in the first place and will undoubtedly cause resentment from the citizens of our adopted countries.

Second, learn the local language. Many Western countries, including the U.S., provide plentiful resources, including many free resources, to help new immigrants learn local languages. Recent immigrants have no excuse for not taking advantage of these resources: numerous studies show that one of the critical success factors for immigrants is the ability to speak the language of their new homeland. Immigrants who can speak the local language typically find better jobs, make more money, and feel much happier than those who do not.

Third, learn to appreciate the local culture. It doesn't mean immigrants have to abandon the culture they were born into entirely. Nor does it mean immigrants have to accept everything the local culture offers. It means that immigrants should make a concerted effort to get to know the local culture, its institutions, and its ideas. For example, I occasionally watch shows like *Family Guy* and *South Park*, but not because I enjoy them. About half the time, I do not understand the metaphors or cultural references these shows use. The other half of the time, when I do get the jokes, I don't find them funny. But I watch them because these shows are part of the popular culture in America, and America is my new home. If I want to join the water-cooler conversations with my colleagues, I ought to at least be familiar with some cultural phenomena or references. That is part of the assimilation process.

I am not suggesting every immigrant watch *Family Guy* and *South Park*. But if new immigrants do not appreciate or understand the local culture, they will feel isolated and lonely. For those immigrants who want to stay in one area and establish a parallel community that resembles the society they left behind, it is worth asking, "Why did you choose to come here in the first place?"

Alexander Hamilton reminded us why assimilation was essential. He said, "The safety of a republic depends essentially on the energy of a common national sentiment; on a uniformity of principles and habits." Without assimilation, immigrants cannot expect to live a happy and fulfilling life in the United States, and a divided population that rejects a shared national identity will put the future of this republic in danger.

As immigrants, we voluntarily leave our birthplace and culture and pick a new home for ourselves and our families. Let's take ownership of our assimilation and become full members of this new homeland.

Summary

Is immigration good for America? History tells us that immigrants who can easily integrate into American society and contribute to our economy and culture are good for America. Charles Murray, an American political scientist, wrote, "the immigrants I actually encounter, of all ethnicities, typically come across as classically American—cheerful, hardworking, optimistic, ambitious."[258] It's in our national interests to continue to roll out the welcome mat for these immigrants to our shores.

CHAPTER 7

Illegal Immigration: History, Issues, and Failed Fixes

For nearly a hundred years since our nation's founding until 1875, the U.S. didn't have an illegal immigration problem. Other than a few requirements for citizenship (i.e., a residency minimum and a demonstration of moral character), there was no immigration law to decide who could or couldn't come to the U.S. All were welcome to stay.

Things began to change in 1875. The Page Act was the first immigration law in U.S. history to restrict certain groups of people from entering the country, including convicts, women "imported for the purposes of prostitution," and Chinese laborers. The Chinese Exclusion Act of 1882 was the first immigration law that prevented immigration and naturalization based on race and nationality. The Act established, for the first time, a distinction between legal and illegal immigration in the U.S. However, it only barred immigration from China; immigration from other countries remained wide open.

The U.S. saw an immigration surge from 1882 to 1920. During that period, more than 23 million immigrants from all over the world came to the U.S. To maintain the ethnic composition of the country (where the Anglo-Saxons were the majority), the U.S. Congress passed the

921 Quota Law, which, for the first time, set a limit on the number of
legal immigrants the U.S. would accept each year. As history shows,
using quotas marked the beginning of an influx of illegal immigrants
that foreshadowed our nation's situation today.

7.1 A Brief History of Illegal Immigration

To understand the history of illegal immigration, we need a quick
overview of the U.S. agricultural industry, a sector of our nation's
economy that has been using imported laborers for centuries.

As early as 1848, following the end of the Mexican-American War
(1846-1848), thousands of Mexican migrants crossed the border and
became farm laborers. The U.S. began importing Chinese laborers as
farmhands when agriculture became a large-scale industry in the late
19th and early 20th centuries. By 1886, seven out of every eight farm
workers in California were Chinese.[259] After the passage of the Chinese
Exclusion Act of 1882, which practically banned the employment of
Chinese workers, the farming industry started to hire more Japanese
and Filipino workers. In the meantime, "Mounted watchmen of the
U.S. Immigration Service patrolled the border [U.S. & Mexico] in an
effort to prevent illegal crossings as early as 1904, but their efforts were
irregular and undertaken only when resources permitted."[260]

During the First World War, the number of immigrants from
Europe declined, and the Immigration Act of 1917 (a.k.a. the Asiatic
Barred Zone Act) restricted the entry of Asian immigrants. Thus, the
demand for migrant workers from Mexico rose. By the 1920s, 75% of
California's 200,000 farm workers were Mexican or Mexican American.
When the United States entered the Great Depression in 1930, and
employment became scarce, sentiment towards foreign workers turned
hostile: they were regarded as unwanted competition that took jobs
away from native-born Americans. Facing intense pressure from
American labor unions, several U.S. states, including California and
Texas, deported between 400,000 and one million[261] Mexican workers
and U.S. citizens of Mexican descent. "Texas's Mexican-born
population was reduced by a third, while Los Angeles lost a third of its
Mexican population."[262]

However, World War II created a labor shortage in the U.S. when many American men were drafted into the Armed Forces. On August 4, 1942, the U.S. and Mexican governments launched a temporary program to bring Mexican agricultural labor into the U.S. The program was officially referred to as the Mexican Farm Labor Program, but most people know it as the Bracero Program (*bracero* in Spanish means "manual laborer"). The Bracero Program wasn't an immigration program, and it simply allowed Mexicans to take temporary agriculture work and, later, railroad work in the U.S. legally, with nonimmigrant status. The Bracero Program was a well-run program in several ways:

First, there was no quota on how many Mexican laborers were allowed into the U.S. Instead, U.S. businesses' needs decided the number of workers. Thus, there was neither a labor surplus nor a labor shortage problem.

Second, the selection process was robust. There were selection/processing centers in Mexico and the U.S. Potential Mexican participants had to first go through interviews and physical examinations at the processing centers in Mexico. Often, they had their hands checked for calluses, indicating whether they were experienced farmhands.[263] When workers came to the U.S., they had to go through interviews again with U.S. employers. The processing centers ensured the quality of the workers and a good match between employers and employees.

Third, each hired Mexican worker signed a contract with beginning and ending dates for employment. At the end of the contract, the worker went back to Mexico. If workers choose, they could apply for the program again. Some Mexican workers came back and forth between Mexico and the U.S. several times a year.

There was some controversy associated with the Bracero Program. Like early Chinese laborers, Bracero workers were willing to take back-breaking jobs at far lower wages than any American worker would. Therefore, American farm workers accused them of driving down farm wages. Some farm owners were accused of taking advantage of Bracero workers by not providing the quality housing and decent meals demanded by their contracts. But overall, the Bracero Program proved so popular in the U.S. and Mexico that the U.S. Congress formalized the program with Public Law 78 in 1951. The program lasted until 1964. Between 1942 and 1964, over 4.6 million Bracero labor contracts were signed.[264]

The legacy of the Bracero Program was twofold: first, it was a win-win for the U.S. and Mexico from an economic standpoint; second (which isn't discussed often), it reduced the influx of illegal immigrants because there were no legal hurdles for Mexican workers to get a work visa in the U.S. There were few compliance requirements for U.S. farmers, and with a guaranteed supply of legal workers, there was limited demand for illegal workers.

In addition, the U.S. Border Patrol was effective at containing illegal immigrants. The Department of Immigration and Naturalization Service (INS) launched Operation Wetback in July 1954. General Joseph May Swing led a quasi-military operation in the search, seizure, and deportation of illegal immigrants in the South. Although his force was small (no more than 700 men), its strength "was exaggerated by border patrol officials who hoped to scare unauthorized workers into flight back to Mexico."[265] The INS and local law enforcement authorities claimed to have removed 1.1 million Mexicans by the end of 1954. But that figure included many illegal immigrants who left voluntarily at the beginning and in the middle of Operation Wetback, for fear of federal apprehension. By 1955, the number of illegal immigrants had been reduced by 90%.[266] The operation ended in 1955 when it ran out of funding.

The twin acts of the Bracero program and enhanced border control and deportation put the illegal immigrant issue under control. But labor unions still opposed the Bracero program because the availability of legal Bracero workers depressed wages for American farm workers. Their accusation wasn't entirely unfounded. The actual wage data showed that "the availability of Braceros held down wages — average farm worker earnings in California rose 41%, from $0.85 an hour in 1950 to $1.20 in 1960, while average factory worker earnings rose 63%, from $1.60 in 1950 to $2.60 in 1960."[267] This data gave people opposing the Bracero Program ammunition. They called for ending it, hoping to save agriculture jobs for American-born workers.

But realistically, by the 1950s, fewer Americans aspired to become agricultural workers because the post-World War II economic boom provided them with much better-paying employment opportunities and better working conditions in many non-agriculture sectors. Farmers could neither raise wages high enough nor change the back-breaking nature of farm work to attract a sufficient number of American workers, so farmers had to import labor from across the border once again. Ignoring this fundamental supply-and-demand issue, the labor unions organized agricultural workers, including Bracero workers, to go on strike and demand higher wages and better working conditions. The frequent wage-related strikes and powerful lobbying from the labor unions gradually convinced the federal government that the low wages of the Bracero workers prevented economic mobility for American and Mexican agricultural workers. Something had to change.

In 1965, the U.S. Congress voted to end the Bracero Program and replace it with the H-2 (changed to H-2A in 1986) temporary agriculture work visa program. The H-2 is an inferior and less flexible program than the Bracero Program. Through the H-2 program, the federal government demands higher wages and a shorter visa duration (120 days), neither of which are desirable to farmers. In addition, farmers must go through a tedious and time-consuming labor certification process. Farmers' reactions were predictable. They began to rely more on machines—"One study predicted that if a fruit or vegetable could not be harvested mechanically, it would not be grown in the United States after 1975"[268]—and on hiring illegal immigrants whenever they could.

In addition to farming, the U.S. construction and housing boom also increased the demand for laborers. When President Gerald R. Ford signed the 1976 Immigration Act, which reduced the quota of legal immigration from Mexico, he predicted that the Act would only increase the volume of illegal immigration. He was proven right. For poor Mexicans, opportunities to work and earn higher wages in the U.S. have always been a big draw. Illegal immigration surges whenever the U.S. government restricts the path to working in the U.S. legally. By 1986, when President Reagan was in office, illegal immigrants in the U.S. numbered 3-5 million. Unlike the Bracero workers, these illegal immigrants chose to stay in the U.S. rather than return to Mexico, fearing apprehension at the border.

In November 1986, President Reagan signed the Immigration

Reform and Control Act of 1986, which he called "the most compre-hensive reform of our immigration laws since 1952." He promised it would fix our broken immigration system. The 1986 Act contained three key provisions:

- Applied sanctions on employers knowingly hiring illegal immigrants or failing to check their paperwork appropri-ately.

- Increased border security.

- Offered legalization or amnesty to around three million illegal immigrants.

The first provision required U.S. companies to employ only individuals who may legally work in the U.S., including U.S. citizens, permanent residents, and foreign nationals with the necessary work authorization. This provision led to the implementation of *Employment Eligibility Verification*, commonly known as Form I-9. It requires "employees to attest to their work eligibility, and employers to certify that the documents presented reasonably appear (on their face) to be genuine and to relate to the individual." The 1996 Illegal Immigration Reform and Immigrant Responsibility Act enhanced the provision by requiring the then-Immigration and Naturalization Service (INS)[269] to conduct pilot programs to determine the best way of verifying an employee's employment authorization.

These pilot programs later evolved into what we today call E-Verify. According to the USCIS website, "E-Verify is an Internet-based system that compares information from an employee's Form I-9, Employment Eligibility Verification, to data from the U.S. Department of Homeland Security and Social Security Administration records to confirm employment eligibility."[270] E-Verify is free for employers and mandatory for federal contractors and most government workers in some states. Outside of that, it's essentially a voluntary system. More than 600,000 employers are enrolled today, and more than 13 million employee verification inquiries are processed through E-Verify annu-ally. Employers and employees who use E-Verify give it high marks for ease of use and a customer satisfaction score in the high 80s on a

100-point scale. It's rare for a government-run program to receive such high customer satisfaction scores. It's not a perfect system. Like any other system, it is only as good as the data it gets. Due to the rampant fraud in Social Security numbers and identity theft, E-Verify has been in a constant battle against data accuracy. But overall, it's a successful program.

Unfortunately, the other provision of the '86 Act, offering three million illegal aliens amnesty, failed to stop the inflow of illegal immigrants as promised. The number of illegal immigrants continued to climb. According to Pew Research, between 1990 and 2007, the illegal immigrant population more than tripled — from 3.5 million to 12.2 million in 2007.

Lack of legal status presents economic costs to many illegal immigrants seeking employment. Illegal immigrants often have to accept employment and wage offers from prospective employers without much negotiating power. Due to their lack of legal status, they may have to subject themselves to harsh working conditions and long work hours without much recourse.

7.2 Where Are We Now?

An estimated 15 million illegal immigrants reside in the U.S. as of 2021, representing about 5% of the nation's labor force. It's worth pointing out that illegal immigrants make up a larger share of the labor force than the total population*.

Although nearly 45% of illegal immigrants come from Mexico, Mexicans' share of illegal immigrants peaked in 2007 and has been declining since. Ana Gonzalez-Barrera from the Pew Research Center estimated that 140,000 fewer Mexicans were living in the U.S. in 2014 than in 2009, and that the net flow from Mexico to the U.S. is now negative. She credited the decline to the U.S.'s economic recession in 2008 and the improving Mexican economy at the same time.[271] Today,

---

* According to the Brookings Institute, As the foreign-born population has grown as a share of the total population, they have grown disproportionately as a share of the labor force. By 2010, immigrants (both legal and illegal) were 16 percent of the labor force, but only 13 percent of the total population. Retrieved from https://www.brookings.edu/research/immigrant-workers-in-the-u-s-labor-force/

as Figure 7.1 shows, while the number of illegal immigrants from Mexico has decreased, the number of unauthorized immigrants from other parts of the world has increased.

Figure 7.1

Increase in recent arrivals from Northern Triangle and Asia, decrease from Mexico

Population of arrivals in previous five years, in thousands

Birth country	2017	Share	2007	Share
Mexico	475	20%	2,050	52%
Northern Triangle	400	17	425	11
Asia	525	23	525	13
Other countries	925	40	925	24
Total	2,350		3,950	

Note: Northern Triangle consists of El Salvador, Guatemala and Honduras. Asia consists of South and East Asia. All numbers are rounded.
Source: Pew Research Center estimates based on augmented U.S. Census Bureau data.

PEW RESEARCH CENTER

In recent years, illegal immigrants have been getting younger, and more travel in family units. Unfortunately, this new trend is the result of our government's policies.

In June 2012, President Obama announced an executive action — the Deferred Action for Childhood Arrivals (DACA) program — giving young adults illegally brought to the U.S. as children temporary deportation relief, even though President Obama admitted DACA is unconstitutional and many legal scholars agreed*. What President Obama and many DACA supporters have failed to appreciate is the relationship between incentives and immigration. Before DACA, about 90 percent of apprehensions along the U.S.-Mexico borders were single

---

* In 2010, when asked about establishing DACA through an executive order, President Obama famously said: "I am not king. . . . With the respect to the notion that I can just suspend deportations through executive order, that's just not the case." But two years later, he did it anyway. Retrieved from https://metrovoicenews.com/obama-said-daca-was-unconstitutional-now-supreme-court-decides/

adults. After DACA was announced, there was a well-publicized surge of unaccompanied minors and families illegally crossing the U.S.-Mexico border. Most of these minors were from Central American countries such as El Salvador, Guatemala, and Honduras. Their journeys were often dangerous, even life-threatening. Many children suffered physical and sexual abuse at the hands of smugglers. In addition, many were at risk of dehydration, heat stroke, and hypothermia when crossing the desert, where it is hot during the day and cold at night.

The Obama administration characterized the surge as the result of worsening criminal activities in Central America, but the truth is that crime in Nicaragua didn't suddenly get so bad in 2013 that many abruptly decided to escape. Rather, these minors and family units were invited to cross the border by their families and relatives who were already in the U.S. That is why the same the *New York Times* reported that many minors who were apprehended "were reunited with their families here and not immediately deported." Consequently, "many Central Americans were left with the perception that the United States was allowing children to stay." DACA has changed the composition of illegal immigration. Today, family units and unaccompanied minors make up about two-thirds of all apprehensions along the U.S.-Mexico border.

In November 2014, President Obama expanded DACA and issued another executive action that shielded U.S. citizens' or legal residents' illegal immigrant parents from deportation and allowed them to work legally. Predictably, illegal crossings rose in the second half of 2015. According to U.S. Border Patrol interviews, of these illegal immigrants, "the vast majority of the family units interviewed heard that if they came to the U.S. they would be allowed to stay. And in fact, most of those interviewed stated that it was the U.S. government's policies that influenced their decision to come to the U.S. in the first place." The Border Patrol also found that "68% of the illegal immigrants interviewed believed that the U.S. was offering some form of either asylum or amnesty. Federal agents found that 64% of the individuals interviewed believed that the U.S. was "granting work permits to those who arrived as a family."[272]

In a way, these illegal immigrants were right because U.S. immigration policy makes it challenging to detain and deport families with children. Once they cross the border, they are allowed to stay while they await court proceedings, a process that can take years. The administration's approach is a "permiso" to come and stay for these illegal immigrants. In conclusion, President Obama's "executive amnesty" offered false hope and incentivized many more illegal immigrants to take on a perilous journey to cross the border.

The Obama administration revived the illegal immigrant catch-and-release policy from the Bush years, with the emphasis on "release," by ordering Border Patrol agents not to arrest or deport many illegal immigrants. According to Brando Judd, president of the National Border Patrol Council, agents were instructed not to ask for proof when an immigrant says he or she has been in the U.S. since 2013, based on the administration's assertion that illegal immigrants who have been in the U.S. for a while are unlikely to be criminals. Of course, once word of this got out, illegal immigrants quickly learned to claim they had been in the U.S. since 2013. Once again, our good-intentioned immigration policies became a magnet for illegal immigrants.

Unlike illegal immigrants, the more than 30 million legal immigrants in the U.S. didn't get any relief even though they dutifully followed the law, paid hefty fees, endured long waits (many in family and employment categories have waited more than a decade), and suffered long separations from their families. To add insult to injury, legal immigrants were pushed further down the line to make room for illegal immigrants. For example, as of January 2015, the Justice Department had delayed thousands of immigrants' court hearing dates for five years until 2019 in order to make room for the courts to process unaccompanied minors and family unit cases.

Texas and 25 other states sued the Obama administration to invalidate the President's executive orders. The Trump administration attempted to end DACA through an executive order. The U.S. Supreme Court ruled in June 2020, saying the Trump administration failed to adequately support its decision to do away with DACA. Still, the justices avoided weighing in on the merits of the DACA program.

Despite President Trump's harsh rhetoric on illegal immigration, apprehension of illegal immigrants during the first two years of his presidency went down only slightly*. Since most illegal immigrants were minors or family units, and claimed asylum, federal immigration authorities released them inside the U.S. as fast as they were taking them in. Seeking to end such "catch-and-release" practices, the Trump administration put the "Remain in Mexico" policy in place in 2019. Illegal immigrants apprehended at the U.S.-Mexico borders were sent back to Mexico to wait for their asylum proceedings in the U.S.

During the 2020 Covid-19 pandemic, the Trump administration invoked Title 42, a public health order that enabled U.S. Border Patrol agents to promptly expel illegal immigrants, instead of allowing them to seek asylum within the country, as had long been the policy before the pandemic. The twin policies of "Remain in Mexico" and Title 42 and the pandemic slowed illegal border crossings. The fiscal year 2020 saw approximately 400,000 encounters with illegal immigrants at our southern borders.

Although Joe Biden was the Vice President under President Obama, Biden didn't learn from Obama's policy mistakes on immigration. Before becoming President of the United States, Biden signaled that he would embrace an open border policy and be lenient with illegal border crossings. Once he became president, Biden ended Trump's "Remain in Mexico" policy. His administration ended the use of Title 42 for unaccompanied minors in March 2022. Biden also sought to end Title 42 for two other groups of illegal immigrants: single adults and people traveling with families, at the end of May 2022, but the U.S. Supreme Court ordered a temporary hold on Title 42's expiration. Like President Obama, Biden's policies and rhetoric on immigration became incentives for illegal border crossings, and encounters at the U.S.-Mexico border surged to historical highs.

---

* Iillegal border crossings was 396,579 in fiscal year 2018, lower than the average over the previous decade (400,751). Retrieved from https://www.politico.com/story/2018/11/02/immigration-crisis-fact-check-916924

Figure 7.2

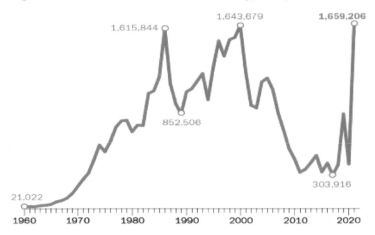

Migrant encounters at U.S.-Mexico border reached their highest level on record in 2021

Migrant encounters at U.S.-Mexico border, by fiscal year

Note: Beginning in fiscal 2020, annual totals combine expulsions and apprehensions into a new category known as encounters. Annual totals before fiscal 2020 include apprehensions only.
Source: U.S. Customs and Border Protection.

PEW RESEARCH CENTER

According to Pew Research*, in fiscal year 2021, the U.S. Border Patrol reported more than 1,659,206 encounters with migrants along the U.S.-Mexico border, more than four times that of fiscal year 2020, exceeding historical highs of 1,643,679 in 2000 and 1,615,844 in 1986. Fiscal 2022's number was even higher, with 2,378,944 encounters as of November 2022. If Title 42 expires as the Biden administration plans to do, the number of illegal crossings at our southern border will be even higher. Sen. Mike Lee (R., Utah) warned: "Title 42 is the one thing standing between us and utter chaos."

Today, our nation faces an unprecedented border crisis. All President Biden has done in his first two years in office is pretending such a crisis doesn't exist. White House Press Secretary Karine Jean-Pierre accuses anyone raising questions about the border crisis of spreading

---

* Retrieved from
https://www.pewresearch.org/fact-tank/2021/11/09/whats-happening-at-the-u-s-mexico-border-in-7-charts/

"misinformation" and helping Mexican cartels*. At the beginning of January 2023, the Biden administration finally realized they could not afford to ignore the border crisis any longer. The administration decided to extract as much political gain as it could from a crisis it had created in the first place.

While the Republicans in the U.S. Congress were tied up in an internal battle, trying to decide who would be the next Speaker of the House, Biden announced his so-called immigration plan. Rather than letting Title 42 expire as he had previously insisted, he kept the rule to expel border-crossing migrants from Cuba, Nicaragua, and Haiti. But more importantly, he would allow 30,000 people from those countries to legally enter the U.S. by air monthly. Migrants who come to the U.S. by air can legally stay for two years if someone in the U.S financially sponsors them, passes background checks, and receives work authorizations. The Biden administration also promised to give $23 million in humanitarian aid to Mexico and Central America, basically paying these corrupt governments to do something to keep their people from leaving.

Converting 30,000 illegal immigrants into legal parolees is amnesty in disguise and an expansion of executive power that the U.S. Congress sought to limit in a 1996 amendment to the Immigration Naturalization Act of 1990, which states the executive branch may grant parole "only on a case-by-case basis for urgent humanitarian reasons or significant public benefit." Biden's plan will not likely reduce the number of illegal border crossings because migrants from those four countries will see the parole plan as an invitation to come to the U.S. through different means, while migrants outside of those four countries who are not eligible for parole will continue to pour in through our southern border. Regardless of how the Biden administration spins its plan, it does little to address the border crisis and will likely turn the current situation from bad to worse.

---

* The exact quote was, "The border is not open. So I want to be very clear about that because we are doing the smuggler's job if we spread misinformation." https://nypost.com/2022/12/19/white-house-claims-its-misinformation-to-say-border-open-when-title-42-ends/

7.3 Why We Should Be Concerned about Illegal Immigration

Fifteen million illegal immigrants have an outsized impact on American society.

Economic impact. Popular opinion holds that illegal immigrants are economic takers, not contributors. That's not entirely accurate. Remember that illegal immigrants make up 3.5% of our nation's population but 5% of the labor force because many of them work. Illegal immigrants also pay taxes, including property tax (which is embedded in rent), sales tax, and some income tax[*]. The Institute on Taxation and Economic Policy (ITEP), a non-profit, non-partisan research organization, published a study on illegal immigrants' tax contributions with the following key findings:

- Illegal immigrants paid about $11.74 billion in state and local taxes in 2017.

- Undocumented immigrants nationwide pay on average an estimated 8 percent of their incomes in state and local taxes (this is their effective state and local tax rate).

- Granting lawful permanent residence to all illegal immigrants and allowing them to work in the United States legally would increase their state and local tax contributions by an estimated $2.2 billion a year.[273]

While acknowledging that many illegal immigrants pay some forms of taxes, we can't shy away from the economic costs these immigrants pose. A Heritage Foundation study shows that "half of the unlawful immigrant households are headed by an individual with less than a high school degree, and another 25 percent of household heads have only a high school degree."[274] This low education level means that the

---

[*] Illegal immigrants often get a tax ID number-- the ITIN (Individual Taxpayer Identification Number) and file through IRS acceptance agents. ITINs are used for foreign nationals and other people who aren't eligible for a social security number.

majority of illegal immigrants are at the bottom of the economic ladder. They compete against low-skilled and less-educated native-born Americans for the same low-skilled and low-paying jobs. Such competition drives down wages in the short run, as discussed in Chapter 6. Professor Borjas's research shows that "in the absence of illegal immigration, immigration would have had little impact on relative wages."[275]

Since illegal immigrants tend to have low-wage jobs and larger households than the native-born, they depend more on welfare per household basis.

The 1996 federal welfare reform law deems that illegal immigrants are not eligible for Social Security, Medicare, Obamacare, federal means-tested social welfare benefits such as food stamps, the refundable Earned Income Tax Credit, etc. But illegal immigrants still receive much social welfare, directly or indirectly, especially at the state and local levels. Because the 1996 welfare reform gave states the responsibility to set state and local welfare eligibility rules for immigrants, many states offer garden variety of welfare benefits to both legal and illegal immigrants. In addition, many illegal immigrants have U.S.-born children who are citizens and have access to all government benefits. Pew Research data shows that about 7% of K-12 students in the U.S. had at least one unauthorized immigrant parent in 2014, and 79% of those children were born in the U.S.[276] Below are a few additional benefits that illegal immigrants have access to:

- All children of illegal immigrants, whether U.S. citizens or not, receive a government-provided K-12 public school education.*

- Illegal immigrant children under 18 receive federally funded free or reduced-price school lunches.

---

* The U.S. Supreme Court ruled in *Plyler v. Doe* (457 US 202 [1982]) that children and young adults who have not been admitted legally into the U.S. have the same right to attend public primary and secondary schools as U.S. citizens and permanent residents.

- Illegal immigrants who are pregnant women are eligible for Medicaid.

- Illegal immigrants can live in public housing if they have U.S.-born children, and their U.S.-born children can also be enrolled in Medicaid.

- As of 2022, twenty states offer in-state tuition to illegal immigrant students, and five even allow them to receive state financial aid.

In addition to these benefits, illegal immigrants, like other residents, enjoy public services such as access to emergency rooms, parks, and roads. Even illegal immigrants in detention centers run by Immigration and Customs Enforcement (ICE) have access to medical care funded by U.S. taxpayers. One can't deny that this ease of access to social welfare benefits has served as an enticement for many illegal immigrants. The Heritage Foundation compared the taxes illegal immigrants paid against the welfare benefits they received in 2010. The analysis showed the average illegal immigrant household paid about $10,334 in taxes and received around $24,721 in government benefits and services. So, on a per household basis, the average illegal immigrant household represents more than $14,000 of the per-year fiscal deficit.

Border towns and cities have felt the most economic impact of illegal immigration. For instance, El Paso, Texas, a border city with less than 700,000 residents, has seen 84,082 immigrants released into its streets between August 22 and December 11, 2022. Border Patrol facilities in the El Paso region were at 162% capacity. The city was forced to turn two vacant schools, the convention center, and part of its airport into shelters to house illegal immigrants. El Paso Mayor Oscar Leeser, a Democrat, announced a state of emergency in December 2022, saying he could no longer keep residents safe.

As the Biden administration lost control of our borders, non-border cities and states felt the burn too. In October 2022, New York City's Mayor Eric Adams, a Democrat, declared a state of emergency due to the influx of more than 17,000 illegal immigrants.* He said the city's shelters were running out of bed space, and the city's public school have taken in 5,500 recently arrived migrant children. The city has converted over 40 hotels into makeshift shelters and planned to set up a tent city on Randall's Island Park. But Adams said the city government had neither the funds nor the shelters to support additional illegal migrants while assisting homeless Americans already in the city. Despite Adam's complaints, another Democrat, Jared Polis, governor of Colorado, announced in late December 2022 that he would also send illegal immigrants from his state to New York City as his way of "helping migrants safely reach their desired final destination." For years, Democrats have denied that the influx of illegal immigrants strains public services and exhausts resources. Finally, they had a dose of their own medicine when illegal immigrants reached their doorsteps.

Security impact. According to U.S. Customs and Border Control, the U.S. shares 5,525 miles of border with Canada and 1,989 miles with Mexico. Most illegal entries come from our southern border with Mexico. The types of barriers between the U.S. and Mexico vary greatly along this long border. In some areas, there is nothing or merely a marker. Only 650 miles along the southern border have some kind of barrier, including cattle fences, pedestrian fences, vehicle barricades, barbed-wire fences, and vertical railroad rails. In some of the more violent areas, there are secondary barriers, such as climb-proof expanded metal fences or concrete columns with mounted cameras. But illegal immigrants have successfully crossed the U.S.-Mexico border through fence-free areas or tunnels, or ladders, and other means to get around those border barriers.

Most of the people crossing our borders illegally are economic migrants who probably don't pose any security threat. But the fact that such large numbers of people can easily cross into the United States shows how our lax border control creates vulnerabilities that can be

---

* Texas and Florida officials have been putting illegal migrants on buses or planes to Democrat-run sanctuary cities such as New York City, Washington, D.C., and Chicago to protest the border crisis caused by the Biden administration's policy and rhetoric.

exploited by those who'd want to harm Americans. General John Kelly, commander of the U.S. Southern Command, called the U.S.-Mexico border security an "existential" threat at a Congressional hearing in 2014.[277] In the same year, the federal government issued a warning bulletin for "an imminent terrorist attack on our borders." According to Judicial Watch, sources revealed that the militant group Islamic State of Iraq and Greater Syria (ISIS) is confirmed to be now operating in Juarez, a famously crime-infested narcotics hotbed located across from El Paso, Texas.[278]

Reality quickly vindicated the feds' concerns. Historically, we have seen mainly migrants from Mexico and Central America cross the border illegally into the U.S. But in recent years, we have seen more migrants come from countries that have not historically been common sources of illegal migration, suggesting that the dysfunction at our southern border has become known and entices people worldwide to seek unlawful entry. Unfortunately, terrorists who seek to harm the United States and Americans are exploiting our broken borders, too. In fiscal year 2022, U.S. border agents arrested over 90 illegal immigrants on the U.S. terrorist watch list. But who knows how many have gotten away and lurk inside the U.S. for opportunities to hurt us?

Figure 7.3

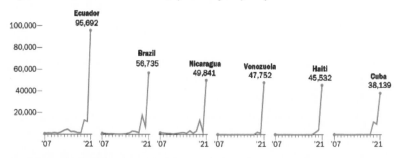

Encounters with migrants from some countries rose dramatically in 2021

Migrant encounters at U.S.-Mexico border, by citizenship and fiscal year

Note: Beginning in fiscal 2020, annual totals combine expulsions and apprehensions into a new category known as encounters. Annual totals before fiscal 2020 include apprehensions only.
Source: U.S. Customs and Border Protection.

PEW RESEARCH CENTER

Mary O'Grady of the Wall Street Journal also noted that historically, some dictatorial regimes in South America have used migrants as a weapon and intentionally encouraged their citizens to flood to the U.S.-Mexico border to destabilize the U.S. economy and national security. Using Cuba as an example. O'Grady noted that the Cuban regime "unleashed three destabilizing crises since taking power in 1959. They occurred in 1965, 1980 and 1994-95, all years when a Democrat was in the White House. During the Obama administration, more than 120,000 Cuban migrants <u>found</u> their way to U.S. ports of entry from 2014-16, mainly via Central America." However, "There was no attempt by Fidel Castro to flood American shores with desperate *balseros* during the presidencies of Ronald Reagan, George H.W. Bush or George W. Bush despite their hardline policies against Cuba."[279] Professor Kelly Greenhill of Tufts University called this type of "coercive engineered migration" a threat to our national security.

Other security concerns involve the ultra-violent Mexican cartels are profiting from the illicit drug trade and human trafficking activities along our southern border.

Fentanyl is a synthetic opioid that is deadly even in small amounts.* According to U.S. government data, between 2020 to 2021, close to 79,000 Americans between the ages of 18 and 45 died of fentanyl overdoses. Fentanyl overdoses have killed more Americans in this age group than any other leading causes of death, including COVID-19, car accidents, cancer, gun violence, and suicide. James Rauh, the founder of Families Against Fentanyl, who lost his son to a fentanyl overdose, said: "This is a national emergency. America's young adults — thousands of unsuspecting Americans — are being poisoned." He called our government to declare "illicit fentanyl a Weapon of Mass Destruction." Most fentanyl in the U.S. is made in China but entered the U.S. through the illicit drug trade from Mexico. In 2022 alone, the U.S. Drug Enforcement Administration (DEA) seized 379 million potentially fatal doses of fentanyl at the U.S.-Mexico border — enough to kill

---

* Owing to its low price and relative ease of production, fentanyl has supplanted prescription opioids and heroin in the illegal drug market. A potentially fatal dose of fentanyl is two milligrams.

Source: https://www.dailymail.co.uk/news/article-11565445/Federal-drug-agents-seized-fentanyl-2022-kill-American.html

every American. This represents is not merely a drug epidemic but a national security crisis as Americans are killed by the most lethal drugs smuggled into the U.S. every day.

Although the illicit drug trade has made Mexican cartels billions of dollars, it's shocking that they have made even more money through human trafficking. In President Biden's first two years in office, nearly five million illegal immigrants crossed the U.S.-Mexico border. Biden's open-border policies lured them, and most of them paid the cartel huge fees for assistance crossing the border. Consequently, human smuggling has become a multi-billion-dollar business for Mexican cartels. U.S. Immigration and Customs Enforcement (ICE) intelligence estimates that before 2018, the cartels treated human smuggling as a side business that provided a supplemental income of about $500 million a year. That financial picture has changed since Joe Biden became President of the United States. ICE estimates that the cartels earned as much as $13 billion from smuggling immigrants in 2022—an increase of $12.5 billion from just four years prior. For the cartels, revenues from human smuggling have surpassed revenues from the illicit drug trade.

The cartels have spent their illicit monetary gains from the drug trade and human smuggling to grow and arm their paramilitaries. A few incidents offered some clues as to how well-armed the cartels are:[280]

- In March 2022, inside four houses controlled by a faction of the Sinaloa Cartel in the northern State of Sonora, the Mexican army recovered 2.8 million rounds of ammunition, 89 hand grenades, 20 machine guns, six .50 caliber sniper rifles, more than 150 handguns and automatic rifles, and bulletproof vests.

- In May 2022, U.S. authorities broke up a Cartel del Noreste scheme to buy $500,000 worth of machine guns, grenades, and rocket-propelled launchers to be smuggled south from the U.S. into Mexico.

- An August 2022 report showed that the state of Tamaulipas seized 257 shop-built armored 'narco-tanks' from the cartels in recent years, so-called 'monsters' made of semis, SUVs, or pickup trucks encased in thick steel with machine-gun ports. Video shows well-kitted masked cartel soldiers filling them."

At this rate, the cartels' paramilitaries will soon be better armed than the Mexican military. When that day comes, the Mexican government won't be able to do anything to contain the cartels' criminal activities. These cartels create economic and national security threats to Mexico and the United States.

Political impact. Although illegal immigrants comprise about a quarter of all immigrants in America, they have an outsized influence on American politics. How to address the illegal immigration problem has sucked all the air out of any discussion on immigration reform. Pew Research shows 72% of Americans—including 80% of Democrats, 76% of independents, and 56% of Republicans—support granting illegal immigrants who are already in the U.S. legal status after certain conditions have been met.[281] But people on the political left and right have different ideas of what granting amnesty means and how to prevent our nation from getting into the same situation again.

People on the left insist on including a path to citizenship for all illegal immigrants. Some will point to a poll by the Pew Research Center showing the majority of illegal immigrants want U.S. citizenship. However, history tells a different story. For those illegal immigrants who received amnesty in 1986, only 35% to 40% of Mexicans who were eligible to become U.S. citizens did so. Thus, these poll results are questionable. Based on anecdotal evidence, citizenship is less desirable than a green card, which gives illegal immigrants all the benefits they seek: the ability to work legally, change jobs, and move around freely. Once illegal immigrants understand this, many will find that a green card is more than sufficient. Some people suspect that the political left's insistence on a path to citizenship has less to do with immigrants' well-being and more with their efforts to turn illegal immigrants into future Democratic voters. "Election is the future's market in stolen properties," said H.L. Menken.

For people on the political right—Republicans, Tea Party members, and Libertarians—there is a wide range of attitudes and proposed solutions on how to deal with illegal immigration. Libertarians are for open borders, the only immigration policy they believe isn't in violation of individual rights and property rights. Here, they borrow the classical property rights definition from John Locke, who famously said, "Every man has a property in his own person."[282] Thus, they see individuals as having the freedom to travel or to take their bodies to wherever they desire. Libertarians do not see illegal immigration as a problem. On the contrary, they see laws restricting immigration by quotas and punishing employers for hiring illegal immigrants as a problem.

Traditional conservatives won't go as far as embracing open borders as libertarians do, but they still have more tolerant views on immigration. They believe America is a land of opportunity where all who work hard can and will thrive. They generally support legal immigration but are against illegal immigration due to their strong belief in the rule of law. Some also use a property rights argument to oppose illegal immigration on the grounds of unlawful trespassing on private property. However, they do not view massive deportation as a practical or humane way to deal with the 15 million illegal immigrants already in the U.S. Thus, they support some form of amnesty to grant illegal immigrants' legal status, but not citizenship. Their thinking is best represented by President Reagan, who said,

> Illegal immigrants in considerable numbers have become productive members of our society and are a basic part of our work force. Those who have established equities in the United States should be recognized and accorded legal status. At the same time, in so doing, we must not encourage illegal immigration.[283]

I consider myself to be in this camp.

But a growing fraction of conservatives do not wish to see any form of amnesty for illegal immigrants and even want to limit legal immigration. The 2016 presidential election gave this group a loud voice through its spokesperson, Donald Trump, a GOP presidential candidate. He began his presidential campaign by taking an anti-illegal immigration stand. He accused Mexico of sending "people that have lots of problems" to America, including rapists, drug runners, and other criminals. He also called for a change to birthright citizenship, an issue dividing Republicans—49% wanted to keep it, while 47% favored a constitutional amendment to bar birthright citizenship.[284]

Trump's rhetoric tapped into the fears and anger of at least a fraction of Americans, who view immigration as undermining their economic opportunities and posing security threats. These people are angry at the government's inability to do anything meaningful about protecting our borders and the safety of Americans.

Trump's solution to illegal immigration was to build a wall along the U.S.-Mexico border and make the Mexican government pay for it. He did manage to build some portions of the border wall when he became President, but Mexico didn't pay for it. President Trump had to pay for his wall by diverting some military construction funds. As I mentioned before, illegal immigrants respond to incentives. Trump's harsh rhetoric on immigration and his border wall served as a disincentive for would-be illegal crossings. Consequently, the number of migrant "encounters" by U.S. Customs and Border Protection had dropped precipitously by 2019.

Convinced by his son-in-law, Jared Kushner, President Trump announced his legal immigration reform proposal in May 2019. He proposed changing our immigration system from emphasizing family reunification to highlighting skill-based immigration. It was a sensible plan, and I will discuss it in more detail in the next chapter. But Trump's past rhetoric on immigration had poisoned the well, and the Democratic majority in the U.S. Congress was determined to oppose anything President Trump proposed, no matter how much sense his ideas made. Thus, Trump's reform proposals went nowhere. When the COVID-19 pandemic hit, it threw any possible national conversation about immigration reform out the window. One good outcome of the pandemic was that illegal border crossings went down even further, partially due to the enforcement of Title 42 and partly due to migrants who were worried about the virus and chose not to risk their lives by crossing the U.S.-Mexico border illegally.

When Biden became president, his approach to everything, including immigration, was to undo every Trump policy. The illegal immigration surge under President Biden has given all Americans a real-life lesson on what an open border policy would do to America. Even some Democrats began having second thoughts about whether an out-of-control border is good. Republicans in Congress prefer to use the border crisis to criticize President Biden while not offering solutions.

As a legal immigrant, I believe immigration is good for America in the long term. I strongly support securing our borders, enforcing immigration laws, and reforming welfare eligibility for immigrants. At the same time, I sympathize with illegal immigrants' desires and efforts to improve their lives and recognize that current immigration laws have drifted away from our nation's founding principles. The history of illegal immigration in this country demonstrates that whenever our legal immigration system becomes restrictive, the number of illegal immigrants increases. Whenever our government offers amnesty, the number of illegal immigrants increases. America has to find a different approach to immigration. Unfortunately, we are running out of time.

CHAPTER 8

A Way Forward

Our nation's immigration system is broken, no longer serves our nation's interests, and has caused anxiety among native-born citizens and immigrant communities alike. We have seen that legal immigrants, who constitute the vast majority of the immigrant community, face long delays and high financial costs due to the very complex and confusing immigration laws. Their experiences offer no motivation for illegal immigrants to participate in the legal immigration process.

The U.S. will never fix its illegal immigration problem unless policymakers fix legal immigration first. Experience shows that effectively addressing criminal immigration issues requires vigorous law enforcement, easy access to work, clear messages, and the right incentives.

The way forward for America is to reform immigration. I do not support improving it with a single comprehensive reform bill because our existing system is too complex, touches too many interest groups, and cannot address all the issues simultaneously. Ultimately, a so-called comprehensive bill would be nothing but special interests-influenced outcomes shoved down lawmakers' throats. It would exacerbate existing problems and create new ones. The U.S. Congress has repeatedly demonstrated that it often hasn't even bothered to read the comprehensive bills it has passed.

For example, in the last week of December 2022, the U.S. Congress passed a 4,155-page omnibus spending bill with members-only having 48 hours to review it. It was reasonable to assume very few lawmakers had time to read it before they voted for it. The bill was full of earmarks—line-item funding for specific pet projects directed by members of Congress, i.e., $3.6 million for a Michelle Obama Trail in Georgia. The $1.7 trillion bill also contains significant policy changes those congressional leaders from both parties purposefully kept their members from debating. As the Wall Street Journal editorial stated, "The political process here is as bad as most of the policy. Major changes in law deserve their own debate and vote. Instead, a handful of powerful legislators wrote this vast bill in a backroom." Glen Reynolds, the founder of the popular Instapundit.com website, referred to comprehensive bills as "Christmas trees on which lobbyists and legislators hang their goodies."

Instead of another comprehensive immigration reform bill, I advocate for a step-by-step approach that will move our nation's immigration system in the right direction; one that will win back the trust and support of the majority of American people and ultimately reach an ideal immigration system. But before I introduce the details, let's discuss what an immigration system should look like.

A sensible immigration policy should reaffirm these founding principles of our nation:

- **All men are created equal**. Immigration policy shouldn't be used as an ideological redistribution tool. No more special programs cater to specific groups. All applicants should be treated the same in the eyes of the law. Suppose two people want to work in the U.S. as temporary workers, one from India and another from Germany. We shouldn't make the one from India wait for decades to get his work visa due to a per-country limit.

- **The rule of law.** Enforcing the law is the only way to ensure the equal protection of everyone's natural rights. If laws are unjust, our founders have given us a process to change them (through the democratic elections of representatives and the legislative process). Simply ignoring a law or finding a way around it will weaken the foundation of our nation and end up hurting the people who need protection the most!

- **Self-reliance**. Since its founding, generations of self-reliant immigrants have come to the nation with next to nothing. They built the most powerful and wealthiest country on this planet with ingenuity and determination. Immigrants want equal opportunities, not handouts.

A sensible immigration policy that rests on these principles would ensure that our immigration system benefits our national interests and immigrants. Our immigration system should be simple and merit-based, balancing border and national security with national interests, market demands, and humanitarian needs, and making America safer and more powerful.

Below, I will lay out the details.

8.1 Enhance Border Security and National Security

We live in an increasingly dangerous world. From 9/11 to the terrorist attack in San Bernardino, enemies of America have never given up and will never give up striking at our homeland and creating terror. We need to know and control who is coming in, who is staying, and who is leaving. The total collapse of our nation's southern border renders any sensible immigration reform impossible unless we secure our border and protect our national security first. We must address physical border control, screening, and nonimmigrant tracking, among other things.

Physical border control. As discussed in Chapter 7, building a wall or fence to run across the entire U.S.-Mexico border is neither practical nor effective and would be tremendously expensive. But that doesn't mean we should maintain the status quo. Since the border runs across many different types of terrain, we should build a strong fence or reinforce existing walls with surveillance cameras at popular entry points or areas where the landscape is easy to cross. For the portions of the border that run across harsh environments—such as mountains, deserts, or large bodies of water—nature can serve as a barricade. However, we should increase human border patrols in areas where we don't have fences because some people will be desperate enough to attempt to cross. More cooperation among local police, border patrols, and the National Guard is necessary to protect our border effectively and enforce immigration laws.

We must enforce existing immigration laws without any ambiguity. Anyone apprehended crossing the border illegally, regardless of age or whether they traveled as a family unit, should be fingerprinted and deported immediately.

Screening. Before issuing any immigrant or nonimmigrant visa, we must enhance the prescreening process. Let's revisit the 2015 San Bernardino terrorist attack.* One of the San Bernardino shooters, Tashfeen Malik, came to the U.S. on a fiancé visa. She didn't encrypt her radical and anti-American thoughts and ideas on Facebook before her visa application; they were posted for anyone to read. But the Secretary of Homeland Security prevented U.S. immigration officials from reviewing social media postings by immigrants like her out of fear of a civil liberty backlash and bad PR. There is no legal basis for the Secretary's concerns. America has no obligation to grant a visa to any non-U.S. citizen who expresses anti-American sentiment. If someone at the Department of Homeland had done a half-hour Google search, 14 lives could have been saved.

Failing to screen Tashfeen Malik adequately was not an isolated case. The leadership at the Department of Homeland Security has a history of "willingness to compromise the security of citizens for the ideological rigidity of political correctness," Philip Haney, a former officer who spent 15 years at the Department of Homeland Security (DHS), disclosed in an essay for *The Hill*. In 2009, he reports, he was

---

* A Pakistani immigrant and his wife in San Bernardino, CA, opened fire on a holiday banquet for his co-workers on December 5, 2015, killing 14 and injuring 21. It was regarded as the deadliest strike by Islamic extremists on American soil since Sept. 11, 2001.

ordered by his supervisor at DHS "to delete or modify several hundred records of individuals tied to designated Islamist terror groups like Hamas from the important federal database, the Treasury Enforcement Communications System (TECS)."[285]

It's not because of a lack of technological know-how or personnel that the government fails to stop terrorists and protect Americans, but because the Department of Homeland Security leadership insists on political correctness and willful ignorance. Therefore, our first step in establishing an effective screening process is to let U.S. immigration officials use the tools and resources already available to the U.S., including social media, without giving in to ideological rigidity and political correctness. We must do this to all visa applicants, not just a select few.

After the San Bernardino shooting, the U.S. Congress tightened the Visa Waiver Program (VWP)* in 2015 by requiring those who hold dual nationality with Iran, Iraq, Sudan, or Syria, as well as any VWP visa waiver member country national who has traveled to or been present in one of those countries within the last five years (except those who have traveled for diplomatic or military purposes in the service of a VWP country), to obtain a visa from a U.S. consulate or embassy in order to travel to the U.S. This represents a step in the right direction. Yet, at the same time, both Secretary of State, John Kerry, and Secretary of Homeland Security Jeh Johnson announced, "The administration could exercise executive authority to waive the VWP limitation for visitors" under certain circumstances—and gave no clear definition of what those circumstances are. This kind of one-step-forward, two-step-back approach from the current administration is very troubling. It creates ambiguity in law enforcement and adds unnecessary burdens to frontline federal customs and border agents who implement the laws.

---

* According to the State Department, "The Visa Waiver Program (VWP) allows citizens of participating (38) countries to travel to the United States without a visa for stays of 90 days or less when they meet all requirements explained below. Travelers must be eligible to use the VWP and have a valid Electronic System for Travel Authorization (ESTA) approval prior to travel." Retrieved from https://travel.state.gov/content/visas/en/visit/visa-waiver-program.html.

More importantly, when we issue and implement laws or regulations but simultaneously carve out exceptions, it sends the wrong message to the rest of the world that we are not serious about enforcing our own laws. A judicious approach is to streamline our visa application and approval processes to make them easier to understand and access, less time-consuming, and more efficient (I will offer ideas on achieving this goal later in this chapter.)

Nonimmigrant tracking. Close to half of the illegal immigrant population here in the U.S. came here legally but overstayed their visas. We need to do a better job at keeping track of nonimmigrant visa holders. It may be time that the U.S. government considers issuing smart identification cards to each nonimmigrant visitor at his or her port of entry. Each smart ID card has embedded integrated circuits that may contain at least the following information:

- **Personal information**. This includes a photo, passport information, and biometric information. According to the Enhanced Border Security and Visa Entry Reform Act of 2002, we have been collecting basic biometric data, such as fingerprints and taking photos of all non-resident aliens at ports of entry, so it shouldn't be too difficult to add this information to a smart card.

- **Visa information**. This includes the type of visa, and visa issuance and expiration dates.

- **Visa holder's U.S. sponsor or contact's information**. This could be an employer, a school or institution, a U.S. citizen, or the organization that sponsored the visa holder's visit. This is the information that current law already requires the State Department to obtain before issuing a visa.

- **Date of entry into the U.S. and expected departure date**. The scheduled departure date should be based on the expiration date of an employment contract for a work visa, the expected graduation date for a student visa, the program end date for a scholar visa, and the date on the round-trip airline ticket for all other visitors. Having this date on the smart card is essential. When the expected departure date arrives, and the visa holder hasn't departed, the USCIS must immediately notify the visa holder and his/her U.S. sponsor. The visa holder's U.S. contact should be held accountable to ensure the visa holder either departs the U.S. on time or files a visa extension. If the U.S. sponsor fails to keep track of his or her sponsored foreign visitors, that sponsor shouldn't be allowed to support anyone else for at least five years.

The State Department and the USCIS currently collect most of this information. Except for the biometric information, most information is collected before the visa holder's arrival. Therefore, storing this information on a smart ID card shouldn't be complicated and can be done before the visa holder arrives in America. At the port of entry, the agent must add a photo and biometric information to the card and hand it to the visa holder. The visa holder should use the smart ID card anywhere within the U.S. where proof of identification is required.

The smart ID card technology has been around for over four decades, and competition has driven down the costs tremendously. Many countries that are typically technically less advanced than the U.S. are already using smart ID cards. For example, Honduras, Zimbabwe, and Nepal have introduced smart ID cards. According to Inverid, a smart card manufacturer, 164 countries have adopted either ePassports or biometric passports, with a contactless (NFC) chip, as of September 2022. Many countries also have identity cards and residence cards with the same chip.

These governments and authorities use smart ID cards not only because of their improved security, better data, and reduced processing costs but also because issuing a smart ID card is a lower-cost option than other traditional means. If the U.S. uses smart ID-based visas for nonimmigrants, it will be able to track who's coming and going and whether anyone is overstaying via high-tech, low-cost means.

8.2 Merit-based System

Our existing immigration system gives overwhelming preference to family reunions with citizens and immigrants already here. This approach needs to be revised on two fronts.

First, it's unfair. It gives preference to blood relationships and family connections. It discriminates against people with no familial connections but who have knowledge, skills, and experience, and can contribute to our economy and be productive citizens. The people our immigration system discriminates against today are the kind of people our nation has attracted since its founding. The current system also overlooks the fact that many people waiting in line for family reunions might qualify to migrate to America based on merit but are instead stuck in a decades-long wait in order to be admitted on a family basis.

Second, this approach doesn't serve our nation's economic needs because (a) the quota for a family reunion is not set based on labor-market demands; and (b) the visa preference hierarchy favors the old (parents of U.S. citizens and permanent residents) and the young (those younger than 21 years of age) but discriminates against the most likely productive ones (people 21 years old or older, and siblings of U.S. citizens and permanent residents). The current system gives preference to people who are more likely to become financial dependents rather than economic contributors. Empirical evidence shows that after admitting immigrants mainly on a family reunification basis in 1965, the U.S. soon opened up the welfare system to immigrants as well.

The current U.S. immigration system has too many programs (see Appendix 8, "Other Ways to Get a Green Card") that were designed to get applicants out of their current less-than-satisfactory situations, while giving little consideration to whether America is the right place for them and how they could have a successful life in America after they got here.

To fix these problems, we need to establish a merit-based system: an immigration system that gives a higher preference to people who have skills and experience to contribute, and to entrepreneurs who want to invest in America to create job opportunities for Americans — in other words, a much more flexible merit-based immigration program to meet our nation's economic needs. We do not have to reinvent the wheel. Canada and Australia have established and successfully operated merit-based immigration systems for years. We can learn from their systems' strengths and weaknesses.

The Canadian immigration system. The Canadians have done several things better than us. First, while the U.S. gives preference to family reunions, Canada gives preference to skilled workers. Canada was the first country to launch a merit-based points system by introducing the Federal Skilled Worker Program (FSWP) in 1967. Today, the Canadian immigration system has ten categories (versus the over two dozen categories in the U.S.), the first seven focusing on attracting skilled workers, also known as economic-class immigrants. These categories are:

Federal skilled workers
Federal skilled trades
Quebec-selected skilled workers
Canadian Experience Class
Start-up visa
Self-employed persons
Live-in caregivers
Family sponsorship
Provincial nominees
Refugees

Canada welcomes about 400,000 new immigrants annually, and 60 percent are skilled workers, compared to only 20% of U.S. legal immigrants. The Canadian immigration system defines skilled workers as "people who are selected as permanent residents based on their ability to become economically established in Canada." People who intend to immigrate as skilled workers do not have to have a job offer at the time of application, but have to pass an automated point system that evaluates their skills, experiences, and education. (We will address the point system in greater detail later.)

The skilled trade category was added in 2013 to address a labor shortage in specific segments of the Canadian economy. An applicant must have a job offer from a Canadian employer, but no educational requirements exist. The only two requirements are minimum language skills (English or French) and at least two years' work experience in the skilled trade the applicant is applying for. These things show that the Canadian immigration system is much more flexible than the U.S.'s. The Canadian government constantly revises its immigration system to reflect Canada's economic needs—something we Americans have failed to do.

Canada's skilled worker programs allow its provinces and territories to participate actively in immigration. Canadian provinces and territories can nominate skilled workers they want to bring in; they have the authority to assess a potential immigrant's work experience and skills to determine if he or she is eligible; and they can issue certificates of qualification after the assessment. In the U.S., by contrast, all immigration-related matters are centralized under the federal government's control, and states have little say.

The Canadian immigration system is much more efficient and objective than the U.S. immigration system because it lets potential immigrants do a self-assessment based on a point system. In contrast, the U.S. immigration system largely relies on federal immigration agents manually reviewing each application (which contributes to the case backlog and turns the USCIS into a giant bureaucracy).

Since January 1, 2015, Canada has improved its point-based system for skilled workers by implementing the Express Entry system. This system covers the Federal Skilled Worker Program, the Federal Skilled Trades Program, and the Canadian Experience Class Program. Express Entry is a web-based system that lets a potential immigrant do an online self-assessment to determine if he or she is eligible to emigrate to Canada. This self-assessment is a point-based system and takes about 15 minutes to complete.

Let's use the Federal Skilled Worker (FSW) Program as an example of how Canada's point-based system attracts self-sufficient skilled workers to contribute to its economy. According to the government of Canada's website, FSW applicants are "chosen as permanent residents based on their ability to settle in Canada and participate in our economy." Applicants must have at least one year's worth of work experience and minimum language skills (a proof-of-language test is required). In addition, applicants are asked to fill out a scorecard online, which will assess each applicant based on six selection categories (see Figure 8.1).

Figure 8.1*

Federal Skilled Worker Scorecard	
Selection Factor	Maximum points
English and/or French skills	28
Education	25
Experience	15
Age	12
Arranged employment in Canada	10
Adaptability	10
Total	100
Pass mark: 67 out of 100 points	

According to the Canada Immigration and Citizenship (CIC) website, if your score is 67 points or higher, you may qualify to emigrate to Canada as a skilled federal worker. The system will ask you to create an online profile within the system, including registration with Canada's job bank, and will place your profile in a candidate pool along with other ranked candidates. Top-ranking candidates will receive an invitation to apply for skill-based permanent residency in Canada and can then fill out an application online. If your score is below 67 points, you will not qualify to emigrate to Canada as a skilled federal worker, and it is better not to apply now.

Several things about this scorecard system stand out. First, Canada has a minimum language requirement for skill-related immigration, while the U.S. doesn't. The Canadian immigration system requires applicants demonstrate listening, speaking, reading, and writing abilities in English or French. An applicant must take a language test, and the results can't be older than two years. The scorecard favors those with a better grasp of English or French because it gives language ability the highest point value. The emphasis on language skills makes

---

* Source: http://www.cic.gc.ca/english/immigrate/skilled/apply-factors.asp

sense because language proficiency has been long associated with an immigrant's successful assimilation and economic well-being.

A 2011 research paper by Sege Nadeau, a professor at the University of Ottawa, shows that immigrants to Canada who are very proficient in either English or French earn as much as 39% more than minimally proficient immigrants.[286] The Washington-based Brookings Institute published a similar study based on immigrants in the U.S. and came up with the same conclusion: "English proficiency is a strong predictor of economic standing among immigrants, regardless of the amount of education they have attained, and it is associated with the greater academic and economic success of the workers' children."[287] Aample research shows that language proficiency is a strong predictor of economic success among immigrants, regardless of the amount of education they have attained. The Canadian system ensures new immigrants can successfully integrate into Canadian society by having a language requirement.

Second, the scorecard gives more weight to education, experience, and age than to arranged employment. As discussed earlier, the skilled worker program is designed to attract people who can contribute to Canada's economy. The odds of finding a job for someone who is young, well-educated, and speaks English or French fluently are high. The U.S. doesn't have a similar program, and Employment-based immigration in the U.S. makes having an arranged job offer a must but gives little consideration to what kind of a job.

Third, the Canadian immigration system gives an immigration applicant autonomy and empowers him or her to do most of the work. Anyone can go online and do a self-assessment. A potential applicant doesn't need a sponsor; all he or she can count on is his or her own ability, knowledge, education, and experience. The process assesses the candidate's self-reliance and merit: a person capable of understanding the instructions, following through, and providing supporting documents is likely someone who can make it in Canada. The U.S. immigration system engenders dependency, whereas the Canadian approach engenders self-reliance.

The Canadian points-based scoring system is straightforward, transparent, simple, objective, and effective. A successful candidate can gain permanent resident status within six months. Canada's merit-based immigration system has been tremendously successful. A 2019 report from the Organization for Economic Co-operation and Development (OECD) found that:[288]

- In 2018, 82% of principal economic applicants aged 25 to 64 were employed, higher than that of non-immigrants (76%).

- Immigration accounted for almost 100% of all labor force growth in Canada and approximately 75% of population growth that year.

- Skilled workers selected through Express Entry are doing very well and establishing themselves in Canada quickly: 95% are working in the year following their admission. Their employment and earnings exceeded Canadian averages soon after landing and continue to increase.

- Most principal applicants admitted through the economic class are classified as high-skilled. In 2019, 85% of economic admissions were in high-skilled occupations.

The Australian immigration system. Australia has a similar scoring-based system (see Appendix 10). Like the Canadian system, Australia's point system evaluates an applicant's age, English language ability, education, and skills. Applicants can take the assessment online. The total points for Australia's system are 120, and the passing grade is 60. Also, like its Canadian counterpart, the Australian government tweaks its point system every couple of years based on new data and to serve its changing economic needs. The most recent tweak took place in 2012.

Australia's point system emphasizes on work experience and an existing employment offer than the Canadian system. The focuse on employment was driven by the Australian government's conscious effort since 2008 to move away from "'supply driven' independent skilled migration towards 'demand-driven' outcomes, in the form of employer and government-sponsored skilled migration."[289]

In addition to meeting the minimum passing score, applicants must select an occupation from the Australian government's Skilled Occupation List (SOL) and have their skills assessed by a recognized authority. The SOL is not static. It was developed by an independent body and is updated annually to reflect occupations in demand in Australia. For example, suppose I claim on immigration application that I have work experience in civil engineering. In that case, I will be directed to contact Australia's civil engineering society to assess my skills and work experience. Only after the engineering society issues a satisfactory assessment result can my immigration application move forward.

In 2011, Australia implemented a two-stage application process called Skill Select for skilled immigrants and investment visas. The process is similar to Canada's Express Entry process (in all fairness, the Canadians probably learned from the Australians), through which applicants submit Expressions of Interest (EOI) for specific skilled immigration visas. Only applicants who receive at least a passing score and demonstrate experience in occupations on the SOL are invited to apply for skill-based immigration. Like Canada, Australia allows its states and territories to nominate skilled immigrants. In addition, Australia allows its residents to nominate their relatives to immigrate to Australia through the skilled immigration program. Consequently, 68% of immigrants to Australia are skill-based, while 31% are family-based. Australia's skilled immigration system is highly successful. A government survey[290] found these impressive statistics:

- The labor force participation rate of independent skilled immigrants is 96%, much higher than the 67% among native-born Australians. 85% of these immigrants work full-time, with a median earning of AUD 79,000.

- Employer-sponsored migrants have a 99% labor force participation rate. 93% are working full-time, with median earnings of AUD 75,000.

- The cumulative fiscal benefit of all Migration and Humanitarian Program (i.e., permanent) visas granted in 2010-11 over the first 10 years of settlement in Australia is over

AUD 10.2 billion, with skilled migrants making the greatest fiscal contribution.

- In 2014, the migrant taxpayers contributed to $84 billion in total personal income? Additionally, the current immigration pattern will add 15.9 percent to the total workforce, generating an additional 5.9 percent in GDP per capita growth in the country.

The Australian point system is so successful that the United Kingdom adopted a similar program in 2003. Canada's and Australia's experiences show us that a country can reap great cultural, social, and economic benefits from the right immigration policy.

It is time for the U.S. to adopt a merit-based immigration system similar to what Canada and Australia have. We shouldn't do away with family-based immigration and immigration based on humanitarian needs, but we should emphasize skill-based immigration by dedicating at least 50% of the annual immigration visa quota to skill-based immigrants (instead of the current 20%). Under the skill-based immigration program, we should have three subcategories:

- Independent skilled workers: those who don't have arranged employment at the time of application.

- Employment-based workers or those nominated by individual U.S. states and territories.

- Entrepreneurs and investors.

To facilitate this skilled immigration program, we need to establish a selection process. Anyone interested in emigrating to the U.S. as a skilled worker should do a self-assessment online. Some critics think the Canadian scoring system favors college graduates, the "good student" type. They argue that someone like Steve Jobs wouldn't pass the scoring system because he was a college dropout. College graduates and productive workers are indeed not synonymous. The U.S. must improve upon Canada's system by up-weighting experience and giving it the same point value as education, yielding a modified score-card like this:

Figure 8.2

Selection Factor	Maximum points
English Skill	22
Education	20
Experience	20
Age	16
Arranged employment in the U.S.	12
Adaptability	10
Total	100

By giving the same weight to education and experience, this pro-posed scorecard ensures that those with little schooling but experience in a skilled trade will have an equal chance to migrate to America. Another feature of this scorecard is "adaptability." Even though it has the lowest weight, it's essential. The adaptability criterion should be structured to test an applicant's civic knowledge and appreciation of the United States. Aspiring immigrants should learn what makes this country great: the rule of law, private property rights, free markets, and limited constitutional government. We only want people who want to be here, love America, appreciate American values, and want to be part of American society.

I recommend this scoring system be entirely web-based. Potential immigrants can navigate and do this self-assessment on their own. A scoring system like this has many benefits. It:

- Increases efficiency.

- Increases transparency.

- Reduces subjectivity and complexity.

- Sets all applicants at an equal starting line with objective measures.

- Prescreens applicants and allows them to easily read through, self-select, and evaluate their eligibility before they flood the system with applications.

- Promotes self-reliance by selecting immigrants based on their language skills, education, meaningful work experiences, and appreciation for what America stands for.

- Enables the U.S. to select skilled migrants who offer the best economic benefits.

- Makes for easy data collection, which will allow the U.S. to fine-tune its immigration policy on a timely basis.

Like Canada, we can set the minimum passing grade at 60. Only those who score 60 or higher will move on to the following stages: building a profile and assessing their skill and experience.

Canada has a government-run national occupation database, while Australia has a non-government entity managing a similar database. I recommend the U.S. follow the Australian model, outsourcing the creation, maintenance, and updating of a national job bank to a private company such as Careerbuilder.com. A private company that makes its living by connecting employers with potential employees has every incentive to keep a national occupation database updated and has the know-how to determine in the private sector is a suitable assessor of specific skill/work experience. Only those who can verify their credentials will be invited to apply for skilled immigration to the U.S. This will help turn a supply-driven immigration system into a demand-driven one.

To truly make our skilled-worker program merit-based, we must eliminate the per-country restrictions. The merit-based system needs to be color-blind and ethnicity-blind. We want the best people to emigrate to the U.S. So, what if we have many engineers and programmers from China and India? Most probably received their higher education at American universities with significant subsidies from the federal and state governments. In other words: as U.S. taxpayers, we have already helped fund their higher education. Why should we send these smart kids back home? It benefits America more if they stay here to start new businesses, invent new medicines, or build rockets.

Canadian and Australian immigration systems allow their provinces and territories to nominate skilled workers they want to bring in. The U.S. should do the same. Individual state governments and entities are more tuned-in to their economies and labor needs than the federal government. Traditionally, states are on the receiving end of the federal government's immigration policy and have borne much of the cost of settling new immigrants. It's only fair that a sensible immigration policy gives states a voice in the skilled workers or entrepreneurs they want to bring in.

Last, I'd like to propose improvements to our entrepreneurs/ investors category. In our current immigration system, we have a category — the EB-5 immigrant investor program — that allocates 10,000 visas a year to investors who invest at least $500,000 in job-creating businesses in "targeted employment areas" — areas suffering from high unemployment. This program was first implemented after the 1990 Immigration Act, and like many visa programs I've discussed, it failed to achieve its intentions. Rather than bringing capital and jobs to areas with high unemployment rates, this program has become a low-cost source of financing for high-end real estate in big cities such as New York and Miami.

In addition, some criticize this program for failing to attract true entrepreneurs committed to building and running businesses in the U.S. Instead, it is a venue for relatively wealthy people from other nations to buy themselves and their families' green cards (by becoming passive investors in sometimes ill-fitting businesses). Since we set the investment threshold relatively low at $500,000, it is affordable for many applicants, and there is a waiting list. Unfortunately, this program has become a magnet for fraudsters. Chinese investors reported that after they gave their funds to supposed immigration representatives, believing they were buying green cards for their families, they found out later they would never see their money again — nor would they get a green card.

Finally, the program does nothing for someone with a brilliant idea but no capital.

The United States is one of many nations that has an investor program. Australia has a similar program, and it does several things better than we do:

1. It requires an investor to be nominated by a state or territory government or the Australian government.

2. It requires investors to pass the same point-based system as all other skilled immigrants to ensure quality.

3. It divides its program into four streams based on business skills and the level of capital an investor brings.

The Australian government requires an investor to maintain business and investment activity in Australia. The Australian program has five streams:[291]

- The **Business Innovation stream** for people with business skills who want to establish, develop, and manage a new or existing business in Australia, with an annual turnover of at least **AUD 500,000.**

- The **Investor stream** for people who want to make a designated investment of at least **AUD 1.5 million** in an Australian state or territory and maintain business and investment activity in Australia.

- The **Significant Investor stream** for people who are willing to invest at least **AUD 5 million** into complying significant investments in Australia and want to maintain business and investment activity in Australia.

- The **Premium Investor stream** for people who are willing to invest at least **AUD 15 million** into complying premium investments in Australia and want to maintain business and investment activity in Australia.

- The **Entrepreneur stream** requires at least an investment of **AUD 200,000.** An applicant must provide a business plan that confirms the economic benefits to the state from innovation and business development in Australia. Permanent residence permit may be granted after 4 years, under the condition of successful business development and creation of new jobs.

All foreign applicants must meet certain requirements of Australian immigration law, including knowledge of English, business experience, clear criminal record, age up to 55 years. Since first implementing its investor program, Australia has attracted AUD \$4.3 billion (U.S. \$3 billion) in investment and handed out 858 residency visas, with another 1,239 applications pending.[292] In 2015, Australia enhanced its investor program by placing a cap on residential real estate investments, demanding investors put more capital into venture capital funds and private equity funds to help stimulate innovation.

Having an investor program is a good idea. With as many problems as we've had with our investor program, it still raised more than \$1.8 billion in fiscal year 2013. The Australian program shows us how to improve our own program, and I propose modeling our investor program after the Australian model like this:

- First, the investor must be nominated by a state or territory government or our federal government.

- Second, the investor has to pass a point-based screening test like the one proposed earlier.

- Third, the investor has to commit to maintaining investments and business in the U.S.

- Fourth, a U.S. green card ought to be more valuable than an Australian green card, and there is a waiting list for the U.S. investor program, so we should increase the investment dollar threshold.

- Fifth, we should exclude real estate investment from being a qualified investment. Instead, demand at least some funds go to a venture capital or private equity firm to stimulate innovation.

Our new investor program should have two streams:

- A **Business Innovation stream** for people with business skills who want to establish, develop, and manage a new or existing business in the U.S. provide a business plan that confirms the economic benefits to the state from innovation and business development in Australia. Permanent residence permit may be granted after five years, under the condition of successful business development and the creation of new jobs.

- An **Investor stream** for people who want to make a designated investment of at least $10 million in a U.S. state or territory, a minimum of $5 million of which has to be invested in a venture capital or private equity fund. Permanent residence permits may be granted after five years, under the condition of successful business development and creation of new jobs.

In summary, a merit-based immigration system would work like this:

- Applicants start by using a point-based web screening tool.

- Private organizations evaluate an applicant's education, experience, and skills.

- The most qualified applicants are invited to emigrate to the U.S. as skilled immigrants.

- Investments are steered towards innovation.

With such a system, we as a nation can ensure that we are rolling out the welcome mat to the kind of immigrants we want, the kind who are willing to work hard and who will contribute to our country.

8.3 Keep it Simple

Leonardo da Vinci once said, "Simplicity is the ultimate sophistication." The U.S. Constitution, one of the most beautiful and magnificent documents in human history, has only four pages containing 4,543 words, including the signatures. If we add up the 27 amendments, the total word count is 7,591.[293] Yet it complements the principles laid out by the Declaration of Independence by creating "a structure of government strong enough to ensure the nation's future strength and prosperity but without sufficient power to threaten the liberty of the people."[294] It's safe to say that we wouldn't live in the most prosperous and free country on Earth if not for our Constitution. So, when it comes to immigration law, we do not need thousands of pages to delineate the rules.

We can keep our immigration system simple by eliminating ineffective and unfair programs. We need only three immigration channels: skilled workers, family reunions, and humanitarian. It's time to cancel the visa lottery program and the more than two dozen special programs (see Appendices 4 and 5). The 50,000-plus annual immigration visa quotas we save from eliminating these programs should be allocated to skilled workers. Replace the 50,000 visa lottery winners with 50,000 investment-based visa holders. With each of those being required to invest $1 million or create 10 jobs in America,* we'll see a $50-billion direct investment in the U.S. or 500,000 new jobs.

Even applicants with family members in the U.S. should be directed to apply as skilled immigrants. Family reunions should be limited to elderly or young relatives of U.S. citizens who are currently unemployable. In such cases, the U.S. citizen who acts as a sponsor should demonstrate the financial capacity to support his or her relatives for five years. As discussed earlier, most immigrants should come through the skilled-worker channel.

For non-immigration visas, we need to do three things:

First, consolidate the currently more than 40 visa categories (see Appendices 4 and 5) into three: temporary workers, students/scholars,

---

* The U.S. requires each investor visa applicant to invest a minimum of $1 million (or $500,000 in a rural area), or create or preserve 10 jobs.

and visitors. There is no earthly reason why we need a separate visa category for "certain 'specialty occupation' professionals from Australia" (E-3 visa) or "fashion models of distinguished merit and ability" (H-1B3). Each category represents an added layer of complexity. We need only one work visa category; let the market decide if our country needs more engineers, professional athletes, or fruit pickers. A temporary worker can travel freely in and out of the U.S. as long as he or she has no criminal record and is currently employed by an American employer. All nonimmigrants should receive an identity card with a smart chip containing their biometric and sponsor-contact information.

Second, better match work visa quotas with economic realities. Let the free-market system tell us how many immigrants it can absorb. The duration of the visa is either the duration of the employment contract or three years, whichever is greater. If the person is still employed when the visa is three months from expiration, the visa can be renewed again for either the duration of the employment contract or three years. The renewal process can repeat itself as long as the applicant is employed.

Third, temporary workers should receive tax IDs that allow them to pay income, Social Security, and Medicare taxes, just like an employed U.S. citizen would. However, since work visas are not immigration visas, work visa holders will not be entitled to government welfare benefits. If later, work visa holders apply and become legal U.S. residents, they will be eligible for governmental welfare benefits after five years. Their Social Security benefits calculation will include the years they spent as temporary work visa holders. This shouldn't be too difficult because they have been paying taxes while being temporary workers, so there will be a track record of their work histories.

Simplifying the visa categories will make it easy for potential immigrants to understand what category they are eligible for, and should apply for, and will speed up the processing time, and reduce the cost (e.g., allow the immigrant to save money on legal counsel). This will help reduce wait times and backlogs. It will make an illegal border crossing a much less attractive option. It will discourage U.S. employers from hiring illegal migrant workers since they can now easily find legal workers. Most importantly, it will free up USCIS resources to focus on vetting potential national security threats.

8.4 Illegal Immigrants

The number of illegal immigrants reached a historical low in the 1950s when the Bracero Program was in place and our nation strictly enforced immigration laws. Therefore, I believe that by securing our border, making it easy to access temporary work visas, and reforming asylum rules, the inflow of illegal immigrants will be reduced.

Additional steps to control the inflow of illegal immigration should include strengthening the E-Verify system. As discussed in Chapter 7, E-Verify is one of the rare successes within our existing immigration system. Since it's free and completely web-based, employers who use E-Verify are generally satisfied with the program and don't consider it burdensome. The USCIS has made a concerted effort to make E-Verify easy to use for employees. On October 6, 2014, USCIS launched myE-Verify, a web-based service for employees to check their work authorization. It was initially rolled out to only five states, including Colorado. On April 12, 2015, myE-Verify became available nationwide. But since E-Verify relies on most private employers' and employees' voluntary participation, it's not as widely used as it should be. Those employers who opt to use E-Verify have been using it not as a prescreening tool but only after hiring an employee; they usually require employees to go through E-Verify on their first day at work.

Is E-Verify an effective tool to deter the hiring of illegal immigrants? We can look to Arizona for a successful case study. According to a Pew Research study, Arizona's illegal immigrant population grew almost fivefold between 1990 and 2005 to about 450,000. But the inflow began to reverse in 2008 after Arizona required all public and private employer to use the E-Verify system. Between 2007 and 2012, Arizona's population of illegal immigrants dropped by 40%. Based on Arizona's experience, I suggest our nation make E-Verify mandatory for all employers nationwide.

The Libertarian Cato Institute published a study in 2015 that opposed making E-Verify mandatory on grounds that "E-Verify nationwide could lead to more identity theft, make legal American workers unemployed."[295] I generally agree with the Cato Institute on its immigration ideas, but on this issue, I disagree. Surveys conducted by an independent organization, Westat—a Rockville, Maryland-based social science research firm—show the accuracy rate of E-Verify has been relatively high, that "96 percent of all E-Verify initial responses were consistent with the person's work authorization status," and only "0.3 percent of applicants received tentative non-confirmations (TNC) that were erroneous but ultimately corrected."[296] In addition, the E-Verify system has made a number of improvements to combat fraud and identity theft,[297] including processes and policies to protect employees' rights. For example, any applicants who receive tentative non-confirmations (TNC) from E-Verify are given time to appeal and provide further evidence to prove their eligibility to work in the U.S. legally.

While the fraud concerns in the Cato Institute's study are valid, and we probably will never eliminate all fraud within the E-Verify system, we can continue to find ways to minimize fraud and identity theft with more sophisticated technology, and increasing cooperation between the private and public sectors. Creating a false identity and using a fraudulent Social Security number are federal felonies. Illegal immigrants who get caught committing such offenses should be deported immediately. Let's not forget that most illegal immigrants are economic migrants. They came here to find better-paying jobs. If we can enforce existing deportation laws and make E-Verify mandatory for employers nationwide, many (if not all) illegal immigrants will be discouraged from crossing the border.

In addition to E-Verify, we must make the "sanctuary jurisdiction" designation illegal. Currently, hundreds of U.S. cities and counties have adopted sanctuary laws or policies that defy federal immigration laws. These sanctuary cities have been drawing illegal immigrants. The idea of establishing a sanctuary city that operates outside of certain laws of the land is very troubling. As Victor D. Hanson, the columnist for *National Review,* rightly points out:

> For every left-wing city that declares immigration statutes inoperative, a right-wing counterpart might do the same with

the Endangered Species Act, gun-registration laws, affirmative action, or gay marriage. The result would be chaos and anarchy, not compassion.[298]

If anything, 2022 was a revealing year. When illegal immigrants were bused in or flown into those self-identified "sanctuary" communities from Martha's Vineyard to Denver, Colorado, sanctuary advocates quickly adopted the "not in my backyard" attitude. They did everything possible to deport those unwelcomed migrants as soon as possible. These advocates' hypocrisy shows that the only sanctuary they really care about is a sanctuary for their virtual signaling. Sanctuary cities or communities do not promote freedom; they promote chaos, and it's time to stop legitimizing them.

Stopping more illegal immigrants from coming is one thing, but what will we do with the 15 million illegal immigrants already here?

The Democrats insist the only way to move forward is to grant them a path to citizenship. On the Republican side, Senators Marco Rubio and Ted Cruz and former Florida's Governor Jeb Bush all supported a path to citizenship at one point but later backed away from it. Now they endorse granting illegal immigrants' legal residency but not citizenship.

The extreme right, however, wants mass deportations. But deporting millions of people is impractical, and the majority of Americans wouldn't support it. Pew Research shows 72% of Americans, including 80% of Democrats, 76% of independents, and 56% of Republicans, say illegal immigrants who are already in the U.S. should be allowed to stay and should be offered some kind of legal status if they meet certain requirements.[299] However, granting them legal residency is a reward for breaking the law and will continue to attract more illegal immigration. A classic example was the Reagan amnesty in 1986. The number of illegal immigrants has more than tripled since then. In addition, our legal immigration system already has a massive backlog. Imagine what would happen if we stuffed 11 million new applications into the pipeline. We cannot keep trying to help illegal immigrants by punishing legal immigrants.

Since we have yet to verify how long an illegal immigrant has been in our country, any policy that tries to give preference to those who have been in the U.S. for a long time or before a specific date will cause fraudulent claims by illegal immigrants. Therefore, I propose granting legal relief to those currently employed in the U.S.

The U.S. government can grant illegal immigrants with jobs and no criminal records temporary work visas after they pay a fine. Each work visa will be good for three years and can be renewed as long as the applicant is employed. Most illegal immigrants are economic migrants who came here to find a better job and life, but not all want to stay in the U.S. for the rest of their lives. A work visa will allow the holder to work legally in the U.S., pay income taxes, and travel in and out of the U.S. with no constraints. These benefits should meet what most illegal immigrants are seeking. But because a work visa is not an immigration visa, the visa holders will still be considered non-resident aliens and, therefore can't access to federal means-tested welfare benefits.

If illegal immigrants bring their families with them, they should also pay a fine for their families. Their family members will get temporary visitor visas, excluding children born here. The length of their visas should be the same as the working visa, and they can renew those visas as long as their primary family member's work visa is valid. Since a visitor visa is also a non-immigration visa, these visa holders can't access to federal means-tested welfare benefits either. If any of these illegal immigrants want to become legal permanent residents, they must go through the same application process as other applicants.

Any illegal immigrant with a criminal record, including creating a false identity or using a fraudulent Social Security number, will be deported immediately and not eligible to apply for any U.S. visa for five years.

8.5 Build a Wall around the Welfare State

One of the biggest concerns of the American public is that legal and illegal immigrants, especially uneducated and low-skilled immigrants, , are overwhelming our nation's already struggling welfare system. Famed economist Milton Friedman once said,

Because it is one thing to have free immigration to jobs. It is another thing to have free immigration to welfare. And you cannot have both. If you have a welfare state, if you have a state in which every resident is promised a certain minimal level of income, or a minimum level of subsistence, regardless of whether he works or not, produces it or not, then it really is an impossible thing.

Even the open-border advocate the Libertarian Cato Institute supports restricting non-U.S. citizen access to federal means-tested benefits such as Medicaid, Supplemental Nutrition Assistance Program (food stamps), Temporary Assistance to Needy Families, and Supplemental Social Security Income. The Cato Institute's late Chairman Emeritus William Niskanen famously said, "Build a wall around the welfare state, not around the country." He was referring tothat it is much more practical and effective to restrict immigrants' access to welfare in order to reduce their economic dependency than to build a wall along the U.S.-Mexico border. A Cato study shows that "preventing noncitizens from accessing means-tested welfare programs will immediately save taxpayers more than $29 billion for the five programs under discussion."[300]

Once again, Arizona set a national example by implementing measures to limit illegal immigrants' access to social welfare programs. For example, illegal immigrants are barred from receiving government benefits, including non-emergency hospital care. They are not eligible for in-state tuition rates. Building a wall around benefits programs, in addition to the E-Verify mandate, helped contribute to the 40% drop in the illegal immigrant population in Arizona between 2007 and 2012.

Some immigration advocates will argue that barring impoverished immigrants from welfare benefits will result in hardships for many. But the same Cato study shows that while cutting access to benefits may negatively impact some immigrant families, the overall impact is minimal because poor noncitizens use less welfare than U.S. citizens. Restricting noncitizen welfare access will also discourage those who come here to get access to the welfare system and will shift the financial burden of supporting future immigrants back to the immigrants themselves and/or to their sponsors. Keep in mind that current immigration laws already require all immigrants to prove that they can either support themselves and their families financially or that someone else (other than the U.S. government) — be it an employer, a family or friend, and/or a charity organization — can support them financially.

To make this happen, we do not need to pass new laws. The policy of not allowing immigrants to receive welfare benefits until they become citizens has been around since our nation's founding. In 1645, Massachusetts disallowed anyone entry to the colony from abroad who could not support him- or herself. Over time until 1965, it was always our nation's policy not to admit people who couldn't support themselves. The policy was loosened up by the Immigration Acts of 1965 and 1996.

The Personal Responsibility and Work Opportunity Reconciliation Act of 1996 (PRWORA), signed by President Clinton on August 22, 1996, effectively prohibited legal immigrants from accessing welfare benefits run by the federal government for the first five years after their legal entry. About 935,000 noncitizens lost benefits due to the passage of PRWORA. Between 1994 and 1999, all major federal public benefit programs saw legal immigrants' usage decline. Unfortunately, PRWORA was undermined by a series of amendments and revisions, as discussed in Chapter 6. An excellent start to building a wall around the welfare system is an amendment to restore the original language and intent of PRWORA — which was not anti-immigration but pro-personal responsibility.

Experience shows that welfare induces dependency. Restricting immigrants' access to welfare helps them depend on themselves to achieve better lives themselves and for their families.

8.6 Reform the Humanitarian Programs

The current U.S. immigration system operates two humanitarian programs: asylum seekers and refugees. The main difference between a refugee and an asylee is the person's location at the time of application. Refugees are outside of the U.S. when they are screened for resettlement, and asylees apply for asylum either at the port of entry or once inside the U.S. At the beginning of each fiscal year, the president, in consultation with Congress, sets a cap on the number of refugees accepted from five global regions. Yet, there is no visa quota for asylees. While both humanitarian programs have been ineffective and abused, the asylum program needs the most urgent reform because it has become a magnet for the illegal immigration surge in recent years.

Since federal law on asylum doesn't define how someone gets inside the United States, even someone in the United States illegally is still eligible to seek asylum. Thus, for illegal immigrants, asylum is the path of least resistance. Unlike previous generations of illegal migrants, today, most illegal immigrants from Asia and Central America surrender voluntarily to U.S. border patrol agents as soon as they cross the U.S.-Mexico border and declare their intention for asylum, even though the vast majority of these migrants are economic migrants. They do not meet the legal definition of asylum[*].

Although many illegal immigrants seeking asylum today understand their applications will likely be denied, they declare their intentions for asylum anyway. They know too well that filing asylum applications will allow them to legally work and live in the U.S. while their cases get stuck in the U.S. immigration courts. It will take years before their cases even get a hearing. Many have no intentions of showing up at their court dates because the goal isn't to pursue legitimate claims but to find work. Their abuses of U.S. laws take up time and resources that rightfully belong to legitimate asylum-seekers. By the end of 2022, more than 1.5 million people in the U.S. were waiting for their asylum claims to be processed.

To solve our border crisis and minimize abuses of the asylum process so legitimate applicants can get the help they need, the U.S. Congress needs to reform the federal statute regarding asylum. Here are suggestions on how to do it:

---

[*] The U.S. legal definition for asylum is someone "who is already in the U.S. who has been persecuted or fear they will be persecuted on account of race, religion, nationality, and/or membership in a particular social group or political opinion." A study by the Syracuse University Transactional Records Access Clearinghouse (TRAC) found a 93% denial rate of asylum cases in the Immigration Court's "Dedicated Docket" for speedy asylum review. Only 7% were awarded asylum from the court.
Retrieved from https://www.washingtontimes.com/news/2023/jan/9/truth-about-so-called-asylum-seekers/

- Impose an annual quota on the number of asylum-seekers the country will absorb.

- Empower border agents to determine asylum seekers' qualifications at the border and turn back those who are not qualified immediately.

- Make asylum seekers admitted into the U.S. wait at least two years before they can legally seek employment.

- Make it easier for economic migrants to apply for temporary work visas so they don't crowd out legitimate applicants.

The refugee program faces a different set of challenges. Besides national security concerns, we must consider whether a refugee resettlement program is the best solution for a migrant crisis. Resettling a few thousand out of the millions of refugees worldwide won't make much of a dent in the refugee crisis. Many believe the most humane way to help most refugees is to establish safe zones with countries that share borders. A coalition of countries, including the U.S., Europe, and others, could jointly provide funding and security protection.

There are at least three benefits to this:

- First, a safe zone can offer many refugees immediate security and meet their humanitarian needs, so they do not have to travel treacherously to other nations.

- Second, once the conflict in their home country is resolved, refugees can quickly return to their homeland.

- Third, the safe zone would be a good place to begin vetting refugees who still desire to immigrate to other countries.

Once refugees do not face imminent threats to their lives, immigration personnel can focus on evaluating whether they are committed to assimilating and accepting laws, cultures, and values that are different from what they are accustomed to. Are refugees determined to build new lives, or are they bent on establishing a replica of their old lives in a foreign land? In addition, immigration officers can evaluate if applicants have any job experience or language skills. The vetting process is crucial to ensuring a win-win outcome for refugees and their host countries. A safe zone will afford both sides the time and place to complete the vetting safely and thoroughly.

These safe zones shouldn't be modeled after the refugee camps currently run by the UN. In addition to basic aid, we need to make these safe zones self-sufficient communities to ensure their lives are as normal as possible by bringing law and order to the refugees. For example, we can hire refugees who have the education to be teachers in schools within these zones; we can employ refugees to provide police work, hire refugees to do janitorial work to keep the zones clean; and we can assist any refugee who aspires to start a new business within the zones with capital and know-how.

Not everyone can or wants to leave their homeland, family, and friends behind. Sometimes, the most effective way to help people is not to get them out but to help them close to home so that they can return when the conflict is over.

Summary

A sensible and principle-based immigration policy should protect our borders, enhance national security, be simple and merit-based, and offer a viable and effective solution to the illegal immigration issue. As mentioned before, there are better approaches than a comprehensive bill. Therefore, what I propose here needn't all happen at once. Some elements are more easily implemented, and some will have broader support. I categorize the proposals below based on the difficulty of implementation and the level of support.

For Border Security:

- **What we should do immediately**: Enforce existing laws. Any individual apprehended crossing the border illegally, no matter their age or whether they traveled alone or as a

family unit, should be fingerprinted and deported immediately.

- **What we should do next**: Build strong fences or reinforce
  existing fences with surveillance cameras at popular entry
  points or areas where the terrain is easy to cross. Increase
  border patrols in portions of the border that run across
  harsh environments. Increase cooperation between local
  police, border patrol, and the National Guard.

For National Security:

- **What we should do immediately**: Enhance the screening
  process for visa applicants. Get rid of political correctness
  and deploy all currently available sources, including social
  media.

- **What we should do next**: Issue a smart identification card
  to each nonimmigrant visitor at his or her port of entry.

Simplification and Merit-based:

- **What we should do immediately**: Get rid of the visa
  lottery program and reallocate its 50,000 annual quotas to
  skill-based immigration. Get rid of out-of-date special visa
  programs.

  o **What we should do next:** *For non-immigration visas.*
  Consolidate all programs into three categories:
  workers, visitors, and students/scholars. Eliminate
  the quota for temporary workers and let the market
  decide what type of workers it needs and how many.

  o *For immigration visas.* Consolidate all programs into
  three categories: skill-based, family-based, and
  humanitarian-based. Allocate at least 50% of the
  annual visa quota to skill-based immigrants. Establish
  a point-based system to prescreen skill-based appli-

cants. Reform the investor program. Make family members financially responsible for family-based immigrants. Combine the refugee and asylum-seeker categories into one humanitarian visa.

Illegal Immigration:

- **What we should do immediately**: Reform the asylum program. Make E-Verify mandatory for all employers nationwide. Deport anyone who has committed a crime while in the U.S.

- **What we should do next:** Give temporary working visas to those who are employed, have no criminal record, and have paid a fine for their illegal entry. Give their family members who are here and who are not employed visitor visas. Build a wall around the welfare system by limiting access to U.S. citizens, based on the original wording of PRWORA.

EPILOGUE

The United States of America has a long and rich immigration history. Our nation has always been and will always be a country of immigrants. Even the loudest opponents of immigration reform can trace their heritage to outside America. Immigrants are Americans by choice because the founding principles of this great nation transcend all cultures. For over two centuries, the influx of immigrants around the world has enriched American culture and helped build the world's wealthiest and strongest nation.

Our nation's strength is not land, natural resources, or a strong military. "More than any other country, our strength comes from our own immigrant heritage and our capacity to welcome those from other lands" (President Reagan).[301] Our nation's history is the best testament that when a human being is set free, when constraints are removed from human minds, "there are no great limits to growth because there are no limits of human intelligence, imagination, and wonder" (President Reagan).

The immigration issue and its controversies are mostly our own doing. Our current immigration policy reflects a more-than-half-century national shift in public policy and culture and a decades-long trend of repudiating our core principles—such as the rule of law, equality before the law, self-reliance, free market economics, and limited government. The law doesn't treat immigrants as assets, as individuals capable of standing independently, but as liabilities that need to be restricted and victims who can only thrive as dependents of our citizens and an ever-growing big government.

Like other government policies, our immigration policy has become an ideological and social justice redistribution tool. We don't do enough to keep those who intend to harm America out, and we make it difficult for hardworking, America-loving, law-abiding people to come, stay, and contribute. Our immigration policy sends a mixed message, creates conflicts between immigrants and native-born Americans, and exacerbates the illegal immigration problem. It does not serve our country's economic needs or national interests.

People will migrate as long as there are different economic and political conditions worldwide. It's human nature to move to a place where a better life is possible. It's the destiny of America to be a beacon of hope for people worldwide. Historian Richard Hofstadter said, "It has been our fate as a nation not to have ideologies but to be one." The only way forward, the only way to make immigrants and native-born Americans one people again, is to find our way back: back to our founding principles; back to being the country where rugged individualism, liberty, and free market economics enable freedom-lovers who are ready to roll up their sleeves to better their lives through their hard work and cleverness. Let's stand firmly on our principles and apply common-sense, incremental policy changes that reaffirm these beliefs and bring tangible benefits. America can again offer a proper welcome mat.

In the towering words of Fredrick Douglas,

> We shall spread the network of our science and civilization over all who seek their shelter whether from Asia, Africa, or the Isles of the sea. We shall mold them all, each after his kind, into Americans . . . all shall here bow to the same law, speak the same language, support the same Government, enjoy the same liberty, vibrate with the same national enthusiasm, and seek the same national end. [302]

APPENDIX 1

Who Was Shut Out?
Immigration Quotas, 1925 to 1927*

Northwest Europe and Scandinavia		Eastern and Southern Europe		Other Countries	
Country	**Quota**	**Country**	**Quota**	**Country**	**Quota**
Germany	51,227	Poland	5,982	Africa (other than Egypt)	1,100
Great Britain and Northern Ireland	34,007	Italy	3,845	Armenia	124
Irish Free State (Ireland)	28,567	Czecho-slovakia	3,073	Australia	121
Sweden	9,561	Russia	2,248	Palestine	100
Norway	6,453	Yugoslavia	671	Syria	100
France	3,954	Romania	603	Turkey	100
Denmark	2,789	Portugal	503	Egypt	100
Switzerland	2,081	Hungary	473	New Zealand & Pacific Islands	100
Netherlands	1,648	Lithuania	344	All others	1,900
Austria	785	Latvia	142		
Belgium	512	Spain	131		
Finland	471	Estonia	124		
Free City of Danzig	228	Albania	100		
Iceland	100	Bulgaria	100		
Luxembourg	100	Greece	100		
Total (Number)	142,483	**Total (Number)**	18,439	**Total (Number)**	3,745
Total (%)	86.5	**Total (%)**	11.2	**Total (%)**	2.3

Total annual immigrant quota: 164,667

APPENDIX 2

Nativity of the Population and Place of Birth of the Native
Population: 1850–1990*

*Indicates sample data.

- Represents zero or rounds to zero.

[1] Starting in 1960, includes population of Alaska and Hawaii. For 1890, excludes population enumerated in the Indian Territory and on Indian reservations (about which, information on most topics, including nativity, was not collected). See Table 6.

[2] Puerto Rico is the only outlying area for which the number has ever exceeded 100,000.

[3] In 1850 and 1860, information on nativity was not collected for slaves. The data in the table assumes, as was done in 1870 census reports, that all slaves in 1850 and 1860 were native. Of the total Black population of 4,880,009 in 1870, 9,645, or 0.2%, were foreign.

* Source: U.S. Census Bureau, Population Division. Authors: Campbell Gibson and Emily Lennon. Retrieved from:
http://www.census.gov/population/www/documentation/twps0029/tab01.html

Year [1]	Total population	Native population						Foreign-born population
		Total	Born in the United States	Born abroad				
				Total	In outlying areas[2]	Of American parents		
1990*	248,709,873	228,942,557	225,695,826	3,246,731	1,382,446	1,864,285		19,767,316
1980*	226,545,805	212,465,899	210,322,697	2,143,202	1,088,172	1,055,030		14,079,906
1970* [3]	203,210,158	193,590,856	191,329,489	2,261,367	891,266	1,370,101		9,619,302
1960* [1]	179,325,671	169,587,580	168,525,645	1,061,935	660,425	401,510		9,738,091
1950*	150,216,110	139,868,715	139,442,390	426,325	329,970	96,355		10,347,395
1940	131,669,275	120,074,379	119,795,254	279,125	156,956	122,169		11,594,896
1930	122,775,046	108,570,897	108,304,188	266,709	136,032	130,677		14,204,149
1920	105,710,620	91,789,928	91,659,045	130,883	38,020	92,863		13,920,692
1910	91,972,266	78,456,380	78,381,104	75,276	7,365	67,911		13,515,886
1900	75,994,575	65,653,299	65,583,225	70,074	2,923	67,151		10,341,276
1890 [1]	62,622,250	53,372,703	53,362,371	10,332	322	10,010		9,249,547
1880	50,155,783	43,475,840	43,475,498	342	51	291		6,679,943
1870	38,558,371	32,991,142	32,990,922	220	51	169		5,567,229
1860 [4]	31,443,321	27,304,624	27,304,624	-	-	-		4,138,697
1850 [4]	23,191,876	20,947,274	20,947,274	-	-	-		2,244,602

APPENDIX 3

Historical Census Statistics on the Foreign-born Population of the
United States: 1850 to 1930 and 1960 to 1990*

* Source: U.S. Census Bureau, Population Division. Authors: Campbell Gibson
and Emily Lennon. Retrieved from:
http://www.census.gov/population/www/documentation/twps0029/tab02.
html

Year	Total	Region of birth reported							Region of birth not reported
		Total	Europe	Asia	Africa	Oceania	Latin America	Northern America	
NUMBER									
1990*	19,767,316	18,959,158	4,350,403	4,979,037	363,819	104,145	8,407,837	753,917	808,158
1980*	14,079,906	13,192,563	5,149,572	2,539,777	199,723	77,577	4,372,487	853,427	887,343
1970*	9,619,302	9,303,570	5,740,891	824,887	80,143	41,258	1,803,970	812,421	315,732
1960*	9,738,091	9,678,201	7,256,311	490,996	35,355	34,730	908,309	952,500	59,890
1930	14,204,149	14,197,553	11,784,010	275,665	18,326	17,343	791,840	1,310,369	6,596
1920	13,920,692	13,911,767	11,916,048	237,950	16,126	14,626	588,843	1,138,174	8,925
1910	13,515,886	13,506,272	11,810,115	191,484	3,992	11,450	279,514	1,209,717	9,614
1900	10,341,276	10,330,534	8,881,548	120,248	2,538	8,820	137,458	1,179,922	10,742
1890	9,249,547	9,243,535	8,030,347	113,383	2,207	9,353	107,307	980,938	6,012
1880	6,679,943	6,675,875	5,751,823	107,630	2,204	6,859	90,073	717,286	4,068
1870	5,567,229	5,563,637	4,941,049	64,565	2,657	4,028	57,871	493,467	3,592
1860	4,138,697	4,134,809	3,807,062	36,796	526	2,140	38,315	249,970	3,888
1850	2,244,602	2,202,625	2,031,867	1,135	551	588	20,773	147,711	41,977

APPENDIX 4

Nonimmigrant Visa Categories*

The chart below contains many different Purposes of Temporary Travel and related nonimmigrant visa categories available on the USCIS website.

Purpose of Travel	Visa Category	Required: Before applying for visa*
Athlete, amateur or professional (competing for prize money only)	B-1	(NA)
Au pair (exchange visitor)	J	SEVIS
Australian professional specialty	E-3	DOL
Border Crossing Card: Mexico	BCC	(NA)
Business visitor	B-1	(NA)
CNMI-only transitional worker	CW-1	(USCIS)

* Source:
https://travel.state.gov/content/visas/en/general/all-visa-categories.html

Crewmember	<u>D</u>	(NA)
Diplomat or foreign government official	<u>A</u>	(NA)
Domestic employee or nanny — must be accompanying a foreign national employer	<u>B-1</u>	(NA)
Employee of a designated international organization or NATO	<u>G1-G5, NATO</u>	(NA)
Exchange visitor	<u>J</u>	SEVIS
Foreign military personnel stationed in the United States	<u>A-2</u> <u>NATO1-6</u>	(NA)
Foreign national with extraordinary ability in Sciences, Arts, Education, Business or Athletics	<u>O</u>	USCIS
Free Trade Agreement (FTA) Professional: Chile, Singapore	<u>H-1B 1 — Chile</u> <u>H-1B 1 — Singapore</u>	DOL
International cultural exchange visitor	<u>Q</u>	USCIS
Intra-company transferee	<u>L</u>	USCIS
Medical treatment, visitor for	<u>B-2</u>	(NA)
Media, journalist	<u>I</u>	(NA)
NAFTA professional worker: Mexico, Canada	<u>TN/TD</u>	(NA)
Performing athlete, artist, entertainer	<u>P</u>	USCIS
Physician	<u>J</u>, <u>H-1B</u>	SEVIS
Professor, scholar, teacher (exchange visitor)	<u>J</u>	SEVIS
Religious worker	<u>R</u>	USCIS
Specialty occupations in fields requiring highly specialized knowledge	<u>H-1B</u>	DOL then USCIS
Student: academic, vocational	<u>F, M</u>	SEVIS
Temporary agricultural worker	<u>H-2A</u>	DOL then USCIS
Temporary worker performing other	<u>H-2B</u>	DOL then USCIS

services or labor of a temporary or seasonal nature.		
Tourism, vacation, pleasure visitor	B-2	(NA)
Training in a program not primarily for employment	H-3	USCIS
Treaty trader/treaty investor	E	(NA)
Transiting the United States	C	(NA)
Victim of Criminal Activity	U	USCIS
Victim of Human Trafficking	T	USCIS
Nonimmigrant (V) Visa for Spouse and Children of a Lawful Permanent Resident (LPR)	V	(NA)
Renewals in the U.S. — A, G, and NATO Visas		(NA)

*What the abbreviations above mean. Before applying for a visa at a U.S. embassy or consulate, the following is required:

- DOL = A U.S. employer must obtain foreign labor certification from the U.S. Department of Labor prior to filing a petition with USCIS.

- USCIS = U.S. Citizenship and Immigration Services (USCIS) approval of a petition or application (The required petition or application depends on the visa category you plan to apply for.)

- SEVIS = Program approval entered in the Student and Exchange Visitor Information System (SEVIS)

- (NA) = Not Applicable. Additional approval by another U.S. government agency is not required prior to applying for a visa.

APPENDIX 5

Temporary (Nonimmigrant) Working Visa Categories*

Temporary (Nonimmigrant) Worker Classifications[303]		
Temporary Worker	Description	Dependent Spouses and Children of a Temporary Worker
CW-1	CNMI—Only transitional workers	CW-2
E-1	Treaty traders and qualified employees	E-1[3]
E-2	Treaty investors and qualified employees	E-2[3]
E-2C	Long-term foreign investors in the	E-2C

---

* Source: *The United States Citizenship and Immigration Services (USCIS) website.* Retrieved from http://www.uscis.gov/working-united-states/temporary-workers/tempoary-nonimmigrant-workers

	CNMI	
E-3	Certain "specialty occupation" professionals from Australia	E-3[3]
H-1B	Workers in a specialty occupation and the following sub-classifications: **H-1B 1** — Free Trade Agreement workers in a specialty occupation from Chile and Singapore **H-1B 2** — Specialty occupations related to Department of Defense Cooperative Research and Development projects or Co-production projects **H-1B 3** — Fashion models of distinguished merit and ability	H-4
H-1C	Registered nurses working in a health professional shortage area as determined by the U.S. Department of Labor	H-4
H-2A	Temporary or seasonal agricultural workers	H-4
H-2B	Temporary non-agricultural workers	H-4
H-3	Trainees other than medical or academic. This classification also applies to practical training in the education of handicapped children.	H-4
I	Representatives of foreign press, radio, film, or other foreign information media	I
L-1A	Intracompany transferees in managerial or executive positions	L-2[3]
L-1B	Intracompany transferees in positions utilizing specialized knowledge	L-2[3]
O-1	Persons with extraordinary ability in sciences, arts, education, business, or athletics and motion picture or TV production	O-3
O-2	Persons accompanying solely to assist an O-1 nonimmigrant	O-3

P-1A	Internationally recognized athletes	P-4
P-1B	Internationally recognized entertainers or members of internationally recognized entertainment groups	P-4
P-2	Individual performers or part of a group entering to perform under a reciprocal exchange program	P-4
P-3	Artists or entertainers, either an individual or group, to perform, teach, or coach under a program that is culturally unique	P-4
Q-1	Persons participating in an international cultural exchange program for the purpose of providing practical training, employment, and to share the history, culture, and traditions of the alien's home country	Not Applicable
R-1	Religious workers	R-2
TN	North American Free Trade Agreement (NAFTA) temporary professionals from Mexico and Canada	TD

[1] Only a few nonimmigrant classifications allow you to obtain permission to work in this country without an employer having first filed a petition on your behalf. Such classifications include the nonimmigrant E-1, E-2, E-3, and TN classifications, as well as, in certain instances, the F-1 and M-1 student and J-1 exchange visitor classifications.

[2] The H-1C nonimmigrant classification expired on December 20, 2009.

[3] E and L dependent spouses may apply for employment authorization.

[4] Though the Immigration and Nationality Act (INA) does not provide a specific nonimmigrant classification for dependents of Q-1 nonimmigrants, this does not preclude the spouse or child of a Q-1 from entering the U.S. in another nonimmigrant classification.

APPENDIX 6

Visa Bulletin for December 2022[304]

Application Final Action Dates for Family-Sponsored Preference Cases

Note: "C" means current; i.e., numbers are authorized for issuance to all qualified applicants. "U" means unauthorized; i.e., numbers are not authorized for issuance.

Family-Sponsored	All Chargeability Areas Except Those Listed	CHINA mainland born	INDIA	MEXICO	PHILIPPINES
F1	1-Dec-14	1-Dec-14	1-Dec-14	15-Nov-00	1-Mar-12
F2A	C	C	C	C	C
F2B	22-Sep-15	22-Sep-15	22-Sep-15	1-Jun-01	22-Oct-11
F3	22-Nov-08	22-Nov-08	22-Nov-08	1-Nov-97	8-Jun-02
F4	22-Mar-07	22-Mar-07	15-Sep-05	1-Aug-00	22-Aug-02

Family-Sponsored Preferences

First: (F1) Unmarried Sons and Daughters of U.S. Citizens: 23,400 plus any numbers not required for fourth preference.

Second: Spouses and Children, and Unmarried Sons and Daughters of Permanent Residents: 114,200, plus the number (if any) by which the worldwide family preference level exceeds 226,000, plus any unused first preference numbers:

- **F2A:** Spouses and Children of Permanent Residents: 77% of the overall second preference limitation, of which 75% are exempt from the per-country limit;

- **F2B**: Unmarried Sons and Daughters (21 years of age or older) of Permanent Residents: 23% of the overall second preference limitation.

- **Third**: (F3) Married Sons and Daughters of U.S. Citizens: 23,400, plus any numbers not required by first and second preferences.

- **Fourth**: (F4) Brothers and Sisters of Adult U.S. Citizens: 65,000, plus any numbers not required by first three preferences.

Application Final Action Dates for Employment-Based Preference Cases

Note: "C" means current; i.e., numbers are authorized for issuance to all qualified applicants. "U" means unauthorized; i.e., numbers are not authorized for issuance.

Employment-based	All Chargea-bility Areas Except Those Listed	CHINA mainland born	EL SALVADOR GUATEMALA HONDURAS	INDIA	MEXICO	PHILIPPINES
1st	C	C	C	C	C	C
2nd	01DEC22	08JUL19	01DEC22	01MAY12	01DEC22	01DEC22
3rd	C	01SEP18	C	01AUG12	C	C
Other Workers	08SEP22	01NOV15	08SEP22	01AUG12	08SEP22	08SEP22
4th	22JUL22	22JUL22	15APR18	22JUL22	15OCT20	22JUL22
Certain Religious Workers	22JUL22	22JUL22	15APR18	22JUL22	15OCT20	22JUL22
5th Unreserved (including C5, T5, I5, R5)	C	01JAN16	C	08DEC19	C	C
5th Set Aside: (Rural—20%)	C	C	C	C	C	C
5th Set Aside: (High Unemploy-ment—10%)	C	C	C	C	C	C
5th Set Aside: (Infrastructure—2%)	C	C	C	C	C	C

Employment-Based Preferences

First: Priority Workers: 28.6% of the worldwide employment-based preference level, plus any numbers not required for fourth and fifth preferences.

Second: Members of the Professions Holding Advanced Degrees or Persons of Exceptional Ability: 28.6% of the worldwide employment-based preference level, plus any numbers not required by first preference.

Third: Skilled Workers, Professionals, and Other Workers: 28.6% of the worldwide level, plus any numbers not required by first and second preferences, not more than 10,000 of which to "*Other Workers".

Fourth: Certain Special Immigrants: 7.1% of the worldwide level.

Fifth: Employment Creation: 7.1% of the worldwide level, of which 32% are reserved as follows: 20% reserved for qualified immigrants who invest in a rural area; 10% reserved for qualified immigrants who invest in a high unemployment area; and 2% reserved for qualified immigrants who invest in infrastructure projects. The remaining 68% are unreserved and are allotted for all other qualified immigrants.

APPENDIX 7

Legal Immigration Roadmap[305]

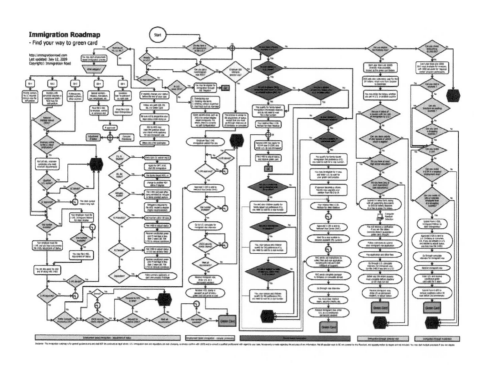

APPENDIX 8

Other Ways to Get a Green Card

Although most immigrants come to live permanently in the United States through a family member's sponsorship, employment, or a job offer, there are other ways a green card (permanent residence) can be obtained, such as the:

- Diversity Immigrant Visa Program (referred to by many as the "Green Card Lottery")

- K Nonimmigrant (includes fiancé[e])

- Legal Immigration Family Equity (LIFE) Act

- Special Immigrant Juvenile (SIJ) Status

Additional programs include:[*]

Special Categories of Family	
Battered Spouse or Child (VAWA)	Widow(er) of a U.S. Citizen
Person Born to a Foreign Diplomat in the United States	V Nonimmigrant
Special Categories of Jobs	
Afghan/Iraqi Translator	Afghan Who Assisted the U.S. Government
Armed Forces Member	NATO-6 Nonimmigrant
International Organization Employee	Physician National Interest Waiver
Iraqi Who Assisted the U.S. Government	Religious Worker
Other Green Card Programs	
Amerasian Child of a U.S. Citizen	Informant (S Nonimmigrant)
American Indian Born in Canada	Indochinese Parole Adjustment Act
Cuban Native or Citizen	Lautenberg Parolee
Haitian Refugee	Nicaraguan and Central American Relief Act (NACARA)
Help HAITI Act of 2010	Victim of Criminal Activity (U Nonimmigrant)
	Victim of Trafficking (T Non-immigrant)

[*] Source: United States Citizenship and Immigration Services (USCIS) website. Retrieved from http://www.uscis.gov/green-card/other-ways-get-green-card

APPENDIX 9

Diversity Visa Program, DV 2019-2021: Number of Entries During
Each Online Registration Period by Region *

Region	# of Entrants			Total
	2019	2020	2021	
Africa	10,877,791	11,315,826	1,776,949	**23,970,566**
Asia	3289665	3,548,165	1,072,234	**7,910,064**
Europe	7,620,677	7,185,456	1,901,468	**16,707,601**
Oceania	39,102	39,608	11,400	**90,110**
Total for South America, Central America, and the Caribbean	594,954	1,090,751	326,793	**2,012,498**
Total	**22,425,053**	**23,182,554**	**5,089,579**	**50,690,839**

* Source: https://travel.state.gov/content/dam/visas/Diversity-Visa/DVStatistics/DV-applicant-entrants-by-country-2019-2021.pdf

APPENDIX 10

Australian Point-based Scorecard for Skilled Immigrants*

Factor	Description	Points
Age at time of invitation	18–24 years (inclusive)	25
	25–32 years (inclusive)	30
	33–39 years (inclusive)	25
	40–44 years (inclusive)	15
	45–49 years (inclusive)	0
English language ability at time of invitation	Competent English – IELTS 6 / OET B	0
	Proficient English – IELTS 7 / OET B	10
	Superior English – IELTS 8 / OET A	20

* Source: Contents copied from Skilled Independent (Subclass 189) Visa, DIAC (SkillSelect),
http://www.immi.gov.au/skills/skillselect/index/visas/subclass-189/ (click on the "Points test" tab).

Skilled employment at time of invitation **Only 20 points can be awarded for any combination of overseas and Australian skilled employment**	Skilled employment outside Australia	5
	At least three but less than five years (of past 10 years)	10
	At least five but less than eight years (of past 10 years)	15
	At least eight and up to 10 years (of past 10 years)	20
Overseas employment in nominated skilled occupation or a closely related skilled occupation **Australian employment in nominated skilled occupation or a closely related skilled occupation**	Skilled employment in Australia for at least one but less than three years (of past 10 years)	5
	At least three but less than five years (of past 10 years)	10
	At least five but less than eight years (of past 10 years)	15
	At least eight and up to 10 years (of past 10 years)	20
Educational qualifications at time of invitation	Doctorate from an Australian educational institution or other Doctorate of a recognized standard	20
	At least a Bachelor degree, including a Bachelor degree with Honors or Masters, from an Australian educational institution or other degree of a recognized standard	15
	Diploma or trade qualification completed in Australia, or qualification or award of recognized standard	10

Australian study requirements at time of invitation	One or more degrees, diplomas or trade qualifications awarded by an Australian educational institution and meet the Australian Study Requirement	5
Other factors at time of invitation	Credentialed community language qualifications	5
	Study in regional Australia or a low population growth metropolitan area (excluding distance education)	5
	Partner skill qualifications	5
	Professional Year in Australia for at least 12 months in the four years before the day you were invited	5
Nomination/sponsorship at time of invitation	Nomination by state or territory government (visa subclass 190 only)	5
	Nomination by state or territory government or sponsorship by an eligible family member, to reside and work in a specified/designated area (visa subclass 489 only)	5

ACKNOWLEDGEMENTS

In the fall of 2014, John Andrews, President of the Centennial Institute, a Colorado-based think tank, asked me to produce a policy brief on immigration issues and free-market-based reform ideas. It was the first policy brief I had ever written, and John was very encouraging and reassuring throughout the process. That policy brief later became the basis for the first edition of this book. A huge thanks to John for believing in me and my ideas.

A special thanks to Deborah Natelson for formatting this book with her usual professionalism and perfection. This is the 5th book we worked on together, and I'm blessed to call her a friend.

I want also to thank my mother-in-law, JoAnne Raleigh, for letting me include Great-Grandpa Gibbon's wedding photo in this book. JoAnne is the Raleigh family's unofficial historian, and she decorates the walls of her house with pictures of several generations of the Raleighs. Without her meticulous record-keeping, I would never have known what Great-Grandpa Gibbon and Great-Grandma May looked like. She and my father-in-law James Raleigh celebrated their 50th wedding anniversary in 2022. Their strong union has always been my inspiration. I owe the greatest debt to my husband, Mike Raleigh. I probably would not have taken on this project without his encouragement and unwavering support. An avid reader, he helped me with my research by recommending many good books. Throughout the book-writing process, he had to review scores of rough drafts, yet he dealt with them with tremendous patience. His insights helped sharpen my focus and allowed me to put my best ideas out there.

Who would have imagined that a girl who grew up in Communist China and a boy descended from an Irish immigrant would someday make a family together? We are both proud Americans. Mike's great-grandfather made that choice for him, and I became an American of my own free will. At home, we celebrate both Chinese New Year and St. Patrick's Day, say the same pledge of allegiance, and sing the same national anthem loud and proud. In a small way, our family is a testament to the strength of this great nation of immigrants.

IMAGE CITATIONS AND REFERENCES

Segar, W. (1598). *Figure 1.1. Portrait of Sir Walter Raleigh*. National Gallery of
Ireland. Retrieved from
https://commons.wikimedia.org/wiki/File:William_Segar_Sir_Walter_R
aleigh_1598.jpg.

Michelangelo (1501-1504). *Figure 1.2. The Statue of David*. Photo was taken by
the author during a trip to Florence, Italy in 2015.

Bradford, W. (1645). *Figure 1.3. The image of the Mayflower Compact*, from
William Bradford's *Of Plimoth Plantation* (created circa 1645, published
1898). Retrieved from
https://commons.wikimedia.org/wiki/File:Mayflower_Compact_Bradfo
rd.jpg.

Trumbull, J. (1806). *Figure 2.1. Portrait of Alexander Hamilton*. Retrieved from
https://en.wikipedia.org/wiki/Alexander_Hamilton#/media/File:Alexa
nder_Hamilton_portrait_by_John_Trumbull_1806.jpg.

Raleigh, M. (2010). *Figure 3.1. Photograph of Irish Brigade Memorial in Antietam.* Raleigh family collection.

Author Unknown. *Figure 3.2. Mary and Gibbon Raleigh wedding photo.* Raleigh family collection.

Author Unknown (1866). *Figure 3.3. Chinese workers working on Transcontinental railroad.* PBS website. Retrieved from http://wwwtc.pbs.org/weta/thewest/resources/archives/images/wimg 630/oc52mnrs.gif

Author and date unknown. *Figure 3.4. Image of an 1892 poster.* Retrieved from https://differenttogether.wordpress.com/2012/06/21/u-s-house-apologizes-for-chinese-exclusion-act

Author and date unknown. *Figure 3.5. Photograph of Wong Kim Ark.* Retrieved from https://commons.wikimedia.org/wiki/File:WongKimArk.gif

Author Unknown (1916). *Figure 4.1. Image of the Cover of Theater Programme for Israel Zangwill's play "The Melting Pot."* Retrieved from https://commons.wikimedia.org/wiki/File:TheMeltingpot1.jpg

Author Unknown (1918). *Figure 4.2. Photograph of Bhagat Singh Thind in his US Army Uniform.* Retrieved from https://commons.wikimedia.org/wiki/File:Bhagatsinghthind.jpg

Lange, D. (1942). *Figure 4.4. Photograph of members of the Mochida family awaiting evacuation.* National Achieve and Record Administration. Retrieved from https://commons.wikimedia.org/wiki/File:Photograph_of_Members_of _the_Mochida_Family_Awaiting_Evacuation_-_NARA_-_537505.jpg

Author Unknown (1936). *Figure 4.5. Image of Albert Einstein's Declaration of Intention card.* Retrieved from http://www.uscis.gov/sites/default/files/USCIS/History%20and%20Ge nealogy/ Our%20History/Historians-Mailbox/EinsteinDeclarationDetail-Large.jpg

Author Unknown (2013). *Figure 4.6. Origins of the U.S. Immigrant Population, 1960-2013.* Retrieved from http://www.pewhispanic.org/2015/09/28/statistical-portrait-of-the-foreign-born-population-in-the-united-states-1960-2013-key-charts/#2013-fb-origin

Daniel Costa, David Cooper, and Heidi Shierholz. *Figure 7.1. Unauthorized immigrant population in the United States, by region of birth, 2008 (in thousands).* August 12, 2014. Retrieved from: http://www.epi.org/publication/immigration-fact

NOTES

[1] Armao, M. (July 28, 2015). Tomb of the Now Known: Jamestown 4. *The Wall Street Journal*. Retrieved from http://www.wsj.com/articles/verdict-in-libya-war-crimes-trial-death-by-firing-squad-1438127477

[2] Miller, Lee (2012). *Roanoke: Solving the Mystery of the Lost Colony* (p. 48). New York, NY: Penguin Press.

[3] Jamestown Colony. Retrieved from http://www.history.com/topics/jamestown

[4] Virtual Jamestown webpage. Retrieved from http://www.virtualjamestown.org/essays/horn_essay.html

[5] Bishop, P. *Martin Luther and the Protestant Reformation*. Retrieved from https://www.hccfl.edu/media/173616/ee2luther.pdf

[6] Luther, M. and Dillenberger, J. (1958). *Martin Luther: Selections From His Writing*. Anchor Publishing. Retrieved from https://books.google.com/books?isbn=030780335X

[7] Calvin, J. translated by Andel, H. (1975). *Golden Booklet of the True Christian Life*. Baker Books.

[8] Study.com website. "Puritan Work Ethic: Definition & Overview." Retrieved from http://study.com/academy/lesson/puritan-work-ethic-definition-lesson-quiz.html

[9] Ibid.

[10] Hanson, M (2015). *Queen Elizabeth I: Biography, Facts, Portraits & Information.* Retrieved from http://englishhistory.net/tudor/monarchs/queen-elizabeth-i

[11] *End Time Pilgrim Website.* Retrieved from http://endtimepilgrim.org/puritans05.htm

[12] *New World Encyclopedia Website.* Retrieved from http://www.newworldencyclopedia.org/entry/Oliver_Cromwell

[13] *End Time Pilgrim Website.* Retrieved from http://endtimepilgrim.org/puritans06.htm

[14] *New World Encyclopedia Website*: Ibid.

[15] James II. *The BBC History website.* Retrieved from http://www.bbc.co.uk/history/historic_figures/james_ii.shtml

[16] Bethl, T. (1999). "How Private Property Saved Pilgrims." *The Hoover Institute website.* Retrieved from http://www.hoover.org/research/how-private-property-saved-pilgrims

[17] Recorded by Nathaniel Morton, keeper of the records of Plymouth Colony, based on the account of William Bradford. Retrieved from http://www.wsj.com/articles/the-desolate-wilderness-1448407070

[18] *May Flower History website.* Retrieved from http://mayflowerhistory.com/voyage

[19] *May Flower History website:* Ibid.

[20] "Great Migration: Passengers of the Mayflower, 1620." *Geni.com.* Retrieved from http://www.geni.com/projects/Great-Migration-Passengers-of-the-Mayflower-1620/8

[21] Recorded by Nathaniel Morton, keeper of the records of Plymouth Colony, based on the account of William Bradford. Retrieved from http://www.wsj.com/articles/the-desolate-wilderness-1448407070

[22] Prince, T. (1736). *A chronological history of New England in the form of annals.* Retrieved from https://archive.org/details/chronologicalhis01prin

[23] It was President Lincoln who declared Thanksgiving a national celebration in 1863.

[24] Bradford, W. (2006). *Of the Plymouth Plantation (Dover Value Editions)* (p. 66). Mineola, NY: Dover Publications.

[25] Bodin, J. (1576). Six Books of the Common Wealth, Book 1. *Constitution website*. Retrieved from http://www.constitution.org/bodin/bodin_1.htm

[26] Bradford, W. *Of the Plymouth Plantation*. p. 162.

[27] *Of the Plymouth Plantation:* Ibid. pp. 162-163.

[28] *History.com website*. Retrieved from http://www.history.com/topics/william-bradford

[29] Wood, S. Retrieved from http://www.pilgrimjohnhowlandsociety.org/john-howland/articles/41-purloined-found-and-recovered-the-history-of-bradfords-history

[30] Madison, J. (1787). *The Federalist Paper, No. 42.*

[31] Ibid.

[32] Hamilton, A. (1787). *The Federalist Paper, No. 32.*

[33] Ibid.

[34] Jefferson, T. (1774). *A Summary View of the Rights of British America*. Retrieved from http://press-pubs.uchicago.edu/founders/documents/v1ch14s10.html

[35] Hamilton, A. (1791). *Report on the Subject of Manufactures*. Retrieved from http://what-when-how.com/the-american-economy/report-on-the-subject-of-manufactures-1791

[36] House of Representatives (1790). *Rule of Naturalization*. Retrieved from http://press-pubs.uchicago.edu/founders/documents/a1_8_4_citizenships8.html

[37] House of Representatives (1790). *Rule of Naturalization:* Ibid.

[38] Washington, G. (1794). *Letter to the Vice President. Retrieved from* http://www.founding.com/founders_library/pageID.2223/default.asp

[39] House of Representatives (1790). *Rule of Naturalization:* Ibid.

[40] House of Representatives (1790). *Rule of Naturalization:* Ibid.

41 Jefferson, T. (1781). *Notes on the State of Virginia.* Retrieved from https://www.thefederalistpapers.org/history/thomas-jefferson-notes-on-the-state-of-virginia

42 Ibid.

43 *University of Pennsylvania website.* Retrieved from http://itre.cis.upenn.edu/~myl/languagelog/archives/000898.html

44 Washington, G. (1794). *Letter to the Vice President.* Retrieved from http://www.founding.com/founders_library/pageID.2223/default.asp

45 Ibid.

46 Alexander Hamilton (Lucius Crassus). *Examination of Jefferson's Message to Congress of December 7, 1801.* Retrieved from https://www.thefederalistpapers.org/current-events/alexander-hamilton-and-immigration

47 McAllister, D.C. (August 18, 2014). "What John Quincy Adams Said About Immigration Will Blow Your Mind." *The Federalist.* Retrieved from http://thefederalist.com/2014/08/18/what-john-quincy-adams-said-about-immigration-will-blow-your-mind

48 House of Representatives (1790). *Rule of Naturalization:* Ibid.

49 House of Representatives (1790). *Rule of Naturalization:* Ibid.

50 House of Representatives (1790). *Rule of Naturalization:* Ibid.

51 House of Representatives (1790). *Rule of Naturalization:* Ibid.

52 Chernow, R. (2014). *Alexander Hamilton,* the Penguin Press, New York, p. 238.

53 United States Congress (March 26, 1790). *An act to establish an uniform Rule of Naturalization.* Retrieved from http://www.indiana.edu/~kdhist/H105-documents-web/week08/naturalization1790.html

54 *The Naturalization Act of 1795.* Retrieved from http://library.uwb.edu/static/USimmigration/1795_naturalization_act.html

55 Rosenthal, N. (2015). *Citizen Sailors. The Wall Street Journal.* Retrieved from http://www.wsj.com/articles/your-papers-please-1445804774

56 *Citizen Sailors:* Ibid.

57 *Alexander Hamilton:* Ibid., p.571.

[58] Alien and Sedition Acts. Retrieved from
http://loc.gov/rr/program/bib/ourdocs/Alien.html.

[59] *Alexander Hamilton*: Ibid., p. 570.

[60] *Alexander Hamilton*: Ibid., p. 571.

[61] *Alexander Hamilton*: Ibid., p. 572.

[62] Cheney, L. (2014). *James Madison*, the Penguin Press, New York, p. 274.

[63] *James Madison:* Ibid.

[64] Jefferson, T. (Dec 8, 1801). *First annual message to congress.* Retrieved from
http://avalon.law.yale.edu/19th_century/jeffmes1.asp

[65] *1802 Naturalization Act.* Retrieved from
https://sites.google.com/site/kmaclubofamerica/1802-naturalization-act. The
three-year notice period was dropped to two years in 1824.

[66] *USCIS.gov website.* Retrieved from http://www.uscis.gov/history-and-
genealogy/our-history/our-history

[67] The federal budget grew from $80 million in 1860 to over $1 billion in 1865.

[68] *1866 Civil Rights Act.* Retrieved from
http://www.pbs.org/wgbh/amex/reconstruction/activism/ps_1866.html

[69] Foner, E. (1988). *A Short History of Reconstruction 1863-1877.* Harper & Row,
New York, p. 113.

[70] Walters, R. (1978). *American Reformers 1815-1860.* HarperCollins Canada Ltd.,
p. 4.

[71] The Germans in America. *The Library of Congress website.* Retrieved from
http://www.loc.gov/rr/european/imde/germchro.html

[72] Engel, P. and Lubin, G. (October 6, 2013). "Here's Why There Are So Many
German-Americans In The US." Retrieved from
http://www.businessinsider.com/german-american-history-2013-10

[73] "Ben Franklin and German Immigrants." Retrieved from
https://almostchosenpeople.wordpress.com/2012/04/12/benjamin-franklin-
on-german-immigrants

[74] Schmidt, C.B. (1906). "Reminiscences of Foreign Immigration Work for
Kansas." *Kansas Historical Collections, 1905–1906.* Retrieved from
https://www.kshs.org/archives/8769

75 *The Homestead Act of 1862.* Retrieved from
http://www.archives.gov/education/lessons/homestead-act

76 Wittke, C. (1939). *We Who Built America: The Saga of the Immigrant.* Retrieved
from http://immigration.procon.org/view.timeline.php?timelineID=000023

77 Shea, W. & Hess J. (1992). *Pea Ridge: Civil War Campaign in the West.* The
University of North Carolina Press Chapel Hill, p. 7.

78 McPherson, J. (1997). *For Cause & Comrades: Why Men Fought in the Civil War.*
Oxford University Press, New York, p. 144.

79 *A Short History of Reconstruction 1863-1877:* Ibid., p.131.

80 *Douglass Papers.* (1869). "Frederick Douglass Describes The 'Composite
Nation.'" Library of Congress, microfilm reel 14. Retrieved from
http://www.blackpast.org/1869-frederick-douglass-describes-composite-
nation#sthash.tSyZiTuA.dpuf

81 *Here's Why There Are So Many German-Americans In The US:* Ibid.

82 "Irish Catholic Immigration to America." The Library of Congress. Retrieved
from
http://www.loc.gov/teachers/classroommaterials/presentationsandactivities
/presentations/immigration/irish2.html

83 *For Cause & Comrades: Why Men Fought in the Civil War:* Ibid., p. 68.

84 *American Reformers 1815-1860:* Ibid., p. 175.

85 McPherson, J. (December 11, 2003). *Battle Cry of Freedom.* Oxford University
Press, p.103.

86 *History Place website.* Retrieved from
http://www.historyplace.com/worldhistory/famine/america.htm

87 *American Reformers 1815-1860:* Ibid., pp. 208-209.

88 *US Commission on Civil Rights website.* Retrieved from
http://www.usccr.gov/pubs/BlaineReport.pdf

89 "Mitchell v. Helms: 530 US 793 (2000)." Retrieved from
https://supreme.justia.com/cases/federal/us/530/793/

90 McPherson, J. (1997). *For Cause & Comrades: Why Men Fought in the Civil War.*
Oxford University Press, New York.

[91] Wittke, C. (1939). *We Who Built America: The Saga of the Immigrant. Retrieved from* http://immigration.procon.org/view.timeline.php?timelineID=000023

[92] Ibid.

[93] Senik, T (2022). *A Man of Iron: The Turbulent Life and Improbable Presidency of Grover Cleveland.* Simon & Schuster. p. 55

[94] *History.com website.* Retrieved from http://www.history.com/topics/u-s-immigration-before-1965

[95] Bradley, J. (2015). *The China Mirage: the hidden history of American disaster in Asia.* Little, Brown and Company, p. 10.

[96] "The Gold Rush of 1849." Retrieved from http://www.history.com/topics/gold-rush-of-1849

[97] Douglass Papers: ibid.

[98] "Chinese Immigrants during the Gold Rush." Retrieved from http://califgoldrush.weebly.com/chinese-immigrants1.html

[99] Ibid.

[100] Takaki, Ronald. *Strangers from a Different Shore: A History of Asian Americans.* Boston: Little, Brown and Company, 1989.

[101] "The Bittersweet Memories of a Happy Dwelling." Retrieved from https://helenraleigh.substack.com/p/the-bittersweet-memories-of-a-happy

[102] *Chinese Americans in the Civil War.* Retrieved from: https://www.battlefields.org/learn/articles/chinese-americans-civil-war

[103] *A Short History of Reconstruction, 1863-1877:* Ibid., p. 134.

[104] The Burlingame-Seward Treaty, 1868. Retrieved from https://history.state.gov/milestones/1866-1898/burlingame-seward-treaty

[105] From remarks by John T. Doolittle, House of Representatives from California on April 29, 1999. Retrieved from http://cprr.org/Museum/Chinese.html

[106] Chang, G. (2019). *The Chinese and the Iron Road.* Stanford University Press, p.15

[107] *Yale University website.* Retrieved from http://ceas.yale.edu/yung-wing

[108] Douglass Papers: Ibid.

[109] *A Short History of Reconstruction, 1863-1877*: Ibid., pp. 217-218.

[110] *The Chinese American Experience from 1857-1892*. Retrieved from http://immigrants.harpweek.com/ChineseAmericans/2KeyIssues/DenisKearneyCalifAnti.htm

[111] Luibheid, E.(2002). *Entry Denied: Controlling Sexuality at the Border*. University of Minnesota Press, p. 31.

[112] *Page Act of 1875*. Retrieved from http://immigrationtous.net/228-page-act-united-states-1875.html

[113] *Page Act of 1875*: Ibid.

[114] *The China Mirage*: Ibid., p. 43.

[115] *Chinese Exclusion Act of 1882*. Retrieved from https://www.mtholyoke.edu/acad/intrel/chinex.htm

[116] *The China Mirage*: Ibid., p. 44.

[117] *A Man of Iron*: Ibid. p. 152

[118] *The China Mirage*: Ibid., p. 45.

[119] *A Man of Iron*: Ibid., p. 154-155

[120] *The Scott Act*. Retrieved from http://immigrationtous.net/266-scott-act-united-states-1888.html

[121] "China's First Yale Man." Retrieved from http://goldsea.com/Text/index.php?id=10719

[122] *The China Mirage*: Ibid., pp. 88-89.

[123] Hirschman, C. (2006). *The Impact of Immigration on American Society: Looking Backward to the Future*. Retrieved from http://borderbattles.ssrc.org/Hirschman/index1.html

[124] Tregarthen, T. and Rittenberg, L. (1999). *Macroeconomics* (2nd ed.). Worth Publishers. p. 177.

[125] Hester, T. *Immigration Act of 1891*. Retrieved from http://immigrationtounitedstates.org/585-immigration-act-of-1891.html.

[126] *Immigration Act of 1891*: Ibid.

[127] *The Constitution of the Immigration Restriction League*. Retrieved from http://pds.lib.harvard.edu/pds/view/5233215

[128] *A Man of Iron:* Ibid. p. 153

[129] *Grover Cleveland's veto message from March 2nd, 1897*. Retrieved from http://www.presidency.ucsb.edu/ws/index.php?pid=70845

[130] Harddow, I. (January, 8, 2008). *When UK GDP last outstripped the US*. Retrieved from http://news.bbc.co.uk/2/hi/uk_news/7174996.stm

[131] Bruner, R. & Carr, S. (2007). *The Panic of 1907: Lessons Learned from the Market's Perfect Storm*. John Wiley & Sons, Inc. New Jersey, p. 58.

[132] Foner, E. and Garraty, J. (editors). *The Reader's Companion to American History*. Retrieved from http://www.history.com/topics/gentlemens-agreement

[133] Ibid. p. 3.

[134] *Immigration Act of 1921 Imposes Quota System, 1921-1924*. Retrieved from http://www.dentonisd.org/cms/lib/TX21000245/Centricity/Domain/535/Immigration%20Act.pdf

[135] Duignan, P. (September 15, 2003). *Making and Remaking America: Immigration into the United States*. Retrieved from http://www.hoover.org/research/making-and-remaking-america-immigration-united-states

[136] Newspaper clip from the *Spokesman Review*, February 15, 1913. Retrieved from https://news.google.com/newspapers?nid=1314&dat=19130215&id=quFVAAAAIBAJ&sjid=ZuADAAAAIBAJ&pg=6711,3831831&hl=en

[137] *Webb-Haney Alien Land Law*. Retrieved from http://www.intimeandplace.org/Japanese%20Internment/reading/constitution/alienlandlaw.html

[138] "Ozawa v. United States." Retrieved from http://encyclopedia.densho.org/Ozawa_v._United_States

[139] Frederick, O. (June 1937). Development of a Eugenic Philosophy. *American Sociological Review*. Retrieved from https://en.wikipedia.org/wiki/Eugenics#cite_note-Osborn1937-6

[140] Grant, M. (1916). *The Passing of The Great Race or The Racial Basis of European History*. Retrieved from http://www.jrbooksonline.com/pdf_books/passingofgreatrace.pdf

141 Retrieved from
https://supreme.justia.com/cases/federal/us/274/200/case.html

142 Witt, J. (December 19, 2015). *Booz and Big Government*. Retrieved from
http://www.wsj.com/articles/booze-and-big-government-1450475211

143 "1917 Immigration Act-Summarized by *Davis Tucker and Jessi Creller*."
Retrieved from
http://library.uwb.edu/guides/USimmigration/1917_immigration_act.html

144 Lombardo, P. *Eugenics Laws Restricting Immigration*. Retrieved from
http://www.eugenicsarchive.org/html/eugenics/essay9text.html

145 *Denton Independent School District website*. Retrieved from
http://www.dentonisd.org/cms/lib/TX21000245/Centricity/Domain/535/I
mmigration%20Act.pdf

146 Shlaes, A. (2007). *The Forgotten Man: A new history of the great depression*.
HarperCollins Publishers, New York, p. 19.

147 *Shut the Door*. Retrieved from http://historymatters.gmu.edu/d/5080

148 *History Matters website*. Retrieved from
http://historymatters.gmu.edu/d/5079

149 *Who Was Shut Out?: Immigration Quotas, 1925–1927*. Retrieved from
http://historymatters.gmu.edu/d/5078

150 Kennedy, J. (1963). *A Nation of Immigrants*. New York, NY: Harper
Perennial, p. 45.

151 Gibson, C. and Lennon, E. (1999). *Historical Census Statistics on the Foreign-
born Population of the United States: 1850-1990*. Retrieved from
http://www.census.gov/population/www/documentation/twps0029/twps0
029.html

152 Johnson, L. (1965). *Remarks at the Signing of the Immigration Bill
Liberty Island, New York*. Retrieved from http://www.lbjlibrary.org/lyndon-
baines-johnson/timeline/lbj-on-immigration

153 Retrieved from http://2012books.lardbucket.org/books/theory-and-
applications-of-macroeconomics/s11-01-what-happened-during-the-
great.html

154 Shlaes, A. (2007) *The Forgotten Man: A new history of the great depression*.
HarperCollins Publishers, New York, p. 352.

155 Chart source: the U.S. Census Bureau

[156] *Alien Registration Act.* Retrieved from http://www-rohan.sdsu.edu/dept/polsciwb/brianl/docs/1940AlienRegistrationAct.pdf

[157] *History.org website.* Retrieved from http://www.history.com/topics/world-war-ii/japanese-american-relocation

[158] Retrieved from http://www.ucs.louisiana.edu/~ras2777/pres/korematsu.html

[159] *Interview of Norman Mineta and Alan Simpson by the Academy of Achievement:* Ibid.

[160] Brown, J. (2021) Face the Mountain: *A True Story of Japanese American Heroes in World War II.* Random House, New York, p. 790.

[161] Reagan, R. (Aug 10, 1988). Remarks on Signing the Bill Providing Restitution for the Wartime Internment of Japanese-American Civilians. Retrieved from http://faculty.history.wisc.edu/archdeacon/404tja/redress.html

[162] Ibid.

[163] *United States Citizenship and Immigration Services (USCIS) website.* Retrieved from http://www.uscis.gov/history-and-genealogy/history-and-genealogy-news/edward-bing-kan-first-chinese-american-naturalized-after-repeal-chinese-exclusion

[164] Repeal of the Chinese Exclusion Act, 1943. Retrieved from https://history.state.gov/milestones/1937-1945/chinese-exclusion-act-repeal

[165] Galston, W. (December 30, 2015). "A Refugee Test of National Honor." *The Wall Street Journal.* Retrieved from http://www.wsj.com/articles/a-refugee-test-of-national-honor-1451430424

[166] Dr. Medoff, R. (October 1, 2015). "US Could Have Done More to Save the Jew." *The Wall Street Journal.* Retrieved from http://www.wsj.com/articles/u-s-could-have-done-more-to-save-the-jews-1443641695

[167] Truman, H. (1952). "Veto of Bill To Revise the Laws Relating to Immigration, Naturalization, and Nationality." Retrieved from http://www.presidency.ucsb.edu/ws/?pid=14175

[168] *A Nation of Immigrants:* Ibid., p. 45.

[169] *Asian Nation website.* Retrieved from http://www.asian-nation.org/1965-immigration-act.shtml

170 Johnson, L. (1965). "Remarks at the Signing of the Immigration Bill Liberty Island, New York." Retrieved from http://www.lbjlibrary.org/lyndon-baines-johnson/timeline/lbj-on-immigration

171 Ibid.

172 *Pew Hispanic website*. Retrieved from http://www.pewhispanic.org/2015/09/28/statistical-portrait-of-the-foreign-born-population-in-the-united-states-1960-2013-key-charts

173 Quotes Retrieved from http://www.vdare.com/articles/so-much-for-promises-quotes-re-1965-immigration-act

174 *President Johnson's Remarks at the Signing of the Immigration Bill:* Ibid.

175 *US Census Bureau website*. Retrieved from http://www.census.gov/population/www/documentation/twps0081/twps0081.html

176 Retrieved from http://www.migrationpolicy.org/article/frequently-requested-statistics-immigrants-and-immigration-united-states#Current and Historical

177 Bush, G. (Nov 29, 1990). *Statement on Signing the Immigration Act of 1990*. Retrieved from http://www.presidency.ucsb.edu/ws/index.php?pid=19117

178 Retrieved from http://ir.lawnet.fordham.edu/cgi/viewcontent.cgi?article=1270&context=ilj

179 *United States Citizenship and Immigration Services (USCIS) website*. Retrieved from http://www.uscis.gov/history-and-genealogy/our-history/organizational-timeline

180 Brown, Anna (2015). "Key takeaways on US immigration: Past, present and future" *Pew Research Center*. Retrieved fromhttp://www.pewresearch.org/fact-tank/2015/09/28/key-takeaways-on-u-s-immigration-past-present-and-future/

181 The United States Census Bureau 2020 Census. Retrieved from: https://www.census.gov/library/visualizations/interactive/race-and-ethnicity-in-the-united-state-2010-and-2020-census.html

182 Saletan, W. (2015). "Our Brothers' Keepers." *The Wall Street Journal website*. Retrieved from http://www.wsj.com/articles/our-brothers-keepers-1445296466

183 *A Nation of Immigrants:* Ibid.

[184] Bier, D. (2019). "Immigration Wait Times from Quotas Have Doubled: Green Card Backlogs Are Long, Growing, and Inequitable." Retrieved from https://www.cato.org/publications/policy-analysis/immigration-wait-times-quotas-have-doubled-green-card-backlogs-are-long

[185] Bier, D. (June 8, 2018). "150-Year Wait for Indian Immigrants With Advanced Degrees." *Cato Institute.* Retrieved from https://www.cato.org/blog/150-year-wait-indian-immigrants-advanced-degrees

[186] Kahn, S and MacGarvie, Megan (October, 2018), "The Impact of Permanent Residency Delays for STEM PhDs: Who Leaves and Why," NBER Working Paper No. 25175.

[187] "Afghan Visa Program Still Riddled with Dysfunction and Delays as Veterans Push for Fixes." Retrieved from https://www.military.com/daily-news/2022/10/21/afghan-visa-program-still-riddled-dysfunction-and-delays-veterans-push-fixes.html

[188] *The Department of State website.* Retrieved from https://travel.state.gov/content/dam/visas/Statistics/AnnualReports/FY20 21AnnualReport/FY21_TableI.pdf

[189] Sullivan, K (March 21, 2013). "Foreign citizens making big investments in US in exchange for green cards." *The Washington Post.* Retrieved from https://www.washingtonpost.com/politics/foreign-citizens-making-big-investments-in-us-in-exchange-for-green-cards/2013/03/21/ecf250d2-8d72-11e2-b63f-f53fb9f2fcb4_story.html

[190] "Get In Line: What it Takes to Legally Immigrate to the United States." Retrieved from https://www.npr.org/2020/01/24/799378739/get-in-line-what-it-takes-to-legally-immigrate-to-the-united-states

[191] Millman, J. (June 13, 2014). "Why Sexual Minorities Have an Inside Track to a U.S. Greencard." *The Wall Street* Journal. Retrieved from http://www.wsj.com/articles/why-sexual-minorities-have-an-inside-track-to-a-u-s-green-card-1402676258

[192] United States Asylum Applications. Retrieved from https://tradingeconomics.com/united-states/asylum-applications

[193] Mehta, S. (August 1st, 2011). "The Asylum Seeker." *The New Yorker.* Retrieved from http://www.newyorker.com/magazine/2011/08/01/the-asylum-seeker

[194] The U.S. *Department of State website.* Retrieved from http://www.state.gov/j/prm/ra/receptionplacement/index.htm

[195] Data retrieved from https://legaljobs.io/blog/green-card-statistics/

[196] Source: https://fraudscrookscriminals.com/2019/06/07/new-rules-to-help-stop-fraud-in-diversity-visa-program/

[197] Source: https://worldpopulationreview.com/country-rankings/us-immigration-by-country

[198] Source: https://blackimmigration.net/5-fast-facts-about-black-immigrants-in-the-united-states/

[199] Source: http://www.uscis.gov/humanitarian/refugees-asylum

[200] "US Brag about Quality Medical Care for Detained Illegal Immigrants." (April, 2012). *The Judicial Watch*. Retrieved from http://www.judicialwatch.org/blog/2012/04/u-s-brags-about-quality-medical-care-for-detained-illegal-immigrants/

[201] *National Conference of State Legislatures website*. Retrieved from https://www.ncsl.org/research/immigration/state-laws-related-to-immigration-and-immigrants.aspx

[202] Raleigh, H(January 14, 2022)."Non-Citizen Voting Cheapens U.S. Citizenship." *Newsweek*. Retrieved from https://www.newsweek.com/non-citizen-voting-cheapens-us-citizenship-opinion-1669095

[203] *The Department of Homeland Security (DHS) website*. Retrieved from https://www.dhs.gov/publication/proposal-create-department-homeland-security

[204] *The Department of Homeland Security (DHS) website*. Retrieved from http://www.dhs.gov/mission

[205] Svvaedra, R. (October 22, 2022). "New Staggering Numbers From Biden's Border Crisis Show Record Highs Across The Board." The DailyWire. Retrieved from https://www.dailywire.com/news/new-staggering-numbers-from-bidens-border-crisis-show-record-highs-across-the-board

[206] "U.S. Immigration Population Hits Record 46.6." Retrieved from https://www.breitbart.com/immigration/2022/02/23/report-u-s-immigrant-population-hits-record-46-6-million/

[207] Ibid.

[208] Seib, G. (December 14, 2015). "The Roots of Republican Fears on Immigration and Trade." *The Wall Street Journal website*. Retrieved from

http://www.wsj.com/articles/the-roots-of-republicans-fears-on-immigration-and-trade-1450107708

209 "How America Middle Class Has Changed in the Last Five Decades." Pew Research. Retrieved from https://www.pewresearch.org/fact-tank/2022/04/20/how-the-american-middle-class-has-changed-in-the-past-five-decades/

210 Hook, J. (December 14, 2015). "New Poll Finds National Security Now Top Concern." *The Wall Street Journal website.* Retrieved from http://www.wsj.com/articles/poll-finds-national-security-now-a-top-concern-1450130463

211 Source: https://fox59.com/news/coronavirus/trump-signs-immigration-order-as-part-of-covid-19-pandemic-crackdown/

212 *United States Citizenship and Immigration Services (USCIS) website.* Retrieved from http://www.uscis.gov/working-united-states/permanent-workers

213 Mises, L. (1919). *Nation, State, and Economy: Contributions to the Politics and History of Our Time* (Lib Works Ludwig Von Mises PB). Liberty Fund Publishing, p.87.

214 Borjas, G. (April, 2013). "Immigration and the American Workers." Retrieved from http://www.hks.harvard.edu/fs/gborjas/publications/popular/CIS2013.pdf

215 Costa, D., Cooper, D. and Shierholz, H. (August 12, 2014). *Economic Policy Institute.* Retrieved from http://www.epi.org/publication/immigration-facts/#5.-are-most-immigrants-employed-in-low-wage-jobs

216 Source: https://www.pewresearch.org/fact-tank/2021/04/29/key-facts-about-asian-americans/

217 Frum, D. (January, 2015). "Does Immigration Harm Working Americans?" *The Atlantic.* Retrieved from http://www.theatlantic.com/business/archive/2015/01/does-immigration-harm-working-americans/384060/

218 Peri, G. (May 2014). "Do Immigrant Workers Depress the Wages of Native Workers." *IZA World of Labor website* Retrieved from http://wol.iza.org/articles/do-immigrant-workers-depress-the-wages-of-native-workers

219 "Immigration and the American Workers." Ibid.

220 Nadler, R. (January, 2008). "Immigration and the Wealth of States." *Immigration works USA website*. Retrieved from http://immigrationworksusa.org/uploaded/file/ImmigrationandWealth.pdf

221 Ibid.

222 Sparshott, J. and Hudson, K. (October 12, 2015). "Labor Shortage Pinches Home Builders." *The Wall Street Journal*. Retrieved from http://www.wsj.com/articles/labor-shortage-pinches-home-builders-1444688976

223 "The Economic Impact and Contribution of the EB-5 Immigration Program in 2013." *Invest in USA (IIUSA) website*. Retrieved from https://iiusa.org/blog/wp-content/uploads/2015/05/Economic-Impacts-of-the-EB-5-Immigration-Program_2013_FINAL-web.pdf

224 "Immigration and the American Workers." Ibid.

225 Sherk, J. (May 6, 2008). "H-1B Workers: Highly Skilled, Highly Needed." *Heritage.org website*. Retrieved from http://www.heritage.org/research/reports/2008/05/H-1B -workers-highly-skilled-highly-needed

226 "Understanding H-1B requirements." *United States Citizenship and Immigration Services (USICS) website*. Retrieved from http://www.uscis.gov/eir/visa-guide/H-1B-specialty-occupation/understanding-H-1B-requirements

227 Source: https://blog.visaexperts.com/h1b-visa-holders-get-whopping-salaries-in-the-u-s/

228 *H1-B Visa Info website*. http://www.h1bvisa.info/h1b_visa_fees

229 Preston, J. (November 10, 2015). "Large Companies Game H-1B Visa Program, Costing the U.S. Jobs."

The New York Times website. Retrieved from http://www.nytimes.com/2015/11/11/us/large-companies-game-H-1B -visa-program-leaving-smaller-ones-in-the-cold.html

230BuzzFeed News. (May 29, 2015). Retrieved from https://www.buzzfeed.com/carolineodonovan/salary-database-shows-the-highs-and-lows-of-silicon-valley-p?utm_term=.igevaGvMAB#.yt6Ov0OAz4

231 North, D. (February, 2011). "Estimating the Size of the H-1B Population in the US." Center for Immigration Study (CIS) website. Retrieved from http://cis.org/estimating-h1b-population-2-11

232 "Reading and Math Scores Plummeted During Pandemic." *The Wall Street Journal*. Retrieved from https://www.wsj.com/articles/education-departments-first-pandemic-era-trend-data-show-worst-reading-math-declines-in-decades-11662004860?page=1&mod=article_inline

233 Abel,J., Deitz, R. and Su, Y. (2014). "Are Recent College Graduates Finding Good Jobs?" Retrieved from https://www.newyorkfed.org/medialibrary/media/research/current_issues/ci20-1.pdf

234 The unemployment rates were higher among some minority groups. According to the Bureau of Labor Statistics' July 2015 report, the unemployment rate for young blacks was 20.7%, and Hispanics 12.7%. Retrieved from http://www.bls.gov/news.release/youth.nr0.htm

235 Brat, I. (August 12, 2015). "On US Farms, Fewer Hands for the Harvest." *The Wall Street Journal website*. Retrieved from http://www.wsj.com/articles/on-u-s-farms-fewer-hands-for-the-harvest-1439371802

236 "College Remediation Needs Revamping." Retrieved from https://medium.com/age-of-awareness/college-remediation-needs-revamping

237 Doar, R. (January 12, 2016). "The Big but Hidden US Jobs Problem." *The Wall Street Journal*. Retrieved from http://www.wsj.com/articles/the-big-but-hidden-u-s-jobs-problem-1452555802

238 Neumark, D. (December 16, 2015). "The Evidence Is Piling Up That Higher Minimum Wages Kill Jobs." *The Wall Street Journal website*. Retrieved from http://www.wsj.com/articles/the-evidence-is-piling-up-that-higher-minimum-wages-kill-jobs-1450220824?mod=trending_now_5

239 *Department of Housing and Human Services website*. Retrieved from https://aspe.hhs.gov/report/personal-responsibility-and-work-opportunity-reconciliation-act-1996

240 Fix, Michael and Jeffrey Passel, "The Scope and Impact of Welfare Reform's Immigrant Provisions," (Washington, D.C: The Urban Institute, 2002). Retrieved from http://www.urban.org/research/publication/scope-and-impact-welfare-reforms-immigrant-provisions

241 Levinson, A. (August 1, 2002). "Immigrants and Welfare Use" Migrant Policy Institute. Retrieved from http://www.migrationpolicy.org/article/immigrants-and-welfare-use

242 Camarota, S. (September, 2015). "Welfare Use by Immigrant and Native Households." Center for Immigration Studies. Retrieved from http://cis.org/Welfare-Use-Immigrant-Native-Households

243 "Immigrant families and Welfare Reform." *The Policy Institute*. Retrieved from https://www.purdue.edu/hhs/hdfs/fii/wp-content/uploads/2015/06/pf_fis41report.pdf

244 Nadler, R. (January, 2008). "Immigration and the Wealth of States." *Immigration works USA website.* http://immigrationworksusa.org/uploaded/file/ImmigrationandWealth.pdf

245 Ousey, G. and Kubrin, C. "Exploring the Connection between Immigration and Violent Crime Rates in US Cities, 1980–2000." *College of Williams & Mary website.* Retrieved from https://www.wm.edu/as/sociology/documents/Ouseydocs/SP5603_04.pdf

246 "From anecdote to evidence: setting the record straight on immigrants and crime." *American Immigration Council website.* Retrieved from http://www.immigrationpolicy.org/just-facts/anecdotes-evidence-setting-record-straight-immigrants-and-crime-0

247 Nowrasteh, A. (July 14, 2015). "Immigration and Crime — What the Research Says." *Cato Institute website.* Retrieved from http://www.cato.org/blog/immigration-crime-what-research-says

248 Rumbaut, R. and Ewing, W. (2007). "The Myth of Immigrant Criminality and the Paradox of Assimilation." *The Immigration Policy website.* Retrieved from http://www.immigrationpolicy.org/sites/default/files/docs/Imm%20Criminality%20(IPC).pdf

249 *The Los Angeles Times.* Retrieved from http://www.latimes.com/local/california/la-me-0705-sf-shooting-20150705-story.html

250 Gzesh, S. (April 1, 2006). "Central Americans and Asylum Policy in the Reagan Era." *Migration Policy Center website.* Retrieved from http://www.migrationpolicy.org/article/central-americans-and-asylum-policy-reagan-era

251 Sahagun, L. and Reyes, E. (July 4, 2015). "The Fatal shooting in San Francisco ignites immigration policy debate." *The Los Angeles Times.* Retrieved from http://www.latimes.com/local/california/la-me-0705-sf-shooting-20150705-story.html

252 Curl, J (September 19, 2022). "Conservatives Eviscerate Sanctuary Liberals Over Hypocrisy of Expelling 50 Migrants." *The Daily Wire*. Retrieved from https://www.dailywire.com/news/conservatives-eviscerate-sanctuary-liberals-over-hypocrisy-of-expelling-50-migrants

253 Washington, G. (1794). *Letter to the Vice President*. Retrieved from http://www.founding.com/founders_library/pageID.2223/default.asp

254 Huntington, S. (2004). *Who Are We? The Challenges to America's National Identity*. New York: Simon & Schuster.

255 GONZALEZ-BARRERA, A., & LOPEZ, M. (February 4, 2013). "Recent Trends in Naturalization, 2000-2011." Pew Research Center. Retrieved from http://www.pewhispanic.org/2013/02/04/ii-recent-trends-in-naturalization-2000-2011-2/

256 Fonte, J. & Nagai, A. (April 2013). "America's Patriotic Assimilation System is Broken." *Hudson Institute*. Retrieved from https://s3.amazonaws.com/media.hudson.org/files/publications/Final04-05.pdf

257 FGM Rates Have Doubled in US. Newsweek. Retrieved from http://www.newsweek.com/fgm-rates-have-doubled-us-2004-304773

258 Murray, C. (February 12, 2016). "Trump's America." *The Wall Street Journal*. Retrieved from http://www.wsj.com/articles/donald-trumps-america-1455290458?mod=trending_now_5

259 Timeline of Agricultural Labor. Retrieved from National Farm Worker Ministry website: http://nfwm.org/education-center/farm-worker-issues/timeline-of-agricultural-labor/

260 Retrieved from http://immigration.procon.org/view.timeline.php?timelineID=000023

261 Retrieved from USCIS.gov website: http://www.uscis.gov/history-and-genealogy/our-history/historians-mailbox/ins-records-1930s-mexican-repatriations

262 Retrieved from Digital History website: http://www.digitalhistory.uh.edu/disp_textbook.cfm?smtID=3&psid=3699

263 Cohen, D. (2011). *Braceros: Migrant Citizens and Transnational Subjects in the Postwar United States and Mexico*. Chapel Hill, NC: University of North Carolina Press, pp. 93, 97.

[264] This estimate double counts individuals who entered the U.S. as a Bracero several times.

[265] Koestler,F. (2015). "Operation Wetback." *Handbook of Texas Online*. Uploaded on June 15, 2010. Modified on November 12, 2015. Published by the Texas State Historical Association. Retrieved from http://www.tshaonline.org/handbook/online/articles/pqo01

[266] Nowrasteh, A. (2014). "Guest Worker Visas Can Halt Illegal Immigration." *Cato Institute website*. Retrieved from http://www.cato.org/publications/policy-analysis/how-make-guest-worker-visas-work

[267] Philip, M. (2003). *Promise Unfulfilled: Unions, Immigration, and Farm Workers*. Ithaca. Cornell University Press. Retrieved from http://www.cornellpress.cornell.edu/

[268] Philip, M. (2003). *Promise Unfulfilled: Unions, Immigration, and Farm Workers*. Cornell University Press: Ithaca, NY. Retrieved from http://www.cornellpress.cornell.edu/

[269] INS became part of the U.S. Department of Homeland Security in 2013.

[270] *USCIS website*. Retrieved from https://www.uscis.gov/e-verify/what-e-verify

[271] O'Grady M. (December 28, 2015). "What Trump Doesn't Know about Mexicans." *The Wall Street Journal*. Retrieved from http://www.wsj.com/articles/what-trump-doesnt-know-about-mexicans-1451258998

[272] Tau, B. (December 10, 2015). "U.S. Is Bracing for Influx of Central American Migrants." *The Wall Street Journal*. Retrieved from http://www.wsj.com/articles/u-s-is-bracing-for-influx-of-migrants-1449795630

[273] Institute on Taxation and Economic Policy. Retrieved from https://itep.org/undocumented-immigrants-state-local-tax-contributions-2017/

[274] Rector, R. & Richwine, J. (May 6, 2013). "The Fiscal Cost of Unlawful Immigrants and Amnesty to the U.S. Taxpayer" *The Heritage Foundation*. Retrieved from http://www.heritage.org/research/reports/2013/05/the-fiscal-cost-of-unlawful-immigrants-and-amnesty-to-the-us-taxpayer

[275] "Immigration and the American Workers." Ibid.

276 "5 Facts about Illegal Immigration in the US." *Pew Research Center.* Retrieved from http://www.pewresearch.org/fact-tank/2015/11/19/5-facts-about-illegal-immigration-in-the-u-s/

277 O'Toole, M. (July 5, 2014). "Top General Says Mexico Border Security Now 'Existential' Threat to US" *Defense One website.* Retrieved from http://www.defenseone.com/threats/2014/07/top-general-says-mexico-border-security-now-existential-threat-us/87958/

278 McCarthy, A. (August 29, 2014). *National Review.* Retrieved from http://www.nationalreview.com/corner/386694/judicial-watch-feds-bulletin-describes-threat-imminent-terrorist-attack-southern

279 O'Grady, M (January 8, 2023). "Biden Bows to Blackmail on Migrants." *The Wall Street Journal.* Retrieved from https://www.wsj.com/articles/biden-blackmail-on-migrants-venezuela-cuba-authoritarian-national-security-border-immigration-11673212207?mod=opinion_lead_pos9

280 Bensman, T (December 22, 2022) "Biden's border crisis is fueling growing cartel armies." *The DailyMail.* Retrieved from https://www.dailymail.co.uk/news/article-11563659/Mexicos-cartels-getting-rich-powerful-Bidens-mass-migration-crisis-TODD-BENSMAN.html

281 Goo, S. (August 24, 2015). "What Americans Want to Do about Illegal Immigration." *Pew Research Center.* Retrieved from http://www.pewresearch.org/fact-tank/2015/08/24/what-americans-want-to-do-about-illegal-immigration/

282 John Locke, Second Treatise, §§ 25 – 51, 123 – 26. Retrieved from http://press-pubs.uchicago.edu/founders/documents/v1ch16s3.html

283 Ronald Reagan: "Statement on United States Immigration and Refugee Policy." July 30, 1981. Online by Gerhard Peters and John T. Woolley, *The American Presidency Project.* Retrieved from http://www.presidency.ucsb.edu/ws/?pid=44128

284 "The Roots of Republican Fears on Immigration and Trade." Ibid.

285 Haney, P. (February 6, 2016). "DHS ordered me to scrub records of Muslims with terror ties." *The Hill.* Retrieved from http://thehill.com/blogs/congress-blog/homeland-security/268282-dhs-ordered-me-to-scrub-records-of-muslims-with-terror

286 Nadeau, S. (May 20, 2011). The Economic Contribution of Immigration in Canada. Retrieved from the University of Ottawa website http://socialsciences.uottawa.ca/grei-rgei/eng/documents/Synthesis_wp_000.pdf

287 Jordan, M. (September 24, 2014). "Limited English Limits Job Prospects." *The Wall Street Journal*. Retrieved from http://www.wsj.com/articles/limited-english-limits-job-prospects-1411531262

288 Source: https://www.canada.ca/en/immigration-refugees-citizenship/corporate/transparency/committees/march-12-2020/economic-immigration.html

289 Mark Cully, *Skilled Migration Selection Policies: Recent Australian Reforms* (2012). Retrieved from http://www.immi.gov.au/media/publications/research/_pdf/skilled-migration-policies.pdf

290 DIAC, The Continuous Survey of Australia's Migrants: Cohorts 1 to 5 Report 2009-11. Retrieved from http://www.immi.gov.au/media/publications/research/_pdf/continuous-survey-aus-migrants.pdf

291 Source: https://international.holdings/en/residency-by-investment/australia/

292 Smyth, J. (September 13, 2015). "Rule Change Hits Demand for Australian Investor Visas." *The Financial Times*. Retrieved from http://www.ft.com/cms/s/0/4e1c1192-57a4-11e5-a28b-50226830d644.html#ixzz3zKlefMkj

293 *Constitution Facts.com website*. Retrieved from https://www.constitutionfacts.com/us-constitution-amendments/fascinating-facts/

294 Justice Joseph Story (1840). *Familiar Exposition of the Constitution*. Retrieved from http://www.heritage.org/research/reports/2009/09/the-meaning-of-the-constitution

295 Alex Nowrasteh and Jim Harper. (July 7, 2015). "Checking E-Verify." Retrieved from http://object.cato.org/sites/cato.org/files/pubs/pdf/pa775_1.pdf

296 *USCIS website*. Retrieved from https://www.uscis.gov/sites/default/files/USCIS/Native%20Docs/Westat%20Evaluation%20of%20the%20E-Verify%20Program.pdf

297 *USCIS website*. Retrieved from https://www.uscis.gov/e-verify/about-program/history-and-milestones

298 Hanson, V. (April, 2013). "What True Immigration 'Reform' Would Look Like." *National Review*. Retrieved from http://victorhanson.com/wordpress/?p=8577

299 Goo, S. (August 24, 2015). *Pew Research Center*. Retrieved from http://www.pewresearch.org/fact-tank/2015/08/24/what-americans-want-to-do-about-illegal-immigration/

300 Nowrasteh, A. & Cole, S. (July 25, 2013). "Building a Wall around the Welfare State, Instead of the Country." *The Cato Institute*. Retrieved from http://object.cato.org/sites/cato.org/files/pubs/pdf/pa732_web_1.pdf

301 Ibid.

302 Douglass Papers, Library of Congress, microfilm reel 14. Retrieved from http://www.blackpast.org/1869-frederick-douglass-describes-composite-nation#sthash.tSyZiTuA.dpuf

303 http://www.uscis.gov/working-united-states/temporary-workers/temporary-nonimmigrant-workers

304 Visa bulletin for December, 2022. *The United States Department of State website*. Retrieved from https://travel.state.gov/content/travel/en/legal/visa-law0/visa-bulletin/2023/visa-bulletin-for-december-2022.html

305 Source: http://www.washingtonpost.com/blogs/wonkblog/wp/2013/01/29/the-path-to-legal-immigration-in-one-insanely-confusing-chart/

Made in United States
Troutdale, OR
09/14/2023

12904147R00170